FORTUNE HUNTERS

A Discourse on The Environmental
Forces Shaping Nigeria's
Political Economy

Dr. Austin Nweze

Vista Press

Vista press
& Distribution Logistics Ltd.

*To all the people who love and believe
in the Nigerian project.*

CONTENTS

Title Page

Copyright

Dedication

PREFACE   3

CHAPTER ONE   7

CHAPTER TWO   36

CHAPTER THREE   55

CHAPTER FOUR   62

CHAPTER FIVE   69

CHAPTER SIX   75

CHAPTER SEVEN   83

CHAPTER EIGHT   95

CHAPTER NINE   103

CHAPTER TEN   123

CHAPTER ELEVEN   129

CHAPTER TWELVE   143

CHAPTER THIRTEEN   156

CHAPTER FOURTEEN   179

CHAPTER FIFTEEN   192

CHAPTER SIXTEEN   231

CHAPTER SEVENTEEN   244

CHAPTER EIGHTEEN   250

CHAPTER NINETEEN   258

CHAPTER TWENTY   262

CHAPTER TWENTY ONE   274

CHAPTER TWENTY TWO   281

CHAPTER TWENTY THREE   288

CHAPTER TWENTY FOUR   296

CHAPTER TWENTY FIVE   312

CHAPTER TWENTY SIX   347

CHAPTER TWENTY SEVEN   362

CHAPTER TWENTY EIGHT   368

CHAPTER TWENTY NINE   374

CHAPTER THIRTY   390

References   416

About The Author   423

ACKNOWLEDGEMNT

This book would not have been possible without the quality contributions of many people of like minds. I will like to begin by thanking Professor Pat Utomi who contributed a couple of chapters (chapter 10 and 15) and gave me the opportunity represent him at some of his numerous speaking engagements. Some of the papers I presented on his behalf have been used in part of this book.

Many thanks go to Taiwo Akerele for contributing a chapter (chapter nine) on the political economy of anti-corruption crusade. The same goes to Akeem Y. for his research contribution in chapters 3, 4, and 5.

I would like to thank the MSc 1 and 2 students of the School of Media and Communication (SMC) of Pan African University where I teach Business Journalism and Economic and Business Environment. The debates we had in class and your quality contributions helped in shaping the idea of this book.

I do appreciate the wonderful work the readers and editors, including Osa Director, as well as the publishers and printer did in getting this book out on time. They all worked tirelessly to produce this book.

There are several other people whose ideas have been used in this book without proper acknowledgement both online and offline. I thank you all for your contributions to this book.

Chris Asoluka, whom I call Chief and Honorable,

1

is another person I would like to appreciate. He recommended resources for me to use and also enlightened me in the course of our several debates in his home library on some topical issues which helped in shaping the ideas in this book.

PREFACE

I didn't set out to write a book by this title. It was really born out of my desire a national and international commentator of political economy. It started over a decade ago when I started feeling this heavy burden about the Nigerian condition. I had the urge to say and do something for posterity sake, and just may be my comments and contributions will be noticed somewhere and some day. I set out sending out my thought on this subject to some national newspapers for publication. Then I started receiving positive reactions from different people. So I said to myself, why not document this into a book so that generations of Nigeria, Africa, and in fact, the world over will benefit from these thoughts.

The work of Dennis C. Mueller in his classical volume (book) *Constitutional Democracy* had a great impact on my thinking about the subject matter. In the opening chapter of his book, Mueller made some profound statements that get ringing in my brain even as I write this preface. I addressed this issue in detail in chapter 1 of this book. Writing on democracy in America, Mueller opined that since the birth of America the nation had remained the "land of dreams". But he was also quick to point to the fact that not all dreams come true in America. That no government can meet up with the aspirations and dreams of all its citizens. The government can only try, but it cannot solve all the problems. As it tries to solve one problem another problem rears up its head.

Still in chapter one, I discussed government failure and the indicators. Some of the signs of a failed state have been listed as high crime rate, dysfunctional education system, high poverty rate, and deficit – "the attraction of buying now and paying later". There is a fifth indicator which I did not discuss at the time of writing that chapter which has been necessitated by the events of the 2008/2009 global financial and economic crises. And that is the issue of debt management. Greece, Italy, Spain, Portugal, and other countries in Europe are bleeding badly due to serious debt overhang. In the business journalism I teach, I gave, as part of the assignment for the semester, the students a book *Debt Threat: How debt is destroying the developing world... and threatening us all,* by Noreena Hertz, an Associate Director for the Center for International Business at the University of Cambridge. I have added the review of that book by Omena Abenabe in chapter 30.

I am grateful to Pat Utomi for helping guide and shape some of the thoughts expressed in this volume. Firstly, for giving me the opportunity by asking me to represent him at seminars and conferences. Secondly, for allowing me use some of the seminal materials as part of this book.
Some of the chapters in this volume have also been contributed by some of my research assistants. I'm indebted to Taiwo Akerele for his contribution of chapter 9.

The book has been structured to stand alone. In other words, the reader can actually find any chapter of interest or for research purposes and read it without necessarily having to read the entire book. But I will suggest that you read the entire book to aid your understanding of the subject matter.

I learned a few secondary school history lessons from Gloria Nweze. in preparing for one her class exams while in class four, she did a summary of her history subject. I stumbled onto it and find it still very useful today as it was many years ago. You will find that in chapter 7.

If you have learned anything from this book, share with others. Let this book be a useful resource to all and sundry. This is one of the many contributions I will be making throughout my life time to building a better nation and continent. What is yours?

Dr Austin Nweze
October 2012

Buddha's Path to Liberation

From right understanding proceeds right thought;
from right thought proceeds right speech;
from right speech proceeds right action;
from right action proceeds right livelihood;
from right livelihood proceeds right effort;
from right effort proceeds right awareness;
from right awareness proceeds right concentration;
from right concentration proceeds right wisdom;
from right wisdom proceeds right liberation.

Author unknown
Culled online

CHAPTER ONE

FORTUNE HUNERS, PREBENDALISTS AND NIGERIA'S DEMOCRACY

The founding fathers of Nigeria had a dream of a nation that will be economically, politically and socially buoyant. A nation where there is no religious and tribal sentiments, where people see themselves as one people- Nigerians – not minding religious or ethnic leaning. Restoring the dignity of the Nigerian was top most in their minds.

Prior to independence in 1960, the few elite leaders were well united to a common cause, not for selfish reason but for common good. Like the biblical apostles, they were with one heart and mind, caring and sharing what they had with one another.

What happened before and during the first elections when suddenly, as though some evil spirits entered the people, they realized that they belonged to one ethnic or religious group or the other rather than

7

first and foremost Nigerians, was the beginning of the balkanization of the nation. The struggle for political power tore what was once a budding nation, full of potentials and endowed with rich mineral, human and other material resources more than any other nation in the world, into several tribal groupings. The tribal interest has been placed before the national interest. What seemed like one nation in the past have become many countries.

The previous attempts by the founding fathers to forge a nation out of Nigeria were scuttled during the military interjection in the 1960s. So, rather than becoming a nation, Nigeria is still struggling to remain a country.

The words "nations" and "country" are usually used interchangeably but they are not really the same. A nation was first a country before becoming a nation. A country talks about the earth or ground or a geographical expression or if you will, a group of people gathered, not together as in holding each other and looking downward. In other words, their main focus is on the resources God endowed them with. They are only interested in whatever they can get out without contributing to the growth and development of the country. They do not have a common goal. A nation on the other hand, to my mind is also a group of people gathered together and looking upward and forward. They are focused on a common goal and common dream. Suffice this to say that while a country focuses on the natural resources, a nation focuses on the people, the citizens of that geographical location. The Nigerian condition can be explained using the country and nation analogies. Nigeria as a country is focused on the exploitation of oil, gas, solid minerals and other natural resources it is endowed with. People are more concerned with what they can take out Nigeria rather than what they can put in. That is why we have the current Niger Delta problem, Boko Haram, Jos crisis, MASSOB and why there is this terrible environmental degradation of the Niger Delta region. A region that produces a large chunk of Nigeria's wealth cannot boast of portable water, good road network or electricity.

Nigeria as a country has no value for human life. It is only in this country that government places premium value on a barrel of oil more than human life. This is quite evident in the events that took place recently. I am talking about political killings, the execution of Ogoni nine, the sack of the entire Odi community by the Olusegun Obasanjo government, and other terrible happenings in the land.

The political hijack of the state by prebendalists and other rent and fortune seekers is a testimony to the state or structure of the country. In 1999 when the Obasanjo administration took over reins, people expected so much from this regime. Many believed that God had finally heard the cries of many Nigerians for a change to a better nation. There was so much expectations, so much excitement about this civilian cum military government.

This was to be short lived when those in the helm of affairs started their policy miss-steps.

Not much was seen in the first stanza of the Obasanjo administration. It was used to settle many political

I.O.Us to the detriment of the common good. The fortune hunters and prebendalists swarmed on the administration like bees and hijacked the system. Many saw politics as a business where they exchange goods and services rather than a process of providing good governance to the people. People saw political power as a tool for settling scores and intimidation of the weak. The police and the military were used for this purpose.

The National Assemble (Senate and House of Representatives) were filled with people with no genuine interest to serve but rather to enrich their pockets. It was and still is awash in scratching of backs and Ghana Must Go bags. It was a big embarrassment watching grown men on a national television fighting and throwing chairs at each other over little disagreement which is common in a democratic set up.

In constitutional democracies like America and Britain, it is never a big deal to disagree in principle with other people's views for as long as everything is geared toward the good of the nation rather than selfish interest. But in Nigeria it is the opposite. People are in government for what they can gain and not to serve the citizens that put them in positions of authority, and also pay the taxes or produce the resources that they use to oppress them. This is a sign of the failure of government.

How do you recognize a failed state or government? Governmental failure results in high crime rates, poverty, collapse in education and lack of government control of deficit or debt management. The most critical in today's knowledge economy is the ability of the leadership to control and properly manage the nation's debt. Greece, once a peaceful and prosperous nation, was thrown into chaos in 2011 due to the inability of the leadership to management its high debt overhang and provide jobs for its citizens. In a desperate effort to rescue the nation's economy they were forced to swallow the IMF bitter pill in form of structural adjustment. A loan package was dispatched but not without the usual internal adjusts on the restructuring the economy. The people of Greece protested the hard economic condition on the streets of Athens and other major cities.

The crime rate in Nigeria has reached an unimaginable rate that the police seemed helpless. There is no security of life and property. Many innocent people lost their lives to armed bandits and political killings since this dispensation. There were several bomb blasts in different parts of the country including Abuja, the seat of the Federal government. The Police Headquarters was bombed and over 100 people lost their lives. Before the country could recover from that and the previous bomb blasts in Suleja, an outskate of Abuja, the UN building that housed several agencies was bombed killing many people.

Even a serving minister, a former Attorney General of the Federation and Minister of Power, was hacked down by the assassins' bullet right in his bedroom in his hometown of Ibadan, Oyo state and the killers have not been brought to book. I am talking about the late Chief Bola Ige.

The high crime rate forced rich Nigerians to providing their own security. People now build high walled houses, buy bullet-proof cars, put street gates, hire private security guards etc., so that they would be able to sleep at night and move around their businesses in the day. But with all these, there was no guarantee of sleeping with your two eyes closed at night.

What is the role of government in all these? According to Wilhelm Von Humbolt, the proper role of the state is the maintenance of security, both against the attack of foreign enemies and internal dissensions. This constitutes the true and proper concern of the state. Certainly, Humbolt continued, no government service is more fundamental than the protection of citizens against crime. Yet there is no day that passes by without hearing of hundreds of people being killed due to violent crimes, especially in the cities. This crime is also being committed against the police. A terrible incident happened in January 2007 at Oshodi, Lagos.

A police officer was attacked by armed bandits at night in her apartment. Invariably the bandits recognized her and told her of her "bad" behavior toward them at one of the police stations located at Akinpelu street, Oshodi, Lagos. The gang of about six armed bandits raped her one after the other. She had a sick younger sister living with her who was just recuperating from a surgery after being discharged from the hospital. The police officer reacted when the armed bandits wanted to rape her sister and told them not to touch her. The bandits felt insulted and shot her and the bullet pierced through her head and she died.

Tell me, is this not a sign of governmental failure – when a government cannot even protect its own citizens not to talk about a serving police officer. Life is equally dangerous in Benin, Asaba, Warri, Port-

Harcourt, Abuja, Aba, Kano, etc.

The only protection people run to now is God. People hold on to the promise of God's protection to His children.

How do you explain the death of Tony Ofuani, the former CEO of Red Star Express and DHL. He had traveled to the United States for a few years to explore other business opportunities. Upon his return toward the end of 2006 to Nigeria he was killed on a Sunday morning on his way to church by unknown bandits.

Education is another government failure. Over the years Nigerians believed that the government should provide a basic education to their children. This expectation had increased overtime to the point that the citizens expected the government to educate their children through secondary school and university. Some religious bodies also set up schools in those days to augment the government's efforts.

After the Nigerian civil war in 1970, the former administrator of the old Eastern region, Ukpabi Asika, decided to take over mission schools. He felt that it was the sole responsibility of the government to provide basic education to the citizens. When other regions heard about the decision to take over mission schools in the eastern region, they decided to follow suit. Lagos State was one of those states that took over mission schools. These schools were not properly run by these governments and there was a total collapse. One of such schools was the new Holy Child College which Lagos State government took over from the Catholic Church. The school was badly run or run down by the government until the eventual hand over back to the church in 2001. As at 2011 the school has been turned around both in physical infrastructure and soft infrastructure. This attracted very rich and not so rich parents to send their children to the school instead of sending them overseas, as was the tradition. Some commentators believed that singular decision by the late Ukpabi Asika to take over mission schools when they had no capacity and capability to run schools successfully was the beginning of the fallen standard of education and moral bankruptcy in schools today.

Who do you blame for the current deteriorating performance of students in all levels of education? Well, the institutions that supposed to be solving the problems should be held responsible. When the governments realized they could not cope with the increasing demand for basic and higher education, they decided to return mission schools back to the original owners as well as encouraged the establishment of privately owned schools at all levels – primary, secondary and university. Today, there is avalanche of privately owned schools.

Government is no longer establishing schools except for some specialized schools like Unity Schools whose management has been transferred to private manager, and some colleges of education and state Universities. Government more or less performs oversight functions and monitors both public and private schools, to ensure that standards are maintained. Even in that role of monitoring, the government has also failed because the schools keep producing poor quality graduates. There is actually a big rut in the system. Students have abandoned their studies to form cults.

Poverty is another indicator of the failure of government. Well, depending on your definition of poverty, a greater percentage of Nigerians live in poverty. Some commentators put it at above 71% of the population that live below or within the poverty level. According to the World Bank, anybody that lives below $1 a day is considered poor.

In his 2003 volume, Obadan defined poverty as a state of deprivation of well-being judged inadequate to live decently. He further stated that poverty connotes social evil or social injustice. It is also antithetical to the developmental objective of any country and the potential for engendering social upheaval. If development is about human welfare, then poverty is a basic structural imbalance that must be adjusted or transformed.

Poverty is a global menace, but it is most devastating in Africa. Nigeria is no exception. The human conditions in Nigeria as well as other parts of Africa have deteriorated within the past decade that it is unimaginable. The rates of malnutrition have been on the rise, food production cannot keep pace with population growth. Also real disposable incomes have declined, and above all, the quality and quantity of health has also gone down greatly.

A visit to Nigeria in 2009 by the US Secretary of State, Hilary Clinton, was quite revealing. She remarked that in 1996, about 40% of Nigerians lived below or within the poverty level. In 2009, that number had increased to 71% of Nigerians who lived within or below poverty level. The question was what went wrong. Did the people become too lazy they could no longer feed themselves, or did the government implement policies that sentenced many Nigerians to the land of the poor?

Poverty threshold in Nigeria, according to UNDP consumption survey of 1991, stood at 45% in terms of expenditure per capita per year. Also the poverty survey of 1995 had Nigeria's relative poverty threshold at 40% of household expenditure. The same UNDP report stated that poverty has often been aggravated by the incapacity of governments and the market to allocate resources efficiently and equitably so that poor people benefit from them. Despite affirmations to the contrary, Nigerian and African governments still have not made poverty reduction a central theme of their policy, as demonstrated by the limited allocation of budget and other resources to assisting the poor. Making basic social services available and accessible has rarely, if even, been a development priority.

Nigeria is far off the mark on the human development index on indicator (HDI) of the UNDP. The human development indicator combines the subsistence and income criteria in order to determine the relative position and relative poverty of countries. HDI is based on the specification of a decent life resulting from the options of people such as long and healthy life; knowledge and access to opportunities for the acquisition of knowledge; and access to financial resources, especially employment income.

When we talk about healthy life we are talking in terms of life expectancy at birth. The life expectancy of the average Nigerian has declined to 42 - 45 years.

Compared to the 1960s and 1970s, the quality of life was better then than it is now. The rate of adult literacy level is still abysmally low, estimated at less than 45%, compared to other emerging nations of South East Asia. As mentioned earlier, the quality of education has declined due to government's weak policies over the years as well as weak institutions caused by long military rule. The per capita income, which relates to the access to financial resources, is still at a low level of between $240 and $1000. Meanwhile Singapore which was below Nigeria in development in the 1960s has a per capita income of $ 8, 000 or more. What has really gone wrong?

Since 2002 Nigeria has been on the list of countries the World Bank considered as fragile states and conflict affected countries. Fragile states are characterized by weak policies, weak institutions and weak governance.

The conflict-affected countries are those that have recently experienced, are experiencing, or are widely regarded as at risk of experiencing violent conflicts.

Nigeria's condition is so critical to be left in the hands of politicians alone. Politicians tell people what they want to hear, and people like to be told they are really "good". So speech lines like these are sure-fire applause - getters.

But good politics can make bad theology, and when we begin to believe our own press releases, we become victims of our own delusion.

The fourth failure of government is in the area of proper management of the economy. A recent CBN report showed that the economy or GDP grew by 7.0% in 2006.

In 2010, a similar growth rate was reported by the CBN. But were growths without providing jobs to the teeming population of Nigerian youths of employable age.

My understanding of economics and how GDP works is that GDP growth is usually accompanied by development. Otherwise it is a negative growth or no growth. There are few nations in the world that are endowed like Nigeria yet the country suffers from Dutch Disease. People live in abject poverty in the midst of plenty. For years Nigeria has experienced double digit inflation rates. In 2006, it was about 10.5%. The manufacturing sector and power sector are in comatose. Prof Pat Utomi once said that the manufacturing sector has become an abandoned baby that no one wants to touch.

In the history of development of nations, there is no nation that has developed without an efficient and effective power sector. How do you explain it when companies like Cadbury, Nestle, Dunlop etc., have to generate their own power in order to run their operations? The cost is quite high which is also passed on to the consumers of the products.

A good management of the economy is a combination of several variables which include operating a balanced budget. Memory fails me to recall the year Nigerian government has not operated a deficit budget. Deficits if not controlled can lead to political instability. The major theme and focus of the 2006 budget was improving the physical infrastructure. Billions of Naira were earmarked to improve NEPA (power), which only succeeded in changing the name to PHCN

(Power Holding Corporation of Nigeria), and road rehabilitation and construction. Well, just like in the power sector, the roads got worse. There was so much carnage on the roads in the past couple of years because of poor road network. In fact more people have died in road accidents than of HIV/AIDS and Malaria and other diseases.

The 2007 budget had as its theme and focus accelerating investments in basic physical infrastructure and human resource capital. The only additions in the 2007 budget flowing from the 2006 budget's focus of power, water, roads and security are education and health. Education and health are the main thrust of human resource capital. The Economist Intelligent Unit forecast for Nigeria's economy in 2007 is as follows: GDP growth of 5.5% in 2005; budget balance of -1.4% of GDP as against -1.0% in 2006 and -1.3%, in 2005; inflation rate for 2007 will be 10.9%. It was 10.5% in 2006 and 17.9 in 2005. oil production in 2007 is estimated at 2.5m b/d as against 2.2m b/d in 2006 and 2.4m b/d in 2005.

According to Dennis C. Mueller, the attraction of "buying now and paying later" is obvious. Many governments have fallen prey to this attraction. Mushrooming deficits, a debt "crisis", or a runaway inflation fed by money printed to cover the deficit have precluded the countries. A responsible government controls deficits and avoids the inter-generational transfers and political instability they can bring. The recent economic and structural reforms of the government are geared toward addressing these failures.

Since the military interregnums in 1984, 1985 and 1993, Nigeria has not known good governance due to the public choices made. There is so much lawlessness that people begin to question the need to have a government. So, why have a government if only a few privileged ones can benefit from government policies or as they say in Nigeria's political parlance, the dividends of democracy. Jean Jacques Rousseau, a French Philosopher once said that what made the establishment of societies necessary was the fact that the interests of individuals clashed. But what made their establishment possible was the fact that those same interests also coincided. In other words, it is the overlap among different interests that creates the social bond so that no society can possibly exist save as there is some point at which all the interests concerned are in harmony. Now society should be governed exclusively in terms of the common interest of its members, Thomas Jefferson also added his voice by saying that the only orthodox object of the institution of government is to secure the greatest degree of happiness possible to the general mass of those associated under it.

What Rousseau said in effect is that government emerged to control the clash of interests that existed in anarchy and satisfy the common interest of the community. Mueller opined that the contractarians' depiction of anarchy as a clash of interests resembles the economist's description of the clash of interests that occurs when individuals meet and compete for scarce resources in the marketplace.

The resultant effect of the political hijack in 1999 by

these fortune hunters and prebendalists are myriad. From fuel scarcity to labor disputes which led to strikes, the Niger Delta crisis and kidnappings, political assassinations and gale of impeachments, air crashes and institutional corruption, the ceding of Bakasi to Cameroun and the Ikeja bomb blast that killed over 5000 people. The list is endless.

The political class seems oblivious of this impending danger to the very existing of Nigeria which Robert Kaplan aptly described as the coming anarchy. Democracy supposed to bring political stability but Nigeria's democracy has caused an upsurge in ethnic violence. The late Claude Ake captured the Nigerian political condition saying that we have essentially relations of raw power in which right tends to be in coexistense with power and security depends on the control of power. The struggle for power, then, is everything and is pursued by every means.

The quest for power tilts towards absolutism rather than an opportunity to serve. The politician's objective is usually to get elected and once elected strives towards being re-elected.

The democratic system encourages the devolution of power from the federal, state and local governments. When this administration took over reins in 1999 we had hoped that this would be an opportunity to practice true federalism. Unfortunately it has not been so. This is just an extension of military rule. The federal has become one behemoth bullying the states and local governments. The EFCC (Economic and Financial Crimes Commission) has become a veritable whip used by the presidency to beat the state and local authorities to do their bidding.

In true federalism, there is separation of power which helps protect the citizens from the government. In Nigeria's democracy the center is too strong and the local government is like a lame duck. The local government is supposed to be the closest to the people in the grass root, but they have been incapacitated. A situation where a government wakes up and fires a local government chairman is not good for democracy. In the words of John Stuart Mill, the very object of local government is in order that those who have any interest in common, which they do not share with the general body of their countrymen, may manage their joint interest by themselves; and the purpose is contradicted if the distribution of the local representation follows any other rule than the grouping of those joint interests. Therefore, the local government is important to the administrating of good governance.

Commenting on the structure of true federalism or federal structure, Thomas Jefferson said that in government, as well as in every other business of life, it is division and subdivision of duties alone, that all matters, great and small can be managed to perfection. First is the general federal republic for all concerns, foreign and federal. Second is that of the state for what relates to its own citizens exclusively. Third is the county republics for the duties and concerns of the county; and finally the ward republics for the small and yet numerous interesting concerns of the neighborhood.

I remember in the 1960s and early 1970s when Nigeria had regional governments, there was a bit of competition between the regions on economic development based on the resources available within the regions.

There was the groundnut pyramid in the North, Cocoa in the West, and Palm oil in the Eastern region. Then oil became the cash cow and all regions abandoned other natural endowments and focus on the revenue that come from oil. Between 1970 and 2000 Nigeria generated over $300 billion from oil sales.

With that kind of money one would have expected to see a lot of developmental projects that will bring comfort to the citizens going on. Unfortunately Nigerian missed that opportunity to develop its infrastructure. Most of what exists today as infrastructure was put in place by General Yakubu Gowon. When he was still the head of state he once said that Nigeria's problem was how to spend her money. This was after the oil windfall resulting from the Yun Kippur war or something like that, when the Arab nations boycotted the sale of oil to the rest of the world.

When Obasanjo took over reins as a result of the death of Murtala Mohammed, he went on a spending spree by organizing FESTAC 77 which did not add any value to the economy or the life of Nigerians. Instead it brought problems to the country that we are still suffering from till date. After that wasteful event, the Obasanjo administration did not have enough money to execute projects. They approached the World Bank or Paris Club who, like a vulture waiting for its prey to die, gave Nigeria loan. It was taken under Decree 30th of February 1978. Cumulatively the money rose to over $ 36 Billion.

It was the same Obasanjo government in 2006 that paid off that debt which was "discounted" to $ 12 Billion.

As earlier mentioned that the first stanza of the Obasanjo administration was more or less used to settle political I.O.Us, the 2003 election was a big fraud, which every Nigerians know. There was not election but allocation of votes to the ruling PDP. This contributed to the apathy people have now toward the 2007 general elections. There was a change of guard at INEC, the body with the arduous task of conducting electrons in Nigeria. Many believe that the present helmsman of INEC is an Obasanjo apologist, and is not capable of conducting free and fair elections akin to the 1993 elections, widely believed to have been the freest election in Nigeria which was won by M.K.O Abiola of blessed memory.

I had the opportunity of listening to INEC helmsman speak on a TV program, Patito's Gang, and I saw his sincere desire and determination to conduct a free and fair even if it would cost him his life.

We had been discussing the Nigerian condition on Patito's Gang since the inception of the program in 2001. Viewers of the program felt and still feel it is the only credible "opposition party" to PDP. Then there was a clarion call from well meaning Nigerians for a change in the way the affairs of the country have been run since independence in 1960. The same people have been recycled several times and they don't seem to have the solution to the Nigeria's problem because they have run out of ideas.

The only way to go about this change is to have a

generational shift and have trusted and credible people come out and run for elective positions. But then who is are those credible people that will go for us and save Nigeria from the coming anarchy? It has been said that the worst thing that could happen to Nigeria is for enough good people to fold their hands and do nothing while evil men and women have their rain.

This is completely unacceptable to the well meaning Nigerians at home and in diaspora.

Pat Utomi's decision to participate in the political process altered the political landscape. It created real panic within the political class. The fortune hunters and prebendalist know that it is no longer business as usual, and that the end has come. So, what they are doing now is fight to make sure the status quo remains. Nigeria's oil wealth has been distributed by the fortune hunters and prebendalists among themselves and their cronies. What this means is that if there is no change in leadership of Nigeria soon, my generation and my children's generation have no share of Nigeria's wealth. It has all been cornered. They know that Pat Utomi is clean and has plenty of ideas and he loves Nigeria very much. He is compassionate and empathic towards the people.

Nigerians love him and believe that he is what Nigeria needs to rescue her from imminent disintegration. The United States released a report recently stating that Nigeria will break up in 15 years if they carry on the affairs of the state in this despicable manner. The political class dismissed it as one of those statements by enemies of Nigeria's progress. Nigeria is standing on the precipice of which if nothing is done by the well meaning people of this country, it will disintegrate right before our eyes.

The Economist magazine in their recent edition had this forecast for Nigeria which I will like to repeat here for emphasis: "African elections are usually one-sided affairs: those in power hate to leave and often don't Nigeria's presidential elections in April will be different. The incumbent, Olusegun Obasanjo, won't be standing and the race to replace him is heating up. That does not mean this will be a model election. This is, after all, Nigeria, with a history of military strongmen, oil-fuel corruption and religious tensions. Patronage, vote rigging and (above all) money will suffuse this election, which will be neither free nor fair. It was about the most bitterly contested election in the world in 2007.

Obasanjo is eager that his People's Democratic Party (PDP) should nominate a candidate who is committed to continuing his reforms. That isn't assured. Mr. Obasanjo is a lame duck, and a candidate who might fit this bill, such as the defacto head of the reforms team, Nasir el-Rufai, has limited power base.

Whoever secures Obasanjo's blessing will have to face the well-resourced network of the current Vice President, Atiku Abubakar, with whom Obasanjo has hardly been on speaking terms. There could also be a challenge from the former military ruler, Ibrahim Babangida, reputedly the country's richest man. As only one person can stand for the PDP either may be forced to jump ship and contest the poll under the banner of another party.

The new president will take over an economy awash

in cash from oil boom. Production, at around 2.2m barrels per day, will rise to 4m within a decade. But even growing oil wealth is unlikely to buy solutions to Nigeria's problems. Poverty is rife, infrastructure dilapidated and government services almost non-existent. The new leader must confront several conflicts: attacks by local militias on oil facilities in the Niger Delta; the Muslim-Christian religious divide; the battle for fertile land; and bitter ethnic rivalries. However, none of this will put off the hopefuls."

The last statement that "none of this will put off the hopeful" is a true talk. Pat Utomi has sounded a warning to these fortune hunters that he will not fold his hands and watch them destroy our future and the future of our lovely children. It is no longer business as usual. That is why he is in the presidential race as a change agent on a rescue mission.

None of Nigeria's past and present leaders has a history of successfully running an enterprise. Pat Utomi has the history as evidenced in his being chairman of several companies. His has good understanding of how to make Nigeria's economy work again. His brand of economics is what Nigeria needs for this hour.

Some skeptics say that he is too young and inexperienced to lead Nigeria. But how old was General Gowon when he ruled Nigeria? How old was General Babangida? Pat Utomi's generation as well as my generation is the generation to rescue Nigeria. His inexperience should actually be a plus because, according to Chris Ngige, the former governor of Anambra State, "Pat doesn't know how to steal money and even if he learns it, will not do it because he is highly principled."

What baffles me is that the professional class, it seems, does not know what they want or what to do. I had expected they will all come out in droves to participate in the political process more than they are doing at the moment. Any way, I expect them to hijack the political process after 2007 elections.

One way of hijacking the political process from these plunderers is for enough good people to come out and take the bull by the horn and participate in politics. It requires a collective effort otherwise people who have no business leading us will be lording it over us, telling us how to live our lives, how to raise our children, how to sleep at night and even how to marry our wives or what to eat.

We want a government that will empower Nigerians to rule their world and not to be enslaved economically and politically. The choices we make in today will determine the kind of future that awaits Nigerians. The leadership must put aside their personal interest and serve the interest of the country if Nigeria is to successfully transit to true democracy. The world is watching and praying that Nigeria will successfully transit from one democratic government to another since independence in 1960.

Just recently the U.S. government expressed fears that Nigeria's democracy is threatened by neglect and corruption. John Negroponte, the US National Intelligence Director opined that the Nigerian government's institutional foundations are hollow from decades of neglect and corruption and will continue to make the country susceptible to recurring crisis in the coming years." This is true talk because the signs are so glaring in the government's inability to stem rising lawlessness and insecurity in the country.

Nigerians are demoralized and sometimes feel helpless every day that passes by. For how long Nigerians can hold their peace, I cannot tell. Many Nigerians don't want war, especially not after the bloody civil war of 1967 – 1970 in which over a million lives were lost. Nigerians want and desire peaceful co-existence or co-habitation with one another. But can the fortune hunters give them that peace? In his volume, "The coming Anarchy," Robert Kaplan quoting the Italian political theorist Gaetano Mosca in "The Ruling Class" (1939) stated that universal peace is something to be feared, because it could come about "only if all the civilized world were to belong to a single social type, to a single religion, and if there were to be an end to disagreements as to the ways in which social betterment can be attained...even granting that such a world could be realized, it does not seem to us a desirable sort of world."

Kaplan further stated that through there is often nothing worse than war and violent death, but a truism that bears repeating is that peace, as a primary goal, is dangerous because it implies that you will sacrifice any principle for the sake of it. He also noted that avoiding tragedy requires a sense of it, which in turn requires a sense of history. "Peace," he noted, "however, leads to a preoccupation with presentness, the loss of the past and a consequent disregard of the future. That is because peace by nature is pleasurable, and pleasure is about momentary satisfaction. In an era of extended domestic peace, those who deliver up pleasures are the power brokers. Because pleasure is inseparable from convenience, convenience becomes the vital element in society."

Democracy cannot be sustained in a country where there is a flagrant disregard for the rule of law. Toni Fine of the Benjamin Cardoso School of Law in New York, USA, defined the rule of law as "having rules that are established, known, accepted and respected by both government and non government actors.

Rule of law invokes a predictable legal system with fair, transparent and effective judicial institutions to protect citizens against the arbitrary use of state authority and lawless acts." Sternford Moyo of the law society of Zimbabwe noted that "the rule of law is the antithesis of the existence of wide, arbitrary and discretionary powers in the hands of the executive or the legislature. The rule of law is a celebration of individual rights and liberties and all the values of a constitutional democracy characterized by the absence of unregulated executive or legislative power. It is a celebration of the concept of separation of powers and the checks and balances that form part of that concept. In a society in which rule of law is observed through the mechanism of judicial review, executive decisions and legislative enactments which are outside the framework of the law are declared invalid, thereby compelling both the executive and the legislature to submit to enjoyment, by the individual, of all rights and liberties guaranteed by the constitution."

There is a catalog of cases of disregard to the rule

of law. It is evident in the political gerrymandering going on in Nigeria. The president, who supposed to show good example, has flouted court orders, the state legislatures have also impeached governors without due process. The list is endless. From the leadership to the led, the story is the same. Right from the military era the judiciary was deliberately weakened by those in authority to enable them carry on with their misrule of the nation. It was the state of lawlessness in the land that gave birth to the celebrated political god fathers in Ibadan, Anambra, Aso Rock, Plateau and other parts of the country.

Where the rule of law is not upheld, there is usually anarchy. Nigeria is in a anarchical state of some sort. People do whatever they like because they know they will get away with it. Innocent people are hacked down on a daily basis on the streets and in their homeland nobody is doing anything about bringing those responsible to book. Simple transaction contracts or agreements are not honored. Even the government is guilty of it. Nigeria is under siege by these fortune hunters and prebendalists.

I believe in democracy and the rule of law. Democracy can only thrive where there is obedience to the rule of law. I have often said that the liberal democracy as practiced in the United States is not suitable to a developing country like Nigeria. It is equally too expensive to maintain. Nigeria needs to evolve its own brand of democracy that will jumpstart real development. Liberal democracy is only effective in maintaining a developed and matured society. America did not start out practicing the liberal democracy it is practicing today. The system evolved over the years as the society developed.

The Asian economies were able to develop, not because thy practiced the liberal democracy akin to American system, but they took what was relevant and adapted it to their cultures. These have evolved over the years to what they now have as a homegrown democracy. Typical examples include Singapore, Malaysia and Indonesia.

A recent survey conducted by Wall Street Journal and the Heritage Foundation ranked Hong Kong and Singapore as the world's freest economies for 2007. Yet they don't exactly practice American brand of democracy. Nigeria comes a distant 88.

Just as liberal democracy is not completely suitable for developing nations; the mainstream economic model has not developed these economies. In Nigeria, neoclassical or mainstream economists parade in the corridors of power. They have come up with different economic models to get Nigeria's economy out of the doldrums. This is basically because of the trainings they received in neoclassical economic schools of thought.

What is wrong with Nigeria's economy is the type of economists we have and the government system. Over the years Nigerian economists, it seems, have employed Harrod-Domar growth models, the Cobb – Douglas production function, the Ricardian theory of comparative advantage and the Keynesian development planning. They overlooked the important role of entrepreneurship in economic development.

In order to explain economic development in a country it requires a dynamic theory which centers on some human agency. This is where the theory of entrepreneurship is required. Though the government's current effort is to operate a private sector-led economy and promote entrepreneurship but there is no serious commitment on their part. Businesses are still heavily dependent on government. There is still too much government and less business. The economy need to be diversified and decentralized beyond Lagos, Port-Harcourt, Kano and Abuja. In my opinion, it seems that the government's efforts are geared more toward promoting what I call "necessity entrepreneurship" rather than real entrepreneurship. Entrepreneurship, we all know, is the factor that can change the given resource situation of an economy.

The government set up different agencies to promote entrepreneurship and alleviate poverty, but most of the functions of these agencies overlap. Setting up many government agencies is not the issue. What we should actually do is to ask ourselves what has been responsible for the dramatic growth of some Asian and Latin American economies? How can their economic models be adapted to grow Nigeria's economy?

Nigeria should look more toward the Kirznerian mode of entrepreneurship. We need to grow more Kirznerian entrepreneurs. Kirznerian entrepreneurs capitalize on the profit opportunities by employing business strategies such as small – scale enterprises, product imitation, subcontracting and spatial arbitrage.

Kirzner in his 1979 volume stated that "for developing

economies, two problems need to be addressed. The first is the determination of the best course of economic development available to the society. It is a matter of comparing alternative possibilities with available resources and technology. The second is to ensure that the opportunities thus computed will be fulfilled. No matter what form of economic organization, whether central planning or market economy, the central issue is to ensure that the opportunities that exist will be discovered and seized."

Nigeria's policy makers are known for coming out with policies that will make the heart of international community leap for joy but fail woefully in the implementation stage. A number of factors are responsible for this, but let me mention a couple of them. The people who are to implement such policies may not have the capacity or capability to implement. They may not be qualified, and even if they are qualified, they may not have the necessary tools to implement them.

It is a case of, for example, sending people to gain computer knowledge because you want them to be able to operate a computer. You have spent money to get them trained, and upon their return back to work there is no computer available for them to use.

Secondly, there might not be alignment of interest between organization or government goals and individual goals. Communication is important to ensure what the government wants to accomplish is clearly understood by those implementing it.

Thirdly, sometimes it could just be that the policy is

weak, as most policies in Nigeria are. Once a policy is weak there is nothing any body can do even if you have the best people and the right tools to implement it.

Fourthly, is the issue of weak institutions. Weak institutions are likened to having a weak foundation for a nice building. Even if you use top grade materials to build the house it will collapse because of the weak foundation.

Suffice this to say that Nigeria's existence is standing on weak foundation. We need to fundamentally rethink and think through certain basic issues. In fact we need to get back to the basis and start building afresh rather than "creaming the market" as we have done since independence.

To be able to do this, we need bold, courageous and committed leadership. We need a leader that is compassionate; a leader with strong emotional competencies; a leader that will serve rather than be served; a leader that will understand that Nigerians today are no longer the same with those of old. Nigerians today argue. They debate and demand their rights and good governance.

They have a sense of self that is "more intricate, acute, detailed, vast, and rich than at any other time in history. But above all, Nigerians are good people, easy to lead and quick to forgive. All they need is a leader who understands and cares of them. Unfortunately, they have not been lucky to have such leader.

May be, just may be such leader will emerge come May 29......

CHAPTER TWO

SYSTEMS AND MECHANISMS FOR THE MANAGEMENT AND ENFORCEMENT OF LAW AND ORDER IN NIGER DELTA

The Niger Delta has played host to oil exploration and extraction by oil multinational for over forty years. This came with severe consequence to its ecological fragile environment. Over 70 percent of Nigeria Oil and Gas production takes place in the Niger Delta, or its adjoining continental shelf.

It was only in the 1970s that oil emerged as the lifeblood of the Nigerian economy. It grew from a mere 0.1 percent in 1959 to 87 percent in the mid 1970s and over 95 percent in the 1990s and 2000s. Ironically, the oil shocks of 1982 and 1986, when the crude prices fell below $15 per barrel, contributed immensely to Nigeria's economic and external debt crisis. With entrenched patron-client network of oil power, the huge wealth that accrued to the nation during the oil boom years had been unscrupulously mismanaged.

This crisis led to increased struggle for the control of the shrinking oil revenues between political and military elites, the ethnic elites and the further marginalization of the Niger Delta region. The oil-fuelled economic crisis exposed the inherent weakness of the contradictions within the Nigerian state and economy. The resultant effect therefore was the introduction of structural adjustment program (SAP) by General Ibrahim Babangida to resuscitate the dwindling economy.

The Niger Delta being the main site of oil production was further exposed to the oil transnational corporations for intensified oil exploration activities. With oil revenues reduced greatly, incentives were offered to these transnational oil corporations to encourage them to invest their capital in the oil-rich Niger Delta region. By so doing the government hoped to revamp its oil earnings, and make structural adjustment less problematic in terms of financing. It was also hoped that the increased oil exports would bring in badly needed foreign exchange to service Nigeria's external debts, fund national reconstruction and a new market-based economic take-off.

This very action of the government facilitated the global control of Nigeria's oil – rich environment and deepened existing contradictions, resulting in the dispossession and marginalization of the Niger Delta. The heightened environmental degradation was followed by conflicts over access to and control of oil rents across the Niger Delta region.

Ownership, Control and Management of Resources

A fierce war has been going on between ethnic and social forces in Nigeria over the control and ownership of oil resources in the Niger Delta.

This has hampered efforts to improve the well-being and economic development of the people and communities in the region. The agitation for self-determination and resource control was a result of the failure of successive Nigerian governments to have as a priority the development of the Niger Delta.

By Law, the ownership, control management of these resources are vested on the Federal Government of Nigeria vide the Petroleum Act, the land use Act, the Exclusive Economic Zone Act and the 1999 Constitution. Most of these laws and legislations have been generated without due consideration for the agitations for the improved well-being of the oil-bearing communities of Niger Delta.

The enactment of NNPC Act which established and authorized the corporation (NNPC) to engage in all commercial activities relating to the petroleum industry and to enforce all regulatory measures relating to the general control of the petroleum sector through its petroleum inspectorate department further consolidated its ownerships of oil in Niger Delta.

The foregoing laws which vested total ownership and control to the Federal Government notwithstanding, the successive military and civilian administrations have made sure that compensations accruable to oil-mineral producing regions or states are based on derivation principles. Currently, the derivation is 13 percent. The question therefore is: have the state and local governments properly utilized the revenues accrued to them to develop the region?

There is no doubt that there is mismanagement of the revenues accrued to the Niger Delta region. This is evident in the poor level of infrastructural and socio-economic development of the region. A number of factors are responsible for this. These range from poor governance, embezzlement by the leadership of the region, to poor tracking of funds. The level of development of the Niger Delta when compared to the funds disbursed to the region shows that there has not been concerted development efforts by both state and local governments.

Government Response and NDDC

The Federal Government, in an attempt to respond to the social and economic crisis in the Niger Delta, established the NDDC. The NDDC was set up to articulate the development needs of the Niger Delta and draw up a master plan for economic and social development of the region.

The structure of NNDC is a recipe for failure. The structure is overloaded with political appointees. In Nigeria's prebendal and clientele political cultures, NDDC still finds it difficult deliver its mission to the people in the region. The practice of separating political leadership from management is the norm in the management reforms of institutions that delivers public goods. In fact, NNDC should have been designed to be less political and more development focused because of the disastrous human condition in the region.

Gaps, Roles and Mechanisms

There is inadequacy of legislative protection of the rights and freedom of the people of Niger Delta. The laws that regulate oil exploration and exploitation business in Nigeria include the following:

Minerals oil Safety Regulation 1963
Oil in Navigable waters Act 1968
Petroleum (Drilling and production) Regulations 1969
Petroleum Act 1969
Petroleum production and distribution (Anti-sabotage) Act 1975
Associated Gas Re-injection Act 1979
Associated Gas Re-injection (Continued flaring of Gas) Regulation
Associated Gas Re-injection (Amendment) Decree 1985
The Harmful waste (Special Criminal Provision) Act 1988
Oil pipelines Act Chapter (CAP.) 338, laws of the Federation of Nigeria (L.F.N) 1990.

Though these laws and regulations exist, there are however problems affecting access to justice and remedies. These include:

Lack of an authoritative act regulating oil operations, unenforceability of some of the Act, clear absence of definite legal authorization and procedures for judicial review, and lack of social realism.

The lack of an authoritative act governing all areas of

oil-related human rights violations and environmental pollution stands as a major barrier to accessibility of justice. This has put communities at a disadvantaged position in the preparation of their cases.

Unenforceability of the law is another problem because of the unchecked discretion in the hands of governmental ministers and lack of enforcement mechanisms.

There are inadequate penalties or sanctions upon failure to comply with the law by oil companies because they are left to the minister in charge. So, most times non – compliance is left unpunished. For example, the requirement by law to pay adequate compensation is left without penalty in case of failure to do so. Also, where penalties are provided, the focus is on remedy to the government without recourse to harm on the communities.

The Nigerian government has contributed to these problems by failing to monitor or regulate oil companies. This could be as a result of their direct role in oil operation. According to a recent World Bank Study, there is no enforcement of environmental sanitation, pollution, forest reserve, or environmental impact assessment regulation.

RECOMMENDED STRATEGIES

The Rule of Law

It is now cliché that human productivity and the related improvement in quality of life have grown much more in the last two hundred and fifty years than in the

5,000 years before. Explanations of how the West grew rich and why a good part of Asia has grown in leaps is myriad. Most focus on the role of technology and knowledge. Some have emphasized the role of institutions. It is important to note that the rule of law and institutions that support the rule of law are at the heart of the enterprise of human progress.

Contentious as several of the issues of globalization may be, one undisputed outcome of the process is that we all can see how others live. Failure to catch up with the pack will undoubtedly produce forms of social anomie and may indeed reach, for some countries, the self fulfilling prophecy of the coming anarchy. When Robert Kaplan wrote the Coming Anarchy he was in fact talking to the possibilities of globalization of what used to be local ethnic and religious conflicts. Countries that cannot create enough wealth or manage wealth well enough for the common Good will find collapse stir them in the face.

It will be much digression to discuss the counterpoint of the proclivity to celebrating Asian traditions that apparently violate the rule of law while delivering material advance. Let us just dispose of the issue for now by noting that prosperity invariably produces a middle class unwilling to be hapless victims of the arbitrariness of individuals of power. In the end rich people cannot but seek to be governed by consistent rules. As the example of "the first new nation" as Seymour Martin Lipset characterizes the United States, and others, indicate, the rule of law and the institutions which support the concept are important for human material advance which, tends also to increase peace and social harmony as a middle class with a stake in prosperity is less inclined to violent disruption of the social order.

What Is the Rule of Law?

This phenomenon which seems to hit us everywhere we look in the media, in this information age, is sometimes assumed to be understood when that may not be the case. In the main the concept of the rule of law deals with experience which has led men to distrust power as it relates to the citizens if the parameters of engagement where not co-defined and the supremacy of that legal code enshrined in the spirit of governance.

The long history of absolute rulers in human experience led those seeking a more just order to articulate the need to be more trustful of laws than the heart or the conscience of man to define the relationship between state and society or power and the citizen. It is perhaps most clearly articulated by the founding fathers of the first new nation. As John Adams, the second President of the United States put it: "The Executive shall never exercise the legislative and judicial powers or either of them, to the end that "it may be a government of laws and not of men" (emphasis mine)

This is the origin of the frequent reference to a government of laws and not of men as the essence of the rule of law. Embedded in this definition is also the idea of separation of powers. As another one of the founding fathers of the American nation, James Madison wrote "the accumulation of all powers, legislative, executive, and judiciary, in the same hands…may justly be pronounced the very definition of tyranny. These views of men seeking to design a modus vivendi that would free them from the monarchist absolutism they were fleeing from in Europe were indeed inspired in such thinking by words written by Thomas Paine in the monograph "Common Sense" which is very usually given credit for sparking off the American Revolution. Paine coined the phrase "the law is king"

Toni Fine who teaches law at the Benjamin Cardoso School of Law in the New York, was guest of the Concerned Professionals to speak on the subject of the Rule of Law and sustainable democracy. In that lecture she defined the Rule of Law as "having rules that are established, known, accepted and respected by both government and non-government actors. Rule of Law invokes a predictable legal system with fair, transparent and effective judicial institutions to protect citizens against the arbitrary use of state authority and lawless acts.

In the African context Mark S Ellis in a paper presented in Abuja in 2004 quotes Sternford Moyo, past president of the law society in Zimbabwe.

"The Rule of Law is the antithesis of the existence of wide, arbitrary and discretionary powers in the hands of the executive or the legislature. The Rule of Law is a celebration of individual rights and liberties and all the values of a constitutional democracy characterized by the absence of unregulated executive or legislative power. It is a celebration of the concept of separation of powers and the checks and balances that form part of that concept. In a society in which rule of law is observed, through

the mechanism of judicial review, executive decisions and legislative enactments which are outside the framework of the law are declared invalid thereby compelling both the executive and the legislature to submit to enjoyment, by the individual, of all right and liberties guaranteed by the constitution."

How Do These All Impact Wealth Creation?

Uncertainty, Institutions and Economic Performance

Where there are no rules or the rules do not govern, there is a high level of uncertainty. The response of economic actors to difficulty to predict outcomes, uncertainty is to either avoid transactions or take steps that mediate likely unfavorable outcome by wedging through such instrumentalities like third party roles, insurance etc. The former, no transactions, means no economic growth, the latter, hedging, means transaction costs. High uncertainty often means high transaction costs which mean challenges for competitiveness.

Uncertainty is reduced by institutions. These Institutions have been defined as rules that set boundaries to human conduct and the structural arrangements for enforcement. Ronald Coarse and other in the Old Institutional Economics School have defined Institutions as settled habits of a community. In effect rules and the sanctions that follow them force compliance at first but with obedience become habitual and may take place without any obvious presence of a sanctions mechanism. In the main, institutions make for uncertainty reduction and high volume transactions and economic growth.

Property Rights, the Mystery of Capital and Economic Performance

One of the challenges with the definitions of Institutions tends to be that property rights are seen as foundational institutions that made the West rich. Economic freedom and rights to property, if we bring Amatya Sen's clear thinking on economic freedom to the table, definitely works together to make for human advance. The situation in the third world that shows why we have not made similar progress is more graphically captured by the Peruvian Economist Hernando de Soto in his discussion of the absence of representational systems capturing ownership and value of property, in the mystery of capital as the root of our poverty.

What is clear is that Nations are poor because of the failings we have in property rights, representational systems that make us collect assets which become dead capital, and ultimately absence of the supremacy of the rule of law which makes for high uncertainty in the arbitrary conduct of people of power.

Ethics, Accountability and Governance in Public Sector

Ethics, accountability and governance are the epi-center of the survival of the public sector and therefore the growth and progress of Nigeria.

Governance can be described as having the capability and capacity to influence, lead, control and/or play a chief role in the administration of country or organization's material and human resources for optimum development.

Governance denotes the utilization of the leader's determination and desire to bring about positive transformation in the lives of the majority of Nigerians. It denotes transparency, honesty, probity, integrity, moral commitment and prudent management of Nigeria's scarce resources.

Governance equally means striving to conscientiously serve humanity and country with the best of one's ability before any personal interest or gain.

Governance also requires vision, competence, knowledge, courage, good intellectual capacity and determination. The function of governance is to ensure the organization, whether public or private, fulfills its obligation or purpose.

Visionary leadership and good governance produce influence which lead to sustainable developments.

What ethics, on the other hand, tries to do is to help in deciding how a person should act in order to achieve a given objective after considering all things. The focus therefore is on determining how to behave so as to ensure a sane life both at home and in the workplace.

UNDP defines accountability as the ability to hold public officials and their representatives to a standard of conduct that is clearly in the public interest. This requires rules and conduct that are transparent, straight forward and broadly accepted in society, as well administrative and legal processes to discipline or remove officials who do not respect such rules.

Governance, being the exercise of authority, direction and control or a system of government or regulation, has ethics and accountability as major elements. The major challenges therefore are the existence of weak public institutions, weak accountability mechanism, low ethical standard and above all absence of good governance.

Institutions are major variables influencing the value of good governance. Institutions are systemic frameworks or value systems used by society to set limits to acceptable conduct. Therefore, institutions exist to constrain behavior in a way that facilitates social intercourse and economic exchange relations. In terms of transactions, for instance, costs are lowered through institutions evolving to bring sanctions to bear on those who defect. These constraints from institutions, or restrained behavior, comes not so much from continuous enforcement which will make transactions costs high but through rules that make informal constraints operational. People restraint themselves because a norm of behavior evolves around the rule policed by the same institution.

Weak accountability mechanisms on the other hand tend to facilitate corruption and other abuses of office and generally undermine governance. In the public sector, accountability is to the citizens of Nigeria. Outside the public sector, accountability is not to the citizen of the country but to the organization or company's stakeholders, as well as to the regulators who act in the public interest.

An understanding of the formal and informal

accountability relationship is important. Let us reflect a little on accountability politics and why Nigeria has a rash of horizontal accountability while vertical accountability is barely a phenomenon of the extant order.

One of the advantages of democratic institutions is that they very often offer opportunities for vertical accountability which are not often exploited in countries like Nigeria.

One of the reasons vertical accountability is as seldom employed as a means of governance in Nigeria is that quality information for the citizens to use in holding accountable the public official who has the weighting in their favor in the information asymmetries that characterize the citizens-public official relationship. In this regard a freedom of information law and think tanks or active knowledge institutions proves helpful.

There can not be good governance without ethical principles or standards and accountability (both vertical and horizontal). The "public value" concept becomes quite useful when considering the unique purpose of public services and their governance in Nigeria. Public value here simply refers to "the things that public services produce, either directly or indirectly using public money". Public value includes such things as "outcomes (such as improved health and improved safety); services (such as primary care services and policing); and trust in public governance.

Unlike the private sector, majority of the users of public services have limited options and sometimes no option at all. They can't get serviced elsewhere. Moreover there is less incentive for the providers of public service compared to the private companies to improve consumers' satisfaction. These not withstanding, additional steps must be taken by organizations that provide public services to ensure high quality services are provided at all times. Nigerian tax payers have "legitimate interest in the value for money provided by organizations that use public money." Therefore, all such organizations that spend public fund (money) directly or indirectly have an important duty to "strive for economy, efficiency and effectiveness in their work."

Good governance can not be fully achieved by compliance with a set of rules and regulations but by shared values or culture in addition to systems and structure. When a shared value is developed it becomes part of the organization's culture.

Good governance builds on Nolan principles of selflessness, integrity, objectivity, accountability, openness, honesty and leadership.

Managing Perceptions

"The problem is never how to get new, innovative thoughts into your mind, but how to get the old ones out." Dee Hock

The problem in the Niger Delta is a perception management problem. The people in the region have the perception of strong injustice by the government.

Not everything that is faced can or must be changed, but just as surely nothing can be changed until it is faced.

Perception Management as an action Framework

The Issue:

Perceptions are real. They color what we see, how we interpret, what we believe, and how we behave. They create or diminish value. They generate or solve problems. So powerful are our perceptions that many psychologists believe that "perception is reality."

We cannot sustain false perceptions (at least not for long), nor should we attempt to communicate them. In the Oil & Gas arena, doing so would be at least unethical, perhaps illegal, and certainly unprofessional.

The Benefits:

Organizations that can crisply communicate that they deliver high value programs to the local communities and other stakeholders will thrive. To this end, perception management is an essential tool for government and its agents.

Influencing the intellectual perceptions of both internal and external audiences significantly impacts your ability to advance the viability, vitality, and visibility of your organization.

Managing perceptions can be just as important as beautiful buildings, and oil being explored. Clearly understand that it doesn't really matter what we say if we have not considered how it will be received.

The Roles:

In today's crisis ridden Niger Delta, we must create motivating communications that break through the sound barrier and have emotional relevance to the individual communities. The communication strategies and tools you wield are the means to manage the perceptions that create the behaviors, which, in turn, lead to success in your relationships with local communities.

Youth Employment in the Niger Delta Region

It was Robert Reich who said: "If we fight for full employment and economic justice, if we fight for better jobs, better wages and decent work for youth we will be fighting the circumstances in which terrorism ("kidnapping and lawlessness" – my own addition) can flourish." It has been stated severally that Nigeria's biggest asset is its youth, which is estimated to be 65 per cent of the population.

Given Nigeria's already high unemployment rates implies that new entrants to the labor market will not be able to enroll in productive employment unless properly equipped with appropriate skills, otherwise will either join the informal sector at increasing rates of underemployment or will remain unemployed.

The main victims of the Niger Delta problem are the youths. This is because institutional support is lacking. Basic structural and institutional reforms are urgently required to enable the youth to become productively employed. The challenges are more difficult for Niger Delta region than other parts of the country if due to the following constraints:
High illiteracy rate;
Deteriorating quality of education;
High unemployment and underemployment rates;

Environmental degradation;
Limited industrial skills;
Limited private sector participation;
Lack of basic infrastructure;

Consequences of Youth Unemployment – if no major Action is taken by Government

Some serious consequences of youth unemployment and insecurity are linked to the exclusion of young people from a productive role in the adult world of work that could demoralize them, undermine social cohesion and lead to social problems such as crime, kidnapping, drug abuse, vandalism, inter-ethnic conflict and general alienation in the vicious circle of poverty.

Critical Areas Requiring Attention

Education and training is a major instrument, if not the instrument for enhancing the employability, productivity and income earning capacity of young people in the Niger Delta. Young people need broad, general, employable skills combined with training in specific skills and exposure to the world of work that will ease transition from school to work. Women also need education and training to give them access to more and better jobs in the labor markets and to overcome the syndrome of poverty and social exclusion.

Skills possessed by young people are significant factor in determining employment of youth. Studies show that employment outcomes are increasingly determined by the level and quality of education and training and by their relevance to labor markets needs and opportunities. The mechanisms deployed to facilitate young people's transition from school to work, such as apprenticeship, alternating training and the involvement of young people in the world of work during their schooling, also play a vital role in their future employability.

As for the rural poor, education policies need to revise the current strategy of basic education for all. The first requirement is to identify the essential employable life skills for today and tomorrow. Secondly, they should develop strategy and approach to enable poor children to acquire the identified competencies through life relevant learning models while avoiding the general emphasis on literacy and numeracy. This will create a learner friendly environment particularly for the children of the poor. Here literacy must be seen through the required social skills, personal skills, intellectual skills, economic skills and the human qualities required for the world of work.

CHAPTER THREE

FISCAL FEDERALISM AND NIGERIA'S ECONOMY

Conceptual exploration
'Fisc' emanated from the Greek word meaning money or resources. In functional usage 'Fiscal' means tax or revenue and in board term it denotes activities of the treasury. Fiscal Policy is defined as "Comprising the deliberate use of taxes, government spending or expenditure and public debt operations to influence economic activity in a desired way".

Federalism is the arrangement of power and resources among the central authority and the other federating units in such a way that each unit contributes its quota to the sustainability of the central government and simultaneously retaining its power and functionality.

Fiscal Federalism in theory and in practice is the constitutional sharing of economy resources among the three tier of government and as stipulated by the organic law of the land. Economics management under a unitary system is an exclusive preserve of the central government, who determines who get what, when and how, not minding the input of other units of government. Thus Fiscal Federalism is the legitimate distribution of economic proceeds among the tiers of government, and in essence the 'electorate' has the power to query the programs of any tier government which fall short of expected performance.

Evolutionary trend of fiscal Vis-à-vis Resources control

The evolutionary trend of fiscal federalism is dated by back to pre-independence Nigeria when Richard constitution was put in place. It gave considerable length of authority to the federating units. Regions were powerful and the central was weaker, hence, it depend heavily on the regions, for articulation of policies, because the federating units had to send resources to the central.

When Nigeria became independent in 1960 the regions maintained the exclusive power of running, and maintaining the resources at their disposal. Resource control was the order of the day, the western region under the able and visionary leadership of Chief Obafemi Awolowo controlled the western resources, and was able to actualize land mark developmental projects such as the first television station, liberty stadium, cocoa house, Obafemi Awolowo university and a host of Oodua group. This became possible through the exportation of cocoa as the Chief Export earner of the western region. In the north the groundnut pyramid was the order of the day and the life wire of the economy, through this the regional government was able to instrument a lot of development such as the prestigious Ahmadu Bello University Zaria, the Bank of the north, Arewa Holdings, and others. In the East palm oil and palm kernel was the mainstay of the economy, the region was able to put in place certain monumental project. Even Malaysia came to Nigeria to get a palm seed and today is the largest exporter of palm oil in the world.

On the assumption of office July 29, 1966, the then head of the state General Aguiyi Ironsi abolished the Functional Federal Structure and replaced it with unitary system of government. He enacted decree 32 which vested all the nation's resources on the central authority. What Hitherto use to be the Fiscal powers of the states and the regions were taking away the Federal Government assumed an almighty power to distribute at will resources to federating units.

The Tripartite Functions of Government

Allocation
Distribution
Stabilization

Allocation
In any economy of the world the government is empowered to allocate resources to cater for diverse economy interest i.e. among the three tiers of governments, and various sectorial demarcations, e.g Energy, Power and Steel, Agriculture, Education, Health, Defence e.t.c.

Distribution
By this, the government has the salient function to distribute equitably the resources among the haves and

haves not. In some text books this has been regarded as unleashing distributive justice.

Stabilization
This function is vested in the power of central bank and some other relevant authorities to effectively stabilize the economy during steep inflation.

4 The Constitutional Sharing Formula among Three Tiers Of Government_

The Constitutional sharing formula among the three among the three tiers of government is a very thorny issue within the Nigerian setting. It has generated a lot of controversies among the citizenry. That is why it has become a bit difficult to state clearly the enduring sharing formula. For the purpose of this paper hypothetical figures will be adopted.

> Federal – 34%
> State – 30%
> Local – 15%
> Derivation – 13%
> Ecological – 3%

5. The Dynamics Of Exclusive, Concurrent And Residual Legislative List of Constitution

Exclusive Legislative List

The Exclusive Legislative list is vested in the powers of federal government, it means only the federal government can legislate on the Nine odd functions, these include , The Armed Forces the printing and control of National Currency, The Foreign Embassies, Energy Aviation oil and Gas, e.t.c.
The afore-stated functions as enshrined in the

constitution could only be legislated upon by the federal government. Except lately when certain amendment were made in the constitution that allowed states and other corporate bodies to set up hydro power plans and refineries to complement those ones set up by the federal government.

The Concurrent Legislative List

In the Concurrent list there are 66 functions in which both State and Federal could simultaneously operate. These include Education, Agriculture Tourism, Commerce, Sport e.t.c.

The Residual Legislative List

The Residual list contain those function exclusively preserve for the local government. It is derived from the functions given to it by the constitution through the state authorities.

The Question of Viability and Sustainability of Each Tier of Government

Each tier of government is vested with some salient functions. But bearing in mind the lopsidedness in the resources available with each tier of government, this has made it practically impossible to meet their responsibilities. And the problem of overhead cost experienced by many local governments has continued to militating against their viability.

The big question therefore is should Responsibilities Breed Revenue? Or Resources Begets Responsibilities? These big questions have been characterized by emergence of resources control argument in the national polity. In Nigeria some State government particularly from south-western and littoral area, have continued to emphasize why it is ideal for them to control their resources at the expense of central government. And again certain tier of government had collected a whooping sum from the federation account without concomitant wellbeing in the lives of the subjects. The big question will continue to generate controversy in both the academia and governmental circles.

The Challenges of Fiscal Federalism

(i) Overlapping Function

In the_federal structure, tiers of government have continued to overlap one another in the area of revenue generation this is caused by concurrent legislative list where state and federal are to operate.

(2) Improper Valuation

This is in connection with the third tier of government, where tenement rates are administered. Many households that should have paid heavily to the coffer of government pay peanuts.

(3) Dearth of Adequate and qualified personnel at the primary tier of the government. Related to the above, competent and qualified personnel are not available at the local government level to expand the revenue base, causing lean purse of the tier of government, and making it depend heavily on the federation account.

(4) Resources Vire

By resources vire, we mean resources that are diverted to private pockets, monies that should have been used to better the lot of many people, are deposited in private account.

(5) Un-control Overhead Cost

In third world setting, government is seen as father Christmas larger Chunk of revenue receipt is used to service salaries, and other overhead expenses.

CHAPTER FOUR

DEREGULATION AND ITS IMPACTS

C onceptual Meaning
De-regulation according to oxford advanced learner Dictionary is the act of freeing from regulation (especially from government regulation) liberation, release, freeing. In economic term Deregulation is allowing capable cooperate bodies to own larger factors of production in a particular sector of the economy.

Deregulation to some economists is defined as the expansion of supply side of the market. This denotes a situation whereby a government of a given economy allows people of wherewithal to own, operate, and engage capital, equipment and labor, to foster enlarged production. Experiences across the globe have shown that certain Deregulated economies where people have been empowered by law to own larger factors of production, created multiple employment opportunities.

Deregulation has been constructed to mean liberation in some economies of the world. In circular flow of income, in a four sector model where government has the reserve power to own strategic economic influence, Government in this scenario plays a vital role in the allocation and distribution of wealth. When the responsibilities of the government reach a plateau height, the government then liberalizes or deregulates key economic sectors so that more wealth could be created, greater employment opportunities, wealth recycle and government will collect tax, and optimum progression in the economy will be ensured.

According to Professor Pat Utomi, Deregulation is an adjunct of economic principle which holds that price mechanism is an efficient allocation of value in a free market situation. In expounding this principle, it will generate competition, scuttle monopoly, create variety of choices, and output expansion.

Rationale behind Deregulation
The Essence of deregulation within Nigerian context is muilt-dimentional considering the sectoral arrangement such as Telecommunication oil and Gas etc. thus deregulation is to maintain a 'reasonable' economic and price stability and a healthy balance of payment. It will minimize existing inequalities in wealth, income and consumption standard which may tend to undermine production efficiency, offend a sense of social justice and endanger political stability. Through creation of multiple employments, it will ensure the desired and inevitable equilibrium of both withdrawal and injections indices necessary to propel the economy further.

Rationalizing deregulation in the oil sector via expansion of supply side of market

Prior to when NNPC was the only agency that control the pipelining, the refining, and sale of petroleum products, it was captured in one of the daily newspaper's editorials thus: "The unprecedented inflow of foreign exchange which started effectively in the '70s' suddenly jerked up the value of naira, making domestically produced goods uncompetitive Agriculture and manufacturing declined sharply as it became far cheaper to import than produce at home. The poor performance of the real sector has crippled the economy's capacity to create jobs and fight crime. Above all, the unhealthy rivalry among the competing factions of the ruling elite to control the oil wealth has fuelled political instability and corruption" In effect if oil and gas is properly deregulated the resultant effect will be enormous and it will positively impact on the generality of the people.

Deregulation as a subset of 'NEEDS' Document

The 'NEEDS' document is a brain child of Professor Charles Soludo and some other eminent economists. NEEDS is an acronym which stands for National Economic Empowerment Development Strategy. The 'NEEDS' document is aimed at rejuvenating Nigeria economy through the instrumentality of the following polices. These include Globalization, Privatization, Commercialization, and Deregulation.

Globalization is an economic principle which holds that economic activities is beyond National boundaries and by extension it denotes movement of superior capital resources and personnel across the globe to compete favorably with that of geographical boundaries.

Privatization is the transfer of public enterprises to the running of the private initiative. It denotes removal of trade restrictions and barriers in the economy. While commercialization, as twin brother of privatization, is the re-arrangement and re-organization of public enterprises so that they do not expect subvention from the government.

Deregulation is the de-nationalization of the economy. It emphasis broaden the sphere of the economy by allowing the investors to own larger factors of production in a particular sector of the economy. In the opposite, nationalization is the optimum control of the economy i.e goods and services by the government.

Successive Governments Policy Thrust on Deregulation
Policy thrust on deregulation is dated back to Babangida regime, when economic policies were anchored toward the path of recovery. It was then envisaged that certain sectors of the economy should be deregulated to actualize free flow of resources down the line. When General Abacha came on board, he formulated deregulation policy in telecommunication which occasioned the introduction of circular phoning to Nigeria.

When Obasanjo came to power in 1999, he retained the policy of Telecomm deregulation, and invited high Networth Corporate leaders to jostle for license. This gave rise to emergence of viable telecommunication companies such as MTN, CELTEL, GLOBACOM, STARCOMM etc. The emergence has given broad opportunities for employment generation.

In the oil and Gas sector, the Obasanjo administration issued what is termed as "approval in principle" to some number of oil magnates who want to run, and manage refineries. But due to certain institutional barriers these oil companies have not started operations.

IMPACTS/BENEFITS

Expansionary Force in Economy

In macro economic analysis, when supply side of the market is broaden. There is tendency for the expansion in the economic system the private sector will invest its resources, generate employment, sell to the public, and pay taxes to the government. The resources will recycle in the economy.

Increase in Foreign Direct Investment

Deregulation will automatically attracts foreign direct investment. Going by the principle of globalization which emphasis movement of superior capital resources and personnel across the globe, it is on record that, when telecomm deregulation became operational, a large chunk of Foreign direct investment had plaid out.

And it is anticipated that if Oil and Gas is properly deregulated, a monumental upward trend, in industrial circles will be achieved. Creating a lot of employment opportunities. Exclusive functions that are being performed by Department of Petroleum Corporation will be shared by the emerging Oil Companies. Only lately Federal government scraps NNPC, and functions were allocated to the emerging regulatory bodies.

Technology Transfer
Closely related to the above, in the event of achievable foreign direct investment, it will create room for technology transfer. Because these foreign companies who are coming to participate in the economic system will bring their technologies, the nationals will have the opportunity to learn from them. And thereafter cyclical wealth will be created.

Creation of Gainful Employment
The situational effect of any deregulation is the creation of more employment for the citizenry. If more funds are employed in the economy, it will broaden the side of business cycles, requiring more hands to be engaged. House holds will have more hands to buy from industrial holdings. This will go a long way to reduce crime waves because they say "an idle hand is the devil's workshop"

Breaking of Monopoly Power
Deregulation is an opposite principle of Nationalization of economy. By nationalization it denotes government optimum control of the economic system. Like NITEL manages telecoms and PHCN (NEPA) shoulders Energy. But with the introduction of the deregulation, monopoly powers are being broken in Telecomm, Oil and Gas. Etc.

Fostering Competition
In a deregulated system, competition is going to be order of the day. This will bring out quality services to the consumers. Experiences in the telecoms have attested to this.

Professorial Support for Deregulation

In a paper delivered at A.B.U Zaria 2002 by Professor Esko Toyo of University of Calabar, he gave his academic nod for deregulation. He said Nigeria government should consider bringing down heavy industrial equipments from Abroad to produce intermediate ad consumer goods.

And Professor Sam Aluko in the 'Sun' Newspaper interview 2002, openly supported deregulation, and even said that, it will create favourite multiplier effect in the economy. What is fundamental to both professors submission is the creation of enabling environment by the government.

CHAPTER FIVE

PRIVATIZATION AND PUBLIC ENTERPRISE

P REAMBLE
The plethora of write-ups and major discourse about privatization of public enterprises in Nigeria today focus on the economic consequence of the exercise alone. This gives the impression that privatization of public enterprise is purely an economic issue. Nothing can be further from the truth than the observation above. In it complete ramification privatization of public enterprises is not an economic revolution, it is an administrative revolution, a political revolution it is indeed a pursuance to a complete social transformation. However, due to a propensity for simplistic analysis of issues in Nigeria, this skewed attention to privatization has obscured the immense benefit that could have come from a more composite study.

Conceptual Meaning of Privatization
Privatization narrowly defined is the Transfer

of government owned shareholding in designated enterprises to private shareholders comprising individual and corporate bodies. Broadly defined privatization is an umbrella term describing variety of policies which encourage competition and emphasis the role of statutory restriction and monopoly powers. This refers to the policy of structural and institutional economic re-adjustment.

Privatization as one of the derivatives of 'NEEDS' document emphasizes private ownership of factors of production. In essence it denotes buy-over or transfer of government parastatals to the running of private initiative. Hence privatization is aiming at re-structuring of the economy, it covers the general spheres of the economy, e.g. Energy, Maritime, Aviation, Telecommunication etc. Privatization dated back to military Era when the then government thought it fit to privatize public enterprises due to inability to meet up with the operating cost. Even General Sani Abacha inaugurated a body named Technical Committee on privatization and commercialization headed by late Hamza Zayyad .

Argument for and against Privatization
(i) Rationale for Privatization
The primary objective of privatization is to remove the state from those activities that are not inherently governmental functions or core business line; to improve the management of remaining economic activities, to reduce the cost of doing business, and to shift greater performance and financial risk to the private sector.

Other reasons, why government has opted for public enterprises privatization, include the following.

Problem of quota system has informed by federal character, this has been abused overtime caused corruption, nepotism, unqualified placement undue under employment under utilization of employees which breeds redundancy.
There is over reliance of rules and regulation governing the conduct of public sector setting.

Personalization of public organization
The managing directors of the public enterprises personalized the organization to achieve their selfish ends. The managing directors become the only determining factor in terms of conduct of the organization and the principle separation of personnel is governed by the whims and caprices of these managing directors - dishonesty, lack of transparency, accountability and corrupt practices. This has caused poor distribution of services, discourtesy to customer, and lack of proper orientation.

These multi-dimensional public enterprises problem rest on the premises that "when the state owns, nobody owns and when nobody owns nobody cares". Therefore general unsatisfactory standard performance of public enterprises has led government to decide for their privatization and commercialization.

Argument against Privatization
It is established in some quarters that the way and manner government transfers public enterprises is shrouded in secrecy. Although enabling laws were enacted to midwife public enterprises conversion to private initiative. Such laws have been contravened. The Antagonists of privatization even said, the keys

beneficiaries of privatization are the custodians of our wealth. What has simply happened is changing of identities of privatize companies.

Privatization has broaden the existing gap among the haves and haves not. In an attempt to privatize public enterprises most of the companies have been grossly under valued to the detriment of the economy.

Conceptual Meaning of Public Enterprises

Public enterprise is a 'Commonwealth' of the nation. Public enterprises are public investments run, manage, and control by government. According to Harrold-Dommer model, government is strategically positioned to manage public enterprises it further stated that government should take it as a point of duty to invest massively in the economy, to achieve full employment. John Maynard Keynes in 1920 stated that, government should fully participate in economic functions that are "technically social" as Aviation, Transportation etc

Rationale for Public Enterprises

In expounding John Maynard Keynes' assertion on public enterprises Government ought to invest massively in "Technically social" services such as Aviation, Maritime, and Transportation. Government in its effort to ensure equitable distribution of goods and services should embark subsidizing certain economic function by way of investing in them.

In Nigeria the underlying objectives of setting up public enterprises include the followings:

(1) To achieve full employment within the context of economic system.
(2) To avert foreign dominance of the economy.
(3) To rescue the economy from the shackles of

foreign capitalist.
(4) To avoid capital flight
(5) To generate cyclical flow of resources within the economy.

Circular Flow of Income in a Four Sector Model

In a circular flow of income, the government provides salient functions of ensuring equitable distribution of income and acting as an arbiter. In a four sector model, the followings are the principal actors.
(a) The Household
(b) The Firm
(c) The Bank
(d) The Government

The household will buy from the firm, the bank will lend money to the industries outlets, The government being the "big brother" in the model will regulate the activities of the household, the firm, and the bank, and go ahead to invest more in the economy through the setting up of public enterprises.

Privatization Matters Arising

Benefit of Privatization

(i) Privatization of public enterprises will help to curb waste. The late Hazma Zayyad once said "Government staff do not create wealth but squander it".
(ii) Privatization will breed efficiency and reduce deadwoodism.
(iii) Privatization will ensure technology transfer given the situation that foreign investors will come with new technologies.
(iv) It will reduce government subsidy, this fund will be used to services other social services.

Demerits of Privatization

As stated earlier in this paper, the transfer was not done with required openness. A larger portion population alleged marginalization.

Most privatized companies were grossly under valued. Even in a story credited to Punch newspaper saying "NITEL Privatization not competitive."

(a) Labor Implication

Transferred employment – It has become a bit difficult for the disengaged employees to be re-absorbed into the privatized companies.

(b) Delay in payment of severance package to the disengaged workers eg Defunct Nigeria Airways.

(c) Expansion of over-saturated labor market.

In conclusion the current regime of President Yar'Adua has reconstituted national privatization council under the headship of Vice president Jonathan Goodluck to examine and make necessary restructuring of the enabling laws i.e privatization and commercialization act 28 1999 and make adjustment where due process is contravened.

CHAPTER SIX

NEWSPAPER, SOCIETY AND NATIONAL GROWTH

I n the beginning

It will do a world of good in this presentation to go back to history and trace the origin of newspapers. Permit me at this point to remind us of what Thomas Jefferson, George Washington and Henry Steel Commager said about the newspaper between 1787 and 1951.

Thomas Jefferson in 1787, commenting on the importance of newspapers stated: "Were it left to me to decide whether we should have a government without newspaper, or newspaper without a government, I should not hesitate a moment to prefer the latter." George Washington added that "For my part I entertain a high idea of the utility of periodical publications; in so much as I could heartily desire, copies of ... magazines, as well as common Gazettes, might be spread through every city, town, and village in the United States. I consider such vehicles of knowledge more happily calculated than any other to pressure the liberty, stimulate the industry, and ameliorate the morals of a free and enlightened people."

Henry Steel Commager on his own part had this to say about the newspaper: "Here is the living disproof of the old adage that nothing is as dead as yesterday's newspaper... This is what really happened, reported by a free press to a free people. It is the raw material of history; it is the story of our own times."

The history of newspaper could be traced back to about five centuries ago in Europe. Information, usually hard-written, about wars, economic conditions of the time, social and human interest features were circulated privately among merchants. What resembled a newspaper as we know it today first appeared in Germany in the late 1400's. This was in the form of news pamphlets and the content was highly sensationalized.

It was not until 1622 before the English-speaking world published their first newspaper titled The Weekly News. These were small pamphlets produced only when note-worthy events occurred. Many other titles came on stream after this. But the London Gazette, published in 1666, was the first true newspaper in English.

In the United States, the first ever newspaper with the title Public Occurrences appeared in 1690 in Boston, Massachusetts. This was short-lived as the colonial masters suppressed and arrested the publishers and the printed copies were destroyed. But in 1704 John Campbell, a postmaster at that time, started the Boston News-Letter heralded to be the first successful newspaper. Other titles were published in both New York and Philadelphia in the 1920's. One important thing to note is that it was the articles published in colonial papers and written by the revolutionary propagandists that actually influenced the American public opinion from reconciliation with England to full independence.

At the end of American Civil War in 1783, 43 newspapers were in print. Many more newspapers were then published afterwards which represented all manners and shades of political opinion. The press played a very important role in the liberation and building of the American nation. It also led to the establishment of the printing industry.

In the beginning of the life of newspapers it was only the wealthy people and the few literate ones that could afford to buy newspapers because of high prices. America was able to achieve universal literacy partly by the sudden availability of cheap and interesting reading materials.

Just like newspapers became established during the American struggle to end colonial rule and the subsequent civil war, Nigeria experienced similar condition which eventually led to the emergence of newspapers between 1920 and 1944. Newspapers were used as tools for propaganda by the founding fathers of Nigeria and the anti-colonists. A typical example was the establishment of the Pilot and Tribune Newspapers by the late elder statesmen, Nnamdi Azikiwe and Obafemi Awolowo respectively. Even though the media generally as wells as individual journalists were suppressed and all manner of punishment meted out on them by the colonial authorities they continued the struggle for national liberation until victory was achieved.

Before the nationalist struggle for independence, the Nigerian Press went through a process of evolution. It started with the early Christian Missionaries like Church Missionary Society (CMS), Catholic Mission, Methodist and Baptist between mid 1840s and late 1880s especially in the Southern part of Nigeria. It was the desire to spread the gospel of the Christian faith to the local people and in their local languages that led CMS to establish the very first newspaper in Abeokuta, the capital of the present day Ogun State. In order to discharge their core responsibilities of spreading their faith, the Christian press was established by mid 1850s and early 1920s. This eventually was used as an instrument against the oppressive rule of the colonialists.

The Press, like in America, helped in establishing the printing industry especially in the South West of Nigeria. Not only that, printing became both a trade and profession first in the South West then other parts of Nigeria such as Onitsha in the present Anambra State, followed. The South West took advantage of their early education and exposure to the Europeans, coupled with the fact that they were the target audience and about the first to embrace the new profession of journalism, dominated and still dominates industry.

During the struggle for independence, the press and the media in general became a potent social force used in promoting the political development of that geographical location that later became Nigeria. The main objective of the media during the nationalistic struggle was hostility toward the colonial suppression and oppression of foreign domination. It was a very big coincidence to see the interest of the media aligns with the national interest. And that seems to have remained the same till date. The media has always been used to promote national interest.

In America, the press is constitutionally regarded as the *"fourth realm or estate"*. In Nigeria, the Press is not only regarded as the "fourth realm", though not constitutionally, but also as the *"watchdog"* of the society. This "watchdog" role rather than hostility toward foreign domination and colonial oppression, the press turned their critical and adversary focus after independence, to the Nigerian government's bad governance.

Media, Law and Democracy

Between 1920's to the period leading to Nigeria's independence in 1960 as the modern Nigerian press, pioneered by Dr. Nnamdi Azikiwe and Chief Obafemi Awolowo evolved, an industry was created at the same time. Also it created a profession for many, especially those in the South West, and became a social force intended to liberate the people of Nigeria. It was during this period that the colonial government came up with some laws and ordinances to guide the press. Interestingly these laws and ordinances facilitated the government and media relationship aimed at fostering Nigeria's democratic process. Rather than continue to work together towards national growth, the press and the government began to perceive each other differently. The press perceived the government as an agent of oppression of the Nigerian people. The government on the other hand enacted laws to checkmate what they perceived as the excesses of the press. This created a big divide between the government and the press. The masses depend on the press to get their views and opinion across to the government.

Though there is no constitutional role for the press except a mention in section 22 of the 1999 Nigerian Constitution, it is still regarded as the fourth realm. In that section 22 of the 1999 constitution, the role of the media, apart from being the "watchdog" in terms of governance and guarding and advancing the freedom and the liberties of the people, it is the "policing institution over the fundamental objectives and direct principles of state policy as well as the citizen's fundamental rights".

Conclusion

The quality of the media determines the quality of life of the people in any society. The media is the fastest growing industry in the world today.

Newspaper provides a platform where government and the people meet on development issues.
Newspaper publication is a business of trust. It is a social contract between the operator and the society. The society depends on the reports of newspaper to order its life, while newspaper reports on activities occurring in the society. It is often said that newspaper or the media is a mirror of the society.

The media (print) is supposed to help set agenda for development. How they report issues of the day determines how the public will respond to development.

The media plays a critical role in informing, educating and entertaining the public.

If development is about people, and government is about driver of the development, then the media should oil the development process by accurately letting government know about the feelings of the citizens, while it also informs the citizens about the government programs and plans.

The media helps hasten development when it publishes truth and not falsehood or half truths.

In democracy, the media plays a central role in the promotion of citizenship participation in the democratic process. How they report events will determine the extent citizens will be ready to participate in sustaining democracy.

It is impossible to talk about national development without full engagement of the media. The irony is that, most times public officials see the media as an enemy instead of an ally in the government process. Particularly during the military regime, there was mutual distrust between the media and the government. But with the onset of democracy, that wall of distrust is coming down gradually. Hopefully with the enactment of Freedom of Information Bill, the media will be better able to serve the society.

Without the media, society will be in the dark, and government will be like someone winking in the dark: you know what you are doing, but no one knows what you are doing.

CHAPTER SEVEN

ECONOMIC AND SOCIAL DEVELOPMENTS IN AFRICA DURING THE COLONIAL PERIOD

The economy of West Africa during the colonial period can be described as dependent economy. Dependent in the sense that West Africa's fortunes were bound up with the export of a small number of primary products, the price of which was determined much more by events elsewhere. This was by changes in demand or in the supply from other countries than by any action or decision of the country itself. Only in the case of cocoa did West Africa supply a substantial proportion of the total world output of a commodity, and even in this case it was proving very difficult for the West African government to alter the price which the world market was prepared to pay.

After the conquest of West African territories, the British discovered that even the skeleton administration could not be established and maintained without some expenditure. The conquest provided the British with a new motive for promoting the economic development of the territories. The British had to create incomes so that they might be taxed indirectly if not directly.

The conquests of these territories coincide with a great change in the market situation. Raw materials were in high demand in Europe and so the territories became very important. The Lancashire cotton manufacturers of England now began to worry more about the price of raw cotton and about the sale of cloth and so they formed the British cotton grow Association in 1902 to promote the cultivation of cotton within the empire, especially in West Africa. The great soap manufacturing firm of Lever Brothers also began to take interest in the sources of its raw materials and entered the West African market in 1906.

The problem of high transport cost which has been the greatest obstacle to African progress was tackled by the colonial masters. They realized that if there were to be any serious agricultural development for exports, transportation system in West Africa had to be improved.

The construction of Railway lines by the British started from Freetown in Sierra Leone in 1896 from Sekandi in Ghana in 1898 and also from Lagos in Nigeria in 1898. Kano railway line did not reach the sea until 1912, while that of Enugu was in 1916. The link between Southern and Northern Nigeria was not effected until 1926. Although Kumasi was linked to Sekandi in 1903, it did not connect Accra until 20 years later. In Nigeria large areas remained without any effective railway service for a long time. To supplement the rail system and to facilitate administration, a considerable effort was also devoted to road construction.

The effects of this investment in transport led to increased exports from West Africa territories. In 1900 and ,1913 the exports from Gold Coast (Ghana) multiplied by about 5 times, those from Sierra Leone about 4 times those from Nigeria about 4 times, while imports from abroad rose in similar proportion. In Gold Coast Cocoa and Gold were exported from there, while cocoa, cotton, groundnut, palm oil, tin, timber from Nigeria. Cocoa, timber and Palm Oil were found in the former Western Region, Tin deposits were found in Jos Plateau, while cotton and groundnut were found in Kano in Northern Nigeria, Coal was found in Enugu.

The West African territories were making a lot of money from exports and by 1915 cocoa became the principal export of Gold coast. Cocoa was also the principal export from Nigeria and it yielded a lot of money for the country. After the 1st World War prices of raw materials rose sharply in world market and the West Africa territories made a lot of money during this time. Gold coast was the richest of the British territories at that time.

In fact, there was a big rise in production for export between 1918 and 1925, but after that, for several years, the volume of exports remained almost static. In 1930, West African territories were struck down by the world slump as prices of most of their exports were halved or more than halved.

The slump was especially disastrous for these countries

which had borrowed heavily from London to construct their Railway and larger exports was now required to pay interest on debts and the pensions of retired officials, but this was not possible at this time.

Social Development in Nigeria during the Colonial Period

Social development means development in education, health and other social activities. The missionaries laid the foundations of the developments in Education and Health in Nigeria. They started formal Education in Nigeria.

The first missionary school was built in 1842 by the Methodists led by Reverend Thomas Birch Freeman. The pupils of this school were taught reading , writing and bible knowledge. While Christians schools developed is the South, Koranic schools developed in the North. The pupils were taught to read and write Arabic and memorize the Koran.

The Christian missions started to provide secondary education as from the 2nd half of the 19th Century.

In 1859, the Church Missionary Society opened secondary school in Lagos while the Methodists and Roman Catholics founded Grammar schools in Lagos in 1878. In 1895 Hope Waddell Training Institute was established at Calabar. St. Andrew's College Oyo was founded in 1896, while Wesley College Ibadan was established in 1905.

The missionaries in fact monopolized education in Nigeria from the beginning, and until 1898 all education was under the direct control of the missionaries. The Christian missionaries also built hospitals, dispensaries and maternity homes in various parts of the country to care for the sick. In this way they helped to alleviate the suffering of the masses who were previously not getting medical care.

After the missionaries had laid the foundations, the government starts to grant aid, inspect them and participate in establishing government schools and state hospitals. The first government secondary school was opened in Lagos in 1899 i.e. King's College. In 1932, Yaba Higher College was founded. In 1948, University College was established in Ibadan and later a teaching hospital was added to the college and this became the first university to be established in Nigeria.

Nationalism in West Africa

Nationalism to some people means National feeling. This can be used to describe the Italian and German nationalism when they fought various wars of unification.

African Nationalism means opposition to foreign rule or a desire to eliminate colonialism. It also means the pride in African customs, traders and institutions.

Nationalism started in West Africa in the 19th Century when the African chiefs resisted the British occupation of their territories.

It is necessary to make two distinctions of nationalism. The first is the traditional nationalism and the second one is modern nationalism. Traditional nationalism refers to easily militant resistance of the African chiefs such as the Delta rulers like the famous King Jaja of Opobo, Nana of Ishekiri and others to the British penetration of the interior of the country. Also the early revolts by Africans were against the operation of foreign political or economic measures. An example was the Aba women's riot of 1929.

While modern nationalism means sentiments, activities opposed to foreign control, and organizational developments which were aimed clearly at attaining independence for West Africa countries. The Educated Africans at that time were the modern nationalist.

Factor Responsible for the spread of Nationalism (West Africa)

There were several factors which assisted the spread of nationalism in West Africa. It is however important to take note of the following internal and external factors like the impact of Western economic forces, impact of Christian missions, development of some African native press, nationalistic writings of some African leaders, the impact of the 1st and 2nd World Wars, etc.

The impact of the western economic forces was very important in the spread of nationalistic feelings in West Africa. In Nigeria for instance, the establishment of British Administration changed the Nigerian society. The changes included the growth of money economy, the drift towards wage employment, leading to the development of urban centers which became the training of Nigerian nationalism.

The western economic forces also led to economic grievances by the natives because the colonial government Europeans traders and expatriate firms controlled the economy of the West African territories. Expatriate firms like the U.A.C. dominated the trading life of many West African countries until recently. In 1930 UAC controlled more than 40% of Nigeria import and exports trade. Europeans also owned and controlled the banking and shipping facilities in Nigeria.

In fact, only petty trades were controlled by the natives, while the overall control of the economy of the West African territories was in the hands of the foreign firms which exploited the Africans.

However, the awareness by the natives of economic exploitation of West African by the British was one of the reasons which associated the spread of modern nationalism in West Africa. Finally, individual grievances led to uprising, local boycotts, strikes and protest movements.

The Christian missionaries also played a critical role in the field of nationalism in West African, by their evangelical activities and long monopoly in the field of Education. Schools were opened by the missionaries in the big towns where pupils were taught how to read and write. They started to provide Secondary Education as from the 2nd half of the 19th Century. The missionaries attacked our customs and old beliefs and gradually a new social system took the place of the traditional systems in the big towns.

By the beginning of the 20th Century, a great number of educated elites had emerged as the products of the Secondary Education. There educated elites were not given employments in the colonial administrative service, and so they antagonized the colonial governments and formed the core of nationalist movement.

The development of African Native Press marked an important stage in the spread of nationalistic feelings in West Africa. It was through the press as well as international conferences those political figures such as Dr. Nnamdi Azikiwe of Nigeria, Dr. J.B. Danquah of Ghana; Mr. Wallace Johnson of Sierra Leone became known. Many newspapers as well established in different parts of West Africa by indigenous Africans. Dr. Zik arrived in Nigeria late in the 1930s from Ghana to establish a series of presses (Newspapers) in the country. The most powerful one was the "West African Pilot" in Nigeria, which served as the medium for the expression and spread of nationalism in West Africa.

Nationalistic writings assumed greater dimensions especially after the 1st World War. Journalists like Caseley Hayfield of Ghana, Herbert Macaulay of Nigeria and a host of others started to write about the economic exploitations, social discriminations in the civil service and other ills of the colonial administration, and the desire to take active part in the guiding of our own national destiny. In their speeches and writings, some men as Leopold Senghor of Senegal, Dr. J.B. Danquah and Dr. Kwame Nkumah both of Ghana, Dr Zik and Awo of Nigeria had all contributed in no small way to the spread of nationalism in West Africa.

The impacts of the 1st and 2nd World Wars were

equally of much significance in aiding the spread of Nationalism in West Africa. The 1st started from 1914 – 1918 while the 2nd World War started from 1939 – 1945. Before and during the wars Africans suffered a lot of racial discriminations. The white men discriminated against blacks in the civil service. Many blacks were not employed and even those employed were treated as 2nd class citizens. Africans also suffered from inferiority complex. The Africans even regarded whites as semi-gods.

However, the 1st World War afforded the Africans the opportunity of knowing a lot about the Europeans. They discovered that the whites were not semi-gods and that there were some of them who were houseboys, labourers, messengers, cleaners etc. in their countries. After the war, the African ex-service men who came back home started revealing to their friends and relations at home those things they discovered about the whites in Europe. This revelation cost the whites dearly because they lost their fame and prestige in the eyes of the African. The enlightened Africans began to form nationalist movements; the most important one was the National Congress of British West Africa which was founded in 1920.

The effect of the 2nd World War also helped to speed up the pace of the nationalist movements in West Africa.

In this economic sphere, the 2nd World War boosted the economy of West African territories. Producers of cash crops gained a lot during this period, while the wage earners suffered greatly as a result of inflation. The influx of displaced soldiers increased unemployment.

There were other external factors like the Atlantic Charter of 1941, especially its famous third clause … "respect the right of all people to choose the form of government under which they live." The American influence of Africa was great because they attacked colonization and imperialism. The British Labour Part also opposed the idea of keeping colonies. It was these huge support from civilized people of the world that encouraged the Africans to rise against their colonial masters and which they did successfully.

National Congress of British West Africa

The rise of W.A. nationalism partially in Nigeria stimulated the formation of National congress of British W. Africa .The congress was found in 1920 in order that the people of African descent should participate in the government of their country.

The members of the congress met at Accra Ghana in 1920 under the championship of Caseley Hayford a well known Gold Coast (Ghana) Lawyer and attended by the representatives of the four B.W.A colonies made of Nigeria, Gold Coast, Sierra Leone and Gambia. It was decided that a delegation be sent to the secretary of state for the colonies in London to demand the following from British governor.

1.   The legislative council for each territory with half the members elected Africans.

2.   Control of taxation by African members of the legislative council.

3.   Appointment of and deposition of chiefs by their

own people.

4. Abolition of racial discrimination in the civil Service.

6. Establishment of a university in West Africa.

The delegation was flatly snubbed by the colonial secretary, Lord Milner when they reached London and after experiencing some financial difficulties they decided to return to Africa. The governor of Nigeria at that time was Sir Hugh Clifford who denounced the members of the congress in Nigerian council on 29th December, 1920 in very strong terms which show that he and his British officers had little sympathy for the African nationalists. He was also critical of the ideal of W. African unity. The demands of congress thought were regarded as fantastic by the British officials yet they exerted some influence on colonial affair in subsequent years. Sir Hugh Clifford who had once violently attacked the congress was also the father of the 1920 constitution, which for the first time in British W. A. provided for elected African members in the legislative council. The new constitution provided for a legislative council which constituted of 46 members, 27 of them officials and 19 of them were unofficial.

The provision of the legislative council in Nigeria and the allocation of three seats to Nigerians in the legislative council led to the emergence of parties and the first political party was called the Nigeria National Democratic party (NNDP). In the election of 1923 into the Nigerian legislative council the NNDP won all the seats as it also did in 1928 and 1933.

It can also be claimed that the activities of the

National Congress of B.W.A. led to the drafting of the New constitution for Ghana in 1925, and also to the establishment of a higher institution in Ghana called Achimota college in 1927. About the same time Fowah Bay College Sierra Leone was upgraded to the status of a higher institution. In Nigeria, Yaba college Lagos was established in 1922 and the other British Colonies later got their higher institutions. Finally, one can conclude by saying that the congress achieved a lot during the brief period of its existence despite the discouragement it got from the British government.

CHAPTER EIGHT

THE POLITICAL ECONOMY
OF HIGH OIL PRICES AND
THE LIBERALIZATION OF THE
DOWNSTREAM SECTOR

I t was 8:15am Monday January 7, 2008 and I was on air at Channels Television, Lagos, Nigeria, being interviewed by Yori and Angela on the implications of the recent high oil prices on the global and especially the Nigerian economy. It was just a 15minutes discussion and I could only say a little of what I would have wanted to say but for time. Anyone familiar with television broadcasting will understand why – time is of essence.

A couple of days earlier the price of crude oil had reached the magic US$100 per barrel, long anticipated by market analysts and speculators. There was great panic and unease across the world because of the attendant consequences to the world economy. Oil is a very important commonly in the world today because of its utility value. It is used in human and material mobility across the globe, land, air and sea. Few industries, if any, can do without it; not to talk about our homes.

Nigeria has been described as a monoeconomy because of oil. Oil constitute about 95 percent of Nigeria's revenue. Every annual budget of the Federal government is based on the expected or projected price of oil in the international market for that year. Government projects are financed with oil revenues. When the price of oil goes higher than the set benchmark, the excess revenue is deposited in the excess crude account or the government – Federal, state and local government – could go on a spending spree.

In the past five years, Nigeria has benefited from rising oil prices both in the domestic and international markets, but more especially in the international arena. In 1999, when the Obasanjo administration came to power the price of oil was around US$10 per barrel. In 2003, the price of oil rose to US$25 per barrel. The world experienced another increase in price of oil in 2005 which more than doubled in August to US$60 per barrel. Prices hovered between US$50 and US$60 in 2006 and early 2007. The price shut up again around July of 2007 to its all time high of US$98 per barrel and has remained within that range for a while until recently when it reached US$100 per barrel for a day or two before it went down again to ninety something dollars.

Between 2006 and 2007, Nigeria's oil production level was 2.2 million to 2.5 million barrels per day, making Nigeria the 6th biggest oil producing nation in the world. For every US$1 increase per year in the price of oil, Nigeria earns revenue equal to US$700 million. Nigeria's domestic consumption of refined crude (PMS) is 26 million liters per day. Since the refineries are not working and no new ones have been built, the refined crude is being imported from different parts of the world by the Nigerian National Petroleum Corporation (NNPC), which has recently been "calibrated" to different autonomous or semi-autonomous units for better "efficiency" (so they made us to believe).

The NNPC has a monopoly over the importation of PMS, AGO, Kerosene and other allied products. This monopoly encourages corruption and the government doesn't want to let go. When General Obasanjo came to power in 1999 he took control of the oil portfolio and refused to appoint a minister to oversee the sector. He held on tightly for the eight years he ruled and the present administration has maintained the status quo. Oil has been used, either in the form of oil blocks licenses or allocation to import or supply refined crude on behalf of NNPC, to sort out political I.O.U.s or to settle friends and party loyalists. No wonder the office of the Group Managing Director of NNPC is constantly besieged by rent seekers looking for oil allocation. These people should realize that the NNPC GMD has a major duty to carry out on a daily basis other than giving out allocation papers, and therefore should be allowed to perform those functions to move the industry forward, especially on the policy level.

Sometimes I wonder why someone has not sued either NNPC or the Federal government for monopolistic tendency or anti-competition behavior for reserving the sole right of importation of oil (refined crude) to NNPC. I hope one day, through the courage of someone, this situation could be tested in the court of law. The oil sector should be completely freed up from the government control. When the sector is completely liberalized, it will curb corruption and benefit the masses. I've often heard that the reason for non liberalization of the oil sector is because it will hurt the masses. My discussions with oil experts pointed otherwise. The corrupt Nigerian elite prefer the system of monopoly to enrich themselves more and impoverish the masses more.

This is what currently obtains. The government would want petrol to sell for N100 per liter, but instead it is being sold for N70 per liter (depending on which city or state you live or buy your petrol). So, the government provides subsidy of N30 per liter of petrol for domestic consumption. Since 26 million liters of petrol are consumed daily in the domestic market, therefore it means that the government spend about N780 million daily on subsidy or N285 billion or US$2.5 billion annually. But for corruption, I would have said this amount could have been invested to develop other sectors of the economy like agriculture or even research and development.

When the oil sector is completely liberalized it will encourage more competition. Even though the pump price of petrol in filling stations will be higher than the prevailing N70 per liter (could be N100 or more), in the short term, but in the long term it will benefit the masses. The pump price will eventually come down to an affordable rate because people will invest in new refineries and existing ones will be put to near capacity utilization. At the prevailing rate of N70 per liter, investors are reluctant to invest. Anybody can import petrol if they so wish rather than the current situation where NNPC has monopoly. One thing we should realize is that government monopoly, or any other form of monopoly for that matter, doesn't not augur well for our economy.

At this point let me take you back to the reasons why oil prices are rising in the global market space. Oil companies are usually blamed for high oil prices. But are they really or solely to be blamed? Several factors contributed to the high oil prices being experienced in the world today. Just like in other markets, demand and supply play a role in determining oil prices. Currently demand has caught up with supply. Be reminded that OPEC controls a huge portion of global oil supply. Production growth outside OPEC members is estimated at one percent or even less.

It is believed strongly by some players in the oil industry that prices will stay high because of growth in the developing economies. We have seen the growth being experienced in China and India. We can also see the impact of population in countries these countries. As the economies of these countries grow more people can afford to buy and drive cars. Also, as mobility increases and more fuel is consumed. As the developing economies grow, large amount of energy is required to drive their industries. Economic growth and development also improves the quality of life of people and that also impacts the demand for oil.

The current global oil consumption is in the region

of 85 million barrels per day. When there is demand pressure OPEC has the production capacity and inventories to handle it or offset it. There is also provision for surplus capacity by OPEC for about 3 million barrels per day. Saudi Arabia which sits on 25 percent of world's oil also holds the surplus production capacity. Apart from the above factors, there is the issue of geopolitical risks which also impacts on the upward swing of oil prices. The Niger Delta crisis in Nigeria has, in more than one occasion, contributed to the high oil price being experienced in the world. The role of oil speculators in the markets and oil politics should not be ruled out.

Implications to Nigeria's Economy

As earlier mentioned, for every US$1 increase in a year in the price of oil, Nigeria makes US$700 million in revenues. The higher the prices of oil in the global market place the more revenue that is accrued to Nigeria. But this gain is diluted or taken away by the subsidy provided by the government for domestic consumption. I mentioned earlier that the Federal government spends up to US$2.5 billion per year in oil subsidy.

Oil money is dollar denominated. So, when there is a slide in the value of the US dollar it impact on the value of oil revenue and Nigeria's foreign reserve. But the upside is that as the dollars slides the Naira firms up (appreciates) and therefore the value of the subsidy for domestic consumption reduces. Generally speaking, high oil price is not good for anybody because it disrupts the economy. If the price of oil gets too high, too quickly, it could lead to global economic recession, which is not healthy.

Alternative source of Energy

The major oil companies are investing in researching alternative sources of energy such as Geothermal, Hydrogen, Biodiesel and Biofuel. Some analysts have even predicted that the end of oil is very near. Others have said that Nigeria's oil well will last only 25 years. Well, I don't want to join issues here by playing God. The person that put oil deposits in different countries of the world knows the quantity and how long it is going to last. But let me say that even though alternative energy sources are currently being sought, the end of oil is not in sight. Statistics shows that between 160,000 and 200, 000 liters of refined crude is consumed per second in the world. This only represents one third of the total global energy system.

The Future

A Woodmark (an energy consulting firm based in Ireland) report showed that the Nigerian Government did not made any investment in the oil sector for exploration in the past five years (2005 - 2010). That means Nigeria has not replenished the oil it exports or uses domestically. The situation is akin to fetching water from a bucket without refilling the bucket hoping that water will remain the same. Experts believe that to maintain the level of 2.2 million barrels a day requires a reinvestment in exploration to achieve about 3.5 million barrels a day. Even though the end of oil is not in sight but it is very dangerous for Nigeria to continue to depend on oil for its economic survival and development. The future of Nigeria's economic growth and development is not in oil. Therefore the economy should be diversified and decentralized by paying attention to other sectors of the economy such as agriculture, manufacturing ICT, etc. Fixing the infrastructure is critical to growth and development. To play in this knowledge economy Nigeria must become competitive in several areas. Other OPEC members like Saudi Arabia are fast divesting from oil as a major source of revenue.

King Abdullah of Saudi Arabia has realized that the future of his country is not oil. So, he is spending US $12.5 billion to establish a graduate research university. This university is being endowed with US$10 billion on day one. This is equivalent to the amount MIT (USA) has as its endowment in its 142 years of existence. The goal of the Saudi Kings is to attract the best researchers in science and technology all over the world.

Nigeria should take a cue from Saudi Arabia, a fellow OPEC member, and restructure the economy. The future is in science and Technology, not oil.

CHAPTER NINE

*THE POLITICAL-ECONOMY OF
ANTI CORRUPTION CRUSADE:
THE NIGERIAN EXPERIENCE
(2003-2007) – Taiwo Akerele*

I ntroduction

The word "corruption" is very popular in Nigerian political and social-economic lexicon due to the high rate of the involvement of the state, the civil society and members of the public in the fight against it in recent times. Corruption in Nigeria became very rampant under the regime of the former military president Ibrahim Babangida between 1986-1993, it was generally believed that this period witnessed the worst form of corruption that continued unabated till the Abacha regime which saw most public wealth been traced to secret accounts in Europe and other parts of the world while the Nigerian state continued to be at the receiving end of the negative effects of this practices. This situation led to the conclusion made by Gboyega (1996) that it was as if the government existed so that corruption might thrive.

The state of corruption in Nigeria before the advent of the Obasanjo regime in 1999 was captured in a speech the former President delivered in 2003 inter alia;

"this process (corruption) was accompanied, as to be expected, by the intimidation of the judiciary, the subversion of due process, manipulation of existing laws and regulations, the suffocation of the civil society, and the containment of democratic processes and institutions....power became nothing but a means of accumulation and subversion as productive initiatives were abandoned for purely administrative and transactional activities...the legitimacy and stability of the state became compromised as citizens began to devise extra-legal and informal ways of survival"[2]

Though some analysts and scholars believe that the incidences of corruption started manifesting in the first republic, the consensus of most observers is that Nigeria and indeed Nigerians started feeling the negative impact of corruption within and outside of Government from the middle eighties.

The above situation of the state of corruption in Nigeria, which the Obasanjo administration met in 1999 made it imperative to embark on a prolonged war and crusade against the scourge; this inevitably led to the establishment of the Economic and Financial Crimes Commission (EFCC) and the independent Corrupt Practices Commission (ICPC) in 2004.

The focus of this paper is to take a critical look at some of the issues arising from the fight against corruption amidst alleged politicization of the whole exercise by a cross section of Nigerians.

What is Corruption?

The word corruption has been defined by various scholars and social scientists as a situation where public trust is abused by individuals entrusted with the responsibilities of carrying out certain duties on behalf of the state. The Swedish International Development Agency (SIDA 2005) defines corruption as when organizations or individuals profit improperly through their position in an activity, and thereby cause damage or loss. Corruption can be found in all countries but is particularly widespread in states where the legal system, mass media and the public administration are weak. In other words, corruption according to this view occurs worldwide, but its prevalence is more pronounced in developing countries as a result of weak or inefficient institutions to the extent of the undeveloped state of those countries involved.

This view is corroborated by Segun Osoba (1996) when he opined that "Corruption is a global phenomenon, intelligible only in its social context. It can been defined as anti-social behavior conferring improper benefits contrary to legal and moral norms, and which undermines the authorities' capacity to secure the welfare of all citizens. In Nigeria it became the principal means of private accumulation during the de-colonization period, in the absence of other means, and came to shape political activity and competition after independence. All subsequent regimes, military and civilian, have been pervaded by corruption. Aided and enhanced by oil revenues, this has created a deepening crisis of kleptocracy, shown in is most extreme form since 1984.

It results in a combination of scandalous wealth among the ruling class with growing poverty, misery and degradation among the mass of Nigerians. Political life has become dominated by winner-take-all factional struggles, political cynicism and violence, while the economy and social institutions have been driven into decay. Corruption has thus become a way of life in Nigeria, one which existing governments neither wish to, nor can, control. Combating corruption requires a popular participatory democracy able to monitor and hold to account those in charge of the state and the treasury"

The department of Ethics of the Taipei Government sees corruption from various definitive angles as follows:

Crime of Making Profits: It means that the public official takes advantage of the business under his authority or supervision to make private profits directly or indirectly, or takes advantage of his authority, opportunity or identification to use the business that is not under his supervision to make profits. This is the most common type of corruption.

Crime of Accepting Bribe: It means that the public official accepts bribe or other illegal interests related his duty. If the public official knows that the process or result does not meet the requirement of the law, but after receiving some benefits from the applicant, the public official illegally handle the application, then he has committed the crime of accepting bribe. Another type of accepting bribe is that the public official accepts the bribe but does not do anything violating his duty. We call such corruption "crime of accepting bribe without violating duty".

Crime of Accepting Commission: It means that when handling public works or purchasing material or supplies for public use, the public official knows that he should pay the supplier but asks the supplier to send him some money in a certain proportion or deduct some money for his private use.

Crime of Occupying Public Properties: It means that the public official occupies the properties handled by him. We also call this type of corruption "embezzlement". After finishing the act of occupation, the crime will be still regarded as committed even if the properties were returned by the public official.

Transparency International (Ireland) defines corruption in a 2006 report as the misuse of entrusted power for private gain". It is a global problem which can take many forms in state, corporate and non-profit sectors. Whatever its guise, corrupt behavior is always determined by ulterior motives, with no concern for the consequences for the wider community. But the Independent Commission against Corruption (ICAC) defines the act of Corruption as involving breaching public trust....corruption leads to inequality, wasted resources and wasted public money. However, Transparency in Palestine differentiates between Corruption according to rule and Corruption against the rule....facilitation payments, where a bribe is paid to receive preferential treatment for something that the bribe receiver is required to do by law, constitute the former. The latter, on the other hand, is a bribe paid to obtain services the bribe receiver is prohibited from providing. (TI. Palestine; 2005)

Corruption is encountered in the routine processes of government both in public and private sectors, and it pollutes the business environment generally. It undermines the integrity of government and public institutions (Aiyede; 2005). The word corruption has gained international dimension owing to its destructive tendencies and its capacity to undermine the common good of the public. In the opinion of Lipset and Lenz (2000) it is an effort to secure wealth or power through illegal means for private benefit at public expense while Sen (1999) defines corruption as the violation of established rules for personal gains and profit. Such an abuse of public power may not necessarily be for one's party, class, tribe, friend or family (Tanzi 1998).

Corruption manifests in several dimension depending on the location where it is perpetuated, in Africa and parts of South America, corruption is measured with the level of development or underdevelopment in terms of access to health facilities by the mass of the people, the state of infrastructures in schools, infant mortality rate, and the state of both state and rural roads. The condition of the people in the Niger Delta region of Nigeria especially the state of shelter is a pure manifestation of the level of official corruption that has characterized governance in the region (Komolafe 2005).

Types, Forms and Dimension of Corruption

Several International agencies including Transparency international (TI) the world bank, Human Rights watch and the Namibia's Zero Tolerance for Corruption Campaign (NTCC) in a unanimous research, identified 14 principal forms of corruption as follows;

BRIBERY: The promise, offer or giving of any benefit that improperly affects the actions or decisions of a public official. A bribe may be given to a public servant (direct), or to another person or entity (indirect). A bribe may consist of money, inside information, gifts, entertainment, sexual or other favors, a job, company shares etc. A variation of bribery occurs where a political party or government is offered, promised or given a benefit that improperly affects the decisions of or actions by the party or government. The word bribe, in Middle English and Old French, meant a piece of bread given as alms.

Embezzlement: Theft of resources by persons entrusted with authority and control over these valuable resources.

Fraud: A criminal deception, involving some form of trick, false pretence or representation to obtain a benefit or gain unjust advantage.

Extortion: Unlawfully and intentionally gaining some advantage, material or immaterial, from another person or entity by placing illegitimate pressure in the form of threats or intimidation to force him/her to hand over the benefit. This coercion can be under the threat of physical harm, violence or restraint and may even be a threat that a third party will suffer injury. The accused must intend his/her words to be interpreted and act as a threat. (S)He must also intend to gain some advantage as a result of the threat while knowing that the threat is illegal.

Abuse of Power: Using one's vested authority to improperly benefit or give undue preferential treatment to any group or individual (or using vested authority to discriminate against any group or individual).

Conflict of Interest: Acting or failing to act on a matter where an individual has an interest, or where another person or entity which stands in a relationship with this individual has an interest.

Insider Trading: Engaging in transactions or acquiring positions or commercial interests that involve the use of privileged information and knowledge that a person possesses as a result of his/her position to provide unfair advantage to another person, entity or to the person him-/herself.

Unlawful Gratuity: The receipt of anything of value as extra compensation for performing official duties from others wishing to conduct business with the agency, institution or organisation.

Favoritism: The provision of services or resources according to personal affiliations such as family ties, party affiliation, tribe, religion, sect and other preferential groupings.

Others are nepotism, illegal contribution, money laundering, identity theft and white collar crime which involve a series of premeditated crimes perpetrated in sophisticated financial environments by an individual or group of individuals with the intention of making a misrepresentation which may prejudice another person or company.

Cost of Corruption

The cost of corruption on the development of a society cannot be estimated. Aside the obvious fact that corrupts practices retard social growth; it engenders social mistrust and breeds violence as a result of social-disconnection. In Nigeria, corruption has been blamed for the level of poverty and wanton neglect of social infrastructures nation-wide. Corruption as it were is a social malaise that leads to the avoidable death of children, women and people in urgent need. Corruption leads to road mishaps, plane crashes and institutional failure. Social polices are haphazardly implemented and therefore leads to inaction on the part of the state due to factors emanating from corruption and corrupt practices.

Transparency in Palestine, in its 2006 report says the cost of corruption can be quantified using different approaches viz ; political, economic, social, and environmental. On the political front, corruption constitutes a major obstacle to democracy and the rule of law. In a democratic system, offices and institutions lose their legitimacy when they are misused for private advantage. Though this is harmful in the established democracies, it is even more so in newly emerging ones. Accountable political leadership can not develop in a corrupt climate. Economically, corruption leads to the depletion of national wealth. It is often responsible for the funnelling of scarce public resources to uneconomic high-profile projects, such as dams, power plants, pipelines and refineries, at the expense of less spectacular but more necessary infrastructure projects such as schools, hospitals and roads, or the supply of power and water to rural areas. Furthermore, it hinders the development of faith in state functions.

The world bank in a report released in 2004, insists that More than $1 trillion dollars (US$1,000 billion) is paid in bribes each year, according to ongoing research at the World Bank Institute (WBI)....the reports says this US$1 trillion figure is an estimate of actual bribes paid worldwide in both rich and developing countries....The $1 trillion figure, calculated using 2001-02 economic data compares with an estimated size of the world economy at that time of just over US$30 trillion...this does not include embezzlement of public funds or theft of public assets...It is extremely difficult to assess the extent of worldwide embezzlement of public funds, but we do know it is a very serious issue in many settings." For example Transparency International estimates that former Indonesian leader Suharto embezzled anywhere between $15-35 billion from his country, while Ferdinand Marcos in the Philippines, Mobutu in Zaire and Abacha in Nigeria may have embezzled up to $5 billion each.

The impact of corruption on the social fabric of a nation is negative in consequences and makes the political stability of the affected society vulnerable and its unity questionable. Corruption weakens democratic institutions. Political costs manifest themselves above all in loss of legitimacy, and of public trust and support, Leads to competitive bribery, instead of fair competition based on price, quality and innovation. This harms trade and investment, Threatens the environment. When environmental protection agencies are corrupt, the very foundations of human development are eroded, Fosters human rights abuse. As corruption increases, regimes become more secretive and desperate...." (TI Ireland 2006).

Fighting The Scourge: The Nigerian Experience

Two fundamental issues that formed the focus of the Obasanjo regime when it came into power in 1999 were the social issues of corruption and energy crisis. In his inauguration speech in 1999, General Obasanjo pointed to pervasive corruption as the biggest problem facing Nigeria. In that speech, he essentially promised Nigerians that he would make fighting corruption a major priority for his government. (Ike Naijaman;2003). This commitment led to the establishment of several panels of enquiry to look into some public policies and actions of past government that tended to be shrouded in controversy or corruption stained. Retired Supreme Justice Nwazota was appointed to lead the investigation of the near-bankrupt national aviation flag carrier *THE NIGERIAN AIRWAYS* In November 2003, the Commission's report was finally made public. The report blamed former top officials of the airline, former members of the Federal cabinet, and former high-ranking civil servants, for the corporation's financial collapse. Among other things, the Commission recommended that the indicted individuals refund varying sums of money they wasted or misappropriated.

Furthermore, in a separate incident in December 2003,

the Government sacked the then Minister for Internal Affairs, Chief Sunday Afolabi who was a very influential member of Government and the ruling party (PDP and some senior members of the civil service and others. These actions were taken in response to revelations of corruption and bribery in connection with the National ID Card Scheme. In another recent scandal, Housing Minister Mobolaji Osomo was sacked for selling government properties in a wealthy Lagos area without due process to government officials and prominent citizens, including close relatives of Obasanjo's wife, a fact that caused the president to express personal embarrassment. Critics allege that the presidency had been aware of the deals and, unlike the other disgraced officials, Osomo faces no charges. (SAIIA; 2005).

To coordinate the fight against corruption, the government in 2003 established the Economic and Financial Crimes Commission otherwise known as the EFCC, the act establishing it was ratified and passed by the national assembly in 2004. What constitutes economic crime and what is the relationship with corruption? Economic and financial crimes are kindred offences with an extremely thin line separating them. All economic crimes are financial crimes but not all financial crimes are economic crimes.

Economic crimes are those crimes that have a damaging effect on the economic and political system of the country. Their damage to the international image of the country is more important than the direct financial loss. These include corruption, embezzlement of public funds, fake currency running, smuggling, drug trafficking, etc. Section 46 of the Economic and

Financial Crimes (Establishment) Act, 2004 defines Economic Crimes which include the non-violent criminal and illicit activity committed with objective of earning wealth illegally, any form of fraud, money laundering, illegal oil bunkering, tax evasion, dumping of toxic wastes, etc. Financial Crimes on the hand are those committed not only with the intention of getting financial benefit but they are targeted directly on funds and financial instruments. These include advance fee fraud, currency trafficking and counterfeiting, etc. From the above, it can be seen that while all economic crimes are financial crimes, not all financial crimes need be economic crimes. Whatever form they take, the objective is to earn wealth illicitly. (Nuhu Ribadu; 2004)

Since the commission came into being, it has waged relentless war against corruption within and outside Nigeria against public officials, conmen otherwise known as "419" and high ranking Nigerian politicians. The arrest of Chief DSP Alamieseigha, the former Governor of Bayelsa state in London and subsequent detention in Nigeria is considered a major break, this is against the backdrop of critics pessimism that he may have been a victim of political rig-marole within the rank and file of the Nigerian political elite.(Akerele; 2006).

The EFCC under the leadership of Nuhu Ribadu has been quite effective in carrying out its statutory roles (Ojewale 2006). It has acquired experience in handling cases of advance fee fraud such as obtaining by false pretence, contract scam, credit card scam, inheritance scam, counterfeiting and religious scam, immigration scam and cases involving banks etc (Aiyede; 2006). In

2006, the EFCC spearheaded the prosecution of a former Inspector General of Police, Tafa Balogun who was alleged to have embezzled several millions of dollars of police funds into his private accounts. In the same vein, former Governor Dariye was intercepted in London by the Metropolitan Police for money laundering, this was done in collaboration with the EFCC. The sum of One Million Pounds cash was recovered from him and his accomplices arrested for interrogation. He was eventually impeached in Nigeria and went into exile until the Supreme Court declared his impeachment illegal in May 2007 (THISDAY; March 9, 2007)

In its bid to fight corruption headlong in Nigeria, several state Governors and their commissioners have been quizzed at one time or the other on corruption charges. While many observers insist that the investigation is selective, the Commission argues that its work is driven by patriotic zeal and within the ambit of the law (see Ribadu; 2004). The Petroleum Technology Development Fund (PTDF) scandal was blown opened by the EFCC in 2005. The involvement of the Vice President Atiku Abubakar made this case a high profile one (Dan Isaacs; 2007). Though the alleged third term ambition of Chief Olusegun Obasanjo and the opposition of the Vice President to it is believed to be the root of the investigation (SAIIA;2006)

In the run up to the 2007 elections, several Nigerian politicians were alleged to have been indicted by the Government based on EFCC report (Thisday April 4, 2007. several leading candidates which cuts across party lines including the leading Peoples Democratic Party were named in the list, However the opposition parties cried fowl as to the casualty rate of its members especially the Action Congress whose platform the Vice President ran (Thisday; March 16, 2007). The indicted candidates list which was timed to coincide with the elections raised serious suspicion as to the non-partisan nature of the activities of the Commission (Thisday February 11, 2007).

The slow process of the Judiciary in Nigeria, made the Commission to take steps in designating special fast-track courts to facilitate prosecution of indicted persons. This is aimed at reducing bottlenecks, legal technicalities and facilitates justice dispensation. This initiative has helped the commission in no small measure in its bid to get justice dispensed. (www.effccnigeria.org)

The Political Fireworks

Although President Obasanjo was often criticized for turning his anti-corruption fight into a political witch-hunt, Nigeria has seen some recent success in trying to minimize corruption...The country is now 18 places above Haiti on Transparency International's global corruption index after occupying last place for years. (Sennan Murray; May 2007). The fears expressed by critics of the anti-corruption crusade, may not be misplaced when a content analysis of Chief Olusegun Obasanjo's body language is put into contextual analysis in his last few years in office. One, the President was quoted to have declared that many of the allegations against some Governors are spurious (Thisday; October 2006) this is against the position of the EFCC Chairman, Nuhu Ribadu who had declared that save for 5 Governors, all the other Governors are undergoing one form of investigation over corruption or the other (Punch; September 27 2006).

Secondly, the President was believed to have shielded the investigation of Peter odili (Rivers), Chimaroke Nnamani (Enugu) and James Ibori (Delta) because of their close affinity to the Presidency (Komolafe; 2006). Beyond officialdom, however, a plausible explanation is that the anti corruption campaign of this administration risks being enmeshed in an intractable politics, and this is the point that the President, EFCC and the public should be wary of.... This is no time to reduce the anti-corruption campaign to politics (Komolafe et al).

The war on corruption in Nigeria has been lauded and described as a right step in the right direction by some analysts, but the reality is that most of the state Governors are upset and angry that under Obasanjo second term, it is no longer business as usual for them. They are no longer free to loot Government treasuries, live in opulence and think they can easily get away with it (Kofarmata ; 2005). Others believe that the war on corruption cannot be fully tackled if the civil society is not actively engaged in the process. The war against graft in Nigeria is yet to begin... it will begin the day civil society organizations (CSO) plan their own programs, source their own funds and take the initiative in executing such programs, it will begin when CSOs can muster enough strength to compel the President and any other senior public official to shed their pretense or immunity and declare their assets publicly and subject themselves to the same kind of probe as anyone else (Asobie, Asisi ; 2005).

Conclusion

In the final analysis, the fight against corruption anywhere in the world is a fight and battle against forces that benefits from its existence. Nicholo Machiavelli captured this situation and social dilemma long ago when he asserted that;

'there is nothing more susceptible to failure than social change, the reformer finds an enemy from those who benefited from the old older and finds lukewarm support from those who may benefit from the new".

This statement is apt when situated within the context of the war against corruption in Nigeria. The anti-corruption war has come under very serious criticism and scathing remarks by members of the civil society Groups on the basis that the operations of the anti-corruption agency lacks respect for human freedom, while legal experts insist that the rule of law is rendered useless by the agency, because of its alleged disregard for court orders. The political class has often argued that the war on corruption is targeted at the opposition, to silence them and render them perpetually powerless. (Tom Zeller; Feb 2007).

The activities of the anti-corruption agency may be described as having been organized in a stage or phase basis. When the commission commenced operations in 2004, it started with Cyber criminals, graduating to international fraudsters who have soiled Nigeria's image abroad for many years. This effort led to the prosecution of several 419 kingpins and others went underground. The commission became controversial when it got to the stage of prosecuting public office holders beginning with civil servants and high profile politicians. Through its anti corruption crusade, the two agencies involved, the ICPC and the EFCC have reportedly saved several billions of naira for the Government which it allegedly recovered from syndicates, criminals and public officer holders (Tom op.cit).

The president, Chief Obasanjo whose style of governance has been described as *imperialistic* (Aluko; 2005), *ruthless, vindictive, unforgiving* (Atiku; 2007), *lawless, dictatorial* (Soyinka), *deceitful, insincere, hypocritical,* (Action Congress), *desperate* (Solomon Lar) *corrupt* (sahara reporters), self serving, *anti-people, anti-democratic* (Kasim Afegbua), all these made the operations of the anti-corruption agencies difficult due to his perceived overbearing influence on the activities of the commission. This posture and the big Government syndrome (Komolafe; op cit) that characterized his eight year rule almost marred and politicized the entire anti-corruption crusade. Other than these, stakeholders in the political –economy of Nigeria, members of the international community and civil society Groups have always been unanimous in commending the political will of the Government in prosecuting the war against what Transparency International refers to as a "scourge against humanity, human growth and development.

CHAPTER TEN

ENTREPRENEURSHIP, DEMOCRATIC TRANSITION AND SUSTAINABLE DEMOCRACY

I can still recall with clarity, even if through the eyes of a child, how on that glorious dawn of October 1 1960 I got off the back of a horse, guided by my father, inspired to believe that the future was a frontier of limitless optimism. As I enter middle age watching a generation that did not behold the enormous hope of the founding fathers, who today look to the future in despair, I cannot reflect on the consequences for our democratic transition after so many failed efforts at building a stable democracy.

The promise of democracy is one in which it is expected that economic freedom and the central place of the dignity of the human person will unleash energies and creativity that will lead to economic growth. That phenomenon, economic growth, has eluded Nigeria with consequent quality of life challenges, large scale unemployment and social strife.

The relationship between democratic life and economic progress often manifested in a robust middle class is remarkably exemplified by the experience of Taiwan where the Gini co-efficient, the measure of income distribution has been altered dramatically from the 1940s to the 1990s when it was established as a newly industrializing country. The difference between a Taiwan that produced such improved quality of life for the broad masses of its citizenry was the enterprise culture. An entrepreneurial Taiwan in which economic freedom bred material progress remains an example for us in Nigeria. Unfortunately leadership culture in Nigeria has not been able to erect a tradition of entrepreneurship, preferring instead a tradition of economic rent-seeking and corruption that has become systemic.

To have a truly sustainable democracy we must have a sturdy middle class and the path to that is a culture of enterprise, Institutional arrangements that reduce corruption and create conditions for economic growth. The alternative, I am afraid, is already manifesting itself in the emerging vision of Nigeria projected in the scenario planning of many. The question we must therefore pose is how Nigeria can get out of this rot. If our democratic transition is not to be a journey down the path to Robert Kaplan's vision of the coming anarchy or down the road to Somalia we mush pay attention to property rights, the mystery of capital, the rule of law and encouraging entrepreneurship.

On The Rule of Law

In the main, the concept of the rule of law deals with experience which has led men to distrust power as it relates to the citizens if the parameters of engagement where not co- defined and the supremacy of that legal code enshrined in the spirit of governance.

The long history of absolute rulers in human experience led those seeking a more just order to articulate the need to be more trustful of laws than the heart or the conscience of man to define the relationship between state and society or power and the citizen. It is perhaps most clearly articulated by the founding fathers of the first new nation. As John Adams, the second President of the United States put it: "The Executive shall never exercise the legislative and judicial powers or either of them, to the end that it may be a government of laws and not of men."

This is the origin of the frequent reference to a government of laws and not of men as the essence of the rule of law. Embedded in this definition is also the idea of separation of powers. As another one of the founding fathers of the American nation, James Madison wrote "the accumulation of all powers, legislative, executive, and judiciary, in the same hands ..... may justly be pronounced the very definition of tyranny. These views of men seeking to design a modus vivendi that would free them from the monarchist absolutism they were fleeing from in Europe were indeed inspired in such thinking by words written by Thomas Paine in the monograph "Common Sense" which is very usually given credit for sparking off the American Revolution. Paine coined the phrase "the law is king"

Toni Fine who teaches law at the Benjamin Cardoso School of Law in the New York, he was guest of the Concerned Professionals to speak on the subject of the Rule of Law and sustainable democracy. In that lecture she defined the Rule of Law as "having rules that are established, known, accepted and respected by both government and non-government actors. Rule of Law invokes a predictable legal system with fair, transparent and effective judicial institutions to protect citizens against the arbitrary use of state authority and lawless acts.

In the African context Mark S Ellis in a paper presented in Abuja in 2004 quotes Sternford Moyo, past president of the law society in Zimbabwe.

"The Rule of Law is the antithesis of the existence of wide, arbitrary and discretionary powers in the hands of the executive or the legislature. The Rule of Law is a celebration of individual rights and liberties and all the values of a constitutional democracy characterized by the absence of unregulated executive or legislative power. It is a celebration of the concept of separation of powers and the checks and balances that form part of that concept. In a society in which rule of law is observed, through the mechanism of judicial review, executive decisions and legislative enactments which are outside the framework of the law are declared invalid thereby compelling both the executive and the legislature to submit to enjoyment, by the individual, of all right and liberties guaranteed by the constitution."

The rule of law and the institutions that support it have been a major consequence for American prosperity.

This is particularly so for the relationship between the rule of law, property rights and entrepreneurial initiative. Critical among these properties is the need to defend the rule of law.

Defending the Rule of Law

Even where the rule of law has become the gradation, power is constantly tempted to turn to arbitrariness. It is in the nature of power not to want to be restrained, after all one of the most enduring definitions of power, by Robert Dahl, says it is the ability of A to make B do what he would not ordinarily want to do.

In recent months the first new nation with its heritage of a nation under law and not man has been going through challenges to the rule of law. Approximately the conscience of America has been aroused in some quarters and some soul searching has been inspired.

Former Vice-President Al Gore in what is perhaps his most impressive speech since losing the Presidential elections in 2000 to George W. Bush recently drew attention to the erosion of the rule of law in America.

Al Gore makes the point of the wire tapping of Martin Luther King Jnr phones by the father fascist-oriented FBI of J Edgar Hoover. He says: "The discovery that the FBI conducted this long-running and extensive campaign of secret electronic surveillance designed to infiltrate the inner workings of the Southern Christian Leadership Conference, and to learn the most intimate details of Dr King's life, was instrumental in helping to convince congress to enact restrictions on wiretapping. And one result of this was the Foreign Intelligence and

Surveillance Act (FISA), which was enacted expressly to ensure that foreign intelligence surveillance would be presented to an impartial judge to verify that there, is indeed a sufficient cause for the surveillance..."

I have argued in the past that we need champions for mentoring and entrepreneurship extension services. We have to broadcast across the land the value of deferred gratification and value creation. The examples of Malaysia's experience with liberating the Malay poor should serve us well.

It is only such a bold vision in a new leadership that can return Nigeria to the promise I saw from under the neem tree after I got off the horse on the Aba Road in Sabon Gari here in Kano in 1960, on that 1st day of October when the potential of our great nation loomed large in a country where though tribe and tongue may differ but in brotherhood we stood.

CHAPTER ELEVEN

CONTROL OF THE COERCIVE
FORCE BACKING THE
AUTHORITY OF GOVERNMENT
– author unknown

(a)Police

The Nigerian federal system is the full-blown type not only because it assigns to both the centre and the states a reasonably adequate area of exclusive power, but also because it established for each a separate and autonomous governmental apparatus for the exercise of its assigned powers – legislature, executive council, civil service, judicature, etc. It is thus unlike the federal arrangement in Kenya under its Independence Constitution which made the regional governments dependent upon the federal civil service for the execution of their law and services.

One important exception to this relates to the Police. The State Governments are not provided with a separate coercive apparatus for the maintenance of their authority and the enforcement of their laws. A single police force, the Nigeria Police, is established for both tiers of government, which is sanctioned by the explicit prohibition of the establishment of any other police force in the Federation (s. 194(1)). While the arrangement of a single police force for the country has existed since Independence, it was supplemented by a provision under the 1960/63 Constitutions which permitted the Regions to have local police forces on a provincial basis. This has made it possible for the northern and western Regional Governments to retain and expand the local police forces established and maintained by some of their native authorities under the Native Authority Ordinance of 1943. No such local police forces existed however, in the Eastern Region before 1960 nor were any established later by virtue of the provision in the 1960/63 Constitution authorizing their establishment.

Unfortunately, the local police forces in the North and West were turned into local arms of the parties in power in the two regions, becoming ready tools for the oppression and harassment of political opponents. In the North, in particular, the native authority police were hardly separable from the party thugs, with whom they closely collaborated in the intimidation, arbitrary mass arrests and detention, lynching and other acts of persecution of party opponents. For this reason, the authority given to the Region by the 1960/63 Constitutions to set up local police forces was, quite rightly, abolished by the military in 1966; the existing local forces were integrated into the Nigeria Police Force under the unified command of the commissioner of police of the State and overall authority of the inspector-general.

The question that arises is whether a single police for both tiers of government is compatible with federalism. There is certainly no inherent incompatibility between them. It all depends on how the control of the force is organized. A single police force has the advantage that it exposes the individual to less risk of oppression than one under the autonomous control of his State Government. This consideration should override all others. What makes the arrangement under the 1979/99 Constitutions objectionable is the fact that the control of the police is unduly centralized in the Federal Government unlike before when the Regional Governments were given a greater participation in its control.

Such participation took the form partly of mandatory consultation with a regional premier in the appointment of a police commissioner for his Region, and partly in the establishment of a police council, with the federal and regional premiers as members, charged with the general supervision of the organization and administration of the force, not being matters relating to the operational control to the force or the appointment, removal and disciplinary control of members, which were vested respectively in an inspector-general and the Police Service Commission. While the vesting of the operational control of the Police in an inspector-general and the appointment, removal and disciplinary control of its members (other than the inspector-general) in a Police Service Commission is retained in the 1979/99 Constitutions, consultation with the state governor in the appointment and removal of the state police commissioner is not. This is a mistake. The 1979/99 Constitutions also err in vesting in the President the appointment and removal of the Inspector-General of Police, instead of it in the Police Service Commission as was the case under the 1963 Constitution.

The appointment of the Inspector-General of Police by the President is clearly incompatible with the constitutional position of the force as an agency common to both the federal and state governments for the enforcement of the authority which they each exercises as a government. It practically nullifies the value of vesting command of the police in a non-partisan, professional police man, the Inspector-General, since he cannot afford to be too independent of the Federal Government in the exercise of his command without, thereby, risking removal. It is certainly incompatible with the autonomy of a state government under a federal system that the only organized coercive force on which it relies to maintain its authority and to enforce its laws should be under the control of the Federal Government through the power to appoint and remove its head and commander. The participation of the State Governments in the exercise of this power is necessary in order that the arrangement of a single police may be reconciled with the autonomy of the State Government. The power should be vested in the Nigeria Police Council whose membership comprises the President, all the State Governors and Chairman, Police Service Commission. The 1999 Constitution now vests in the Police Council, the organization and administration of the Force and all other matters relating thereto (not being matters relating to the use and operational control of the Force or the appointment, disciplinary control and dismissal of the members), thus remedying a shortcoming in the 1979 Constitution which did away with the Police Council altogether.

The failure of the 1979 and 1999 Constitutions to provide, as did the 1963 Constitution, that the State Governor must be consulted by the Police Service Commission on the appointment and removal of the state police commissioner is also incompatible with federalism in needlessly undermining the authority of the Governor vis-à-vis the police commissioner. Indeed, the appointment, removal, transfer and disciplinary control of a state police commissioner should require the approval of the Governor, not just consultation with him.

The vesting of the command or the control of the operational use of the Nigeria Police Force in non-partisan, professional policeman is, however, qualified by the power given to the President or a State Governor to give "lawful" directions to the Inspector-General or the State Police Commissioner respectively with respect to the use of the Police Force for maintaining and securing public safety and public order without thereby making the President or the State Governors part of the command structure of the Force in the sense in which that term is understood within an organized, disciplined force.

It is necessary to set out the provision in section 215(4) in its precise wording:
"(4) Subject to the provision of the section, the Governor of a State or such Commissioner of the

Government of the State as he may authorize in that behalf may give to the Commissioner of Police of that State such lawful directions with respect to the maintenance and securing or public safety and public order within the State as he may consider necessary, and the Commissioner of Police shall comply with those directions or cause them to be complied with.

Provided that before carrying out any such directions under the foregoing provisions of this subsection the Commissioner of Police may request that the matter be referred to the President or such Minister of the Government of the Federation as may be authorized in that behalf by the President for his directions." (Emphasis supplied.) Section 215(3) empowers the President, in more or less identical terms (but without the qualification in the proviso in section 215(4), to give the same directions to the Inspector-General.

The critical question arising from the constitutional arrangement regarding the control of the operational use of the police force is as to the extent of the control embraced in the power of a State Governor to give directions to the State Police Commissioner with respect to the use of the police for maintaining and securing public safety and public order within the State. The extent of the power is delimited primarily by its purpose as expressed in section 215(4) quoted above, viz the use of the police for maintaining and securing public safety and public order within the State.   A direction by the Governor with respect to the use of the police force for a purpose other than the maintenance and securing of public safety and public order is outside the scope of the power and may be refused. Such a direction is not a "lawful" direction within the meaning of that word as used in section 215(3) and (4).

But the maintenance and securing of public order is a very wide and elastic term, especially considering that the word "public" in the term "public safety and public order" refers to the state, its government and the nation or people; it is the safety, peace and stability of the government and people of the state that is meant. So long as the Governor's direction is directed to this purpose, and provided it is not unlawful on any other grounds, the State Commissioner of Police must carry it out as a matter of constitutional duty; he is not at liberty to refuse to do so. Section 215(4), in the main part of its provision, is explicit, clear and emphatic that he shall comply with those directions or cause them to be complied with" (emphasis supplied).

The provision in the proviso enabling the State Commissioner of Police, before complying, to "request that the matter be referred to the President....... for his direction" must be construed in the light of the duty to comply cast on him in the preceding part of the subsection (section 215(4)). The spirit of the proviso does not contemplate a refusal to comply at the arbitrary whim or caprice of the State Commissioner of Police or the President. The words "may request", in the context of the provision in section 215(4) taken in its entirety, rule out such arbitrary, high-handed refusal, as had happened in Anambra State; they suggest a supplication by a subordinate to a superior. They imply a recognition that, in the matter of the maintenance and securing of public safety and public order in a State, the Governor, as the chief executive and chief security of the State, is the boss, the controlling authority, and that the State Commissioner of Police is subordinate to him. Liberty in the State Commissioner of Police to comply or not to comply, at his arbitrary pleasure or that of the President, is a contradiction of the relationship between him and the State Governor envisaged by the provision; it is antithetical to the letter and spirit of the arrangement of a single police force as an agency common to both the Federal and State Governments for the maintenance of their respective existence and authority and the enforcement of their respective existence and authority and the enforcement of their laws, and is a recipe for trouble and the eventual collapse of the arrangement.

The proviso is intended to be used in cases of extreme gravity and sensitiveness, and to check the use of the police at the state or local government levels as an instrument of oppression, harassment and victimization for partisan political federal governments to undermine the position of the state government in relation to the police force, the proviso should be deleted from the Constitution.

It is an error to think of the Nigeria Police Force as an agency of the Federal Government alone, and subject as such to its complete control, merely because police is listed as an item on the exclusive legislative list (item 45) or because the execution powers vested in the President are stated in section 5(1) to extend to the execution of "all matters with respect to which the National Assembly has, for the time being, power to make laws". This definition of the extent of the President's executive powers in expressly made "subject to the provisions of this Constitution", while the exclusion of the State Governments from exercising legislative or executive powers with respect to matters on the exclusive legislative list has effect only insofar as it is not "otherwise provided in this Constitution" (section 4(3)).

As regards the police, the Constitution does provide otherwise in two important respects. There is, first, the provision empowering both the Federal and State Governments by law to confer powers and duties on the police (section 214(2) (b)). There are numerous state laws conferring functions or imposing duties on the police, notably the Criminal Code (or the Penal Code in the northern States) which is largely a state law. This would not have been constitutionally permissible if the position had been that the Nigeria Police Force is an agency of the Federal Government alone, since neither the Federal not the State Governments can confer functions or impose duties on the agencies or functionaries of the other: see Attorney-General of Ogun State & Others v. Attorney-General of the Federation & Others (1982) 3 NCLR 583. To regard the police force as an agency of the Federal Government alone would make nonsense of the arrangement of a single police force as a coercive force for maintaining and securing the existence and authority of both the Federal and State Government and enforcing their laws.

There is, secondly, the provision creating a Nigeria Police Council composed of the President as chairman, the Governor of each State in the Federation, the Chairman of the Police Service Commission and the Inspector-General of Police, and vesting in it responsibility wit respect to "(a) the organization and administration of the Nigeria Police and all other matters relating thereto (not being matters relating to the use and operational control of the Force or the appointment, disciplinary control and dismissal of members of the Force; (b) the general supervision of the Nigeria Police Force.

Interestingly, the police was not an item in either the Exclusive or Concurrent Legislative List in both the 1960 and 1963 Constitutions. It was only brought into the Exclusive Legislative List by the 1979 and 1999 Constitutions, and should be deleted therefrom. The provisions in the body of the Constitution relating to the police are enough.

The choice before us is either to retain the single police force with the reforms here suggested or to permit the establishment by the Regional Constitutions of regional should exist side by side with the Nigeria Police. Our choice should be informed by the recognition of the contradiction in speaking of government not backed by force. "States exist or not according as they have the force to impose their commands."[1]

(b) **Armed Forces**

All the constitutional arrangements for power sharing between the National Government and the Governments of the component units of the Federation designed to make the Centre less attractive and thereby lessen the intensity of the struggle for its control as well as those for making executive leadership equally accessible to the various groups might be stultified unless some answer is found to the frequent incidence of military coups. The division of powers with respect to the armed forces under the Swiss Constitution seems to me well suited to answer our need for constitutional safeguards against military coups.

It (i.e. the Swiss Constitution) prohibits the maintenance of a standing army by the Federal Government; only the cantons are allowed to maintain a standing army, provided that the approval of the Federal Governments must be obtained for a standing army larger than 300 men in strength (art. 13). In practice of course each Canton, with the approval of the Federal Government, maintains an army well in excess of the prescribed minimum of 300 men. The troops maintained by each Canton shall be made up of men from that Canton, unless there are objectives to this on military grounds (art.21). In addition, military service is compulsory for all Swiss citizens (art. 18). The armies maintained by the Cantons within their respective territories together with all Swiss citizens subject to military service constitute the federal army (art. 19).

Laws relating to military organization and the protection defence of the civilian population against the consequences of acts of war are made by the Federal Government, and executed by the Governments of the Cantons within the limits laid down by federal legislation and under the supervision of the Federal Government (art. 20 and 22).

Control of the operational use and deployment of the armed forces and of war materials rest with the Federal Government and, insofar as it is not inconsistent with the federal Constitution or federal legislation, with the

Governments of the Cantons as a concurrent power (art. 19). In time of danger, either from within or without, the armed forces maintained by the Cantons are immediately placed under federal command (art. 17). Armament and military training and likewise a federal concern; however, the supply and maintenance of clothing and equipment are for the Cantons but they are entitled to be reimbursed for such expenses by the Federal Government according to regulations laid in federal legislation (art 20). The composition of the troops, their care and upkeep, the selection and promotion of officers are cantonal concerns subject to such general regulations as the Federal Government may lay down (art. 21).

The Nigerian armed forced should be re-structured along the lines of the Swiss system. All officers and men presently employed in the armed forces should move to their Regions of origin (or States of origin is the structure of six Regions or Zones is not adopted) to constitute the armies to be maintained by the Regions (or States). The regulation of military organization, the control of the operational use of troops, control of arms and ammunition for use by them, etc shall, with such modifications as may be necessary, be as outlined above under the Swiss Constitution.

5. Common Revenue and its Sharing

The provisions of the 1999 Constitution bearing on common revenue and its haring are contained in section 162(1), (2) and (3), which states as follows:-

162 – (1) The Federation shall maintain a special account to be called "the Federation Account" into which shall be paid all revenues collected by the

Government of the Federation, except the proceeds from the personal income tax of the personnel of the armed forces of the Federation, the Nigeria Police Force, the Ministry or department of government charged with responsibility for Foreign Affairs and the residents of the Federal Capital Territory, Abuja.

(2) The President, upon the receipt of advice from the Revenue Mobilization Allocation and Fiscal Commission, shall table before the National Assembly proposals for revenue allocation from the Federal Account, and in determining the formula, the National Assembly shall take into account, the allocation principles especially those of population, equality of States, internal revenue generation, land mass, terrain as well as population density; Provided that the principle of derivation shall be constantly reflected in any approved formula as being not less than thirteen per cent of the revenue accruing to the Federation Account directly from any natural resources.

(3) Any amount standing to the credit of the Federation Account shall be distributed among the Federal and State Governments and the local government councils in each State on such terms and in such manner as may be prescribed by the National Assembly.

The proviso to section 162(2) gives rise to two interpretative questions, viz (a) whether it entitles a mineral producing State to be paid 13 per cent pending when the National Assembly determines what the percentage payable should be, not being a percentage less than 13 per cent; (b) whether the percentage payable covers revenue from on-shore natural resources as well as revenue from off-shore natural resources. The Supreme Court in Att-Gen of the Fedn v. Att-Gen of Abia & 35 Ors (2002) 4 S. C. pt. 1) p. 1; (2002) 6 NWLR (pt 764) 542 answered both questions in the negative; i.e., as regards the second question, that it does not entitles a mineral producing State to be paid any percentage at all in respect of revenue derived from off-shore natural resources.

The reasoning behind the negative answer to the first question is stated as follows in the Judgment:

"In the absence of any legislation by the National Assembly pursuant to section 162(2)of the Constitution which fixes a figure that is not less than 13 per cent (but which may be more than that figure) in calculating the amount due to a State affected by the principle of derivation in the proviso to the subsection, it is for the President, as the prescribed authority, to modify Cap 16 (as amended) to bring it in conformity with the provisions of the Constitution, particularly section 162 thereof. Unless and until either is done, the 3rd Defendant cannot, as of legal right, lay claim to 13 per cent.

CHAPTER TWELVE

*RE-STRATEGIZING THE
CURRENT FEDERAL
GOVERNMENT ECONOMIC
AND POLITICAL REFORM
PROGRAMS*

The 2005 edition of the population Datasheet published by the U.S-based Population Reference Bureau puts Nigeria's population at 132million, making Nigeria the Ninth (9th) most populous country in the world. The same publication predicts that with the current growth rate of 2.8 per cent it is expected that Nigeria's population will increase to 258million, making it the 7th most populous country by the year 2050.

This figure is very startling as well as revealing. With the current state of affairs – weak institutions, poor economic performance and almost non-existent infrastructures – the task ahead is herculean and challenging as well. Since independence in 1960,

Nigeria's economic growth performance has been very poor and has not impacted or improved the standard of living of the citizens. The real economic growth in the past 42years (1960-2002) averaged about 3percent. Nigerians are worse off today than they were in 1960. Poverty has worsened since 1960 as revealed by socio-economic indicators including real per capita consumption, literacy, real per capita income, access to clean water, and income distribution. As a matter of fact, a recent report by BusinessDay newspaper stated that 96 percent of Nigeria's wealth are controlled by 1percent of the population. The per capital income in 2002 was much lower than 1975. Having been endowed with abundant natural resources yet Nigeria is rated as one of the poorest countries in the world.

Today, Nigeria's economy is heavily dependent on oil. In the 1960s, Nigeria's economy was agrarian. Agriculture contributed over 60 percent of GDP, was a major employer of labor and accounted also for the bulk of export earnings. It was one of the major exporters of key cash crops in the world. In 2005, Nigeria is a net importer of food. The decline of agricultural exported is attributed to the impact of Dutch disease, weak infrastructure, and misguided sectoral policies.

The story is the same in the manufacturing sector. Manufacturing only contributes 5 percent to the GDP, which makes Nigeria one of the least industrialized countries in both Sub-Sahara Africa and the world. According to IMF country report, Nigeria's economy has been highly volatile and unstable. Most macro economic indicators – terms of trades, real exchange rate, government investment per capita, real per capita

GDP growth – display higher volatility than the average for developing countries. It further stated that the volatility stems from the country's heavy dependence on oil as a major source of government revenue and export earnings, highly uncertain policy environment and weak economic management, socio and political conflicts, and ineffective financial system.

The Oil Economy

Current levels of perception of misery in the Nigerian population are such that you could tell Nigeria has been earning more, far much more, in oil revenues since 1999. If this third oil boom leaves any legacy, it seems that will be one of struggle to rein in public sector expenditure, which has ballooned in the meanwhile, with consequences of structural distortions that are likely to negatively affect economic growth.

It used to be that possibilities of national well-being were predicted on acumen for industry, adaptation of technology and natural resource endowments. Natural resources were considered one of the keys to the wealth of nations by the fathers of economics like Adam Smith. Besides the puzzle of the thriving Switzerland and the other countries having natural resources or access to it through colonial conquest, few natural resources have attained the centrality in value that oil has, as a source of energy, to power a world that has been in a revolution of production based on power. Crude oil as a source of fossil fuel has been on great demand. But Nigeria, a country much gifted with natural resources, of which oil is dominant, remains hostage of poverty and strife that generally comes with deprivation. By contrast to this experience many resource poor developing countries have out-performed resource rich Nigeria by far. World Bank published in 1995 a study indicating that resources-poor countries tended to outperform natural resource rich countries, thus reversing the traditional notion of what drives National Wealth.

In recent months there has been much call for increased local content in an industry that is operated by global giants who by the sophistication of the technology and the need for competitiveness can employ a very limited number of people relative to the importance of the sector in Nigeria. The key to that sector pulling its due weight therefore, lies in how much local content it can create. The local content issue spans the spectrum from input supplies by indigenous companies to facilitating joint venture efforts between foreign firms that have expertise in sophisticated services with understudy local partners.

There is also the fact that the oil industry, which is increasingly offshore, is almost totally disconnected from the Nigerian economy except for royalties and taxes that go to government. Even financing is almost exclusively foreign. While we acknowledge the absence of financial deepening in Nigeria, an effort to encourage syndications in which Nigerian financial institutions play a role is important. Evidence of this disconnect is abundant in the example of events that followed Shell announcing it would invest billion of dollars in Nigeria beginning 2001/2002 financial year.

British ministers made speeches about how many thousand new jobs those investments would create in the UK. No figure of new job in Nigeria that would result from those investments came from Nigerian officials. It did not take much genius to recognize that they would be marginal. That cannot be the path to sustainable prosperity. The challenge therefore is to encourage entrepreneurship, a culture of a deferred gratification, and a determination on the part of the entrepreneurs to build competencies in specific areas. This would be beneficial to both parties as it should reduce costs for the oil companies, create jobs and skills in Nigeria and make wealth for the entrepreneurs. Beyond this though there remains a failure of national strategy to add value locally to the hydrocarbons value chain flowing from the exploration of crude oil in Nigeria.

Non-Oil Private Sector
The state of affairs in Nigeria's economy has not spared the non-oil private sector. The sector has experienced, very significantly, poor investment performance and loss of productivity. Between 1960 and 2000 total factor productivity contribution was negative. This was largely due to the economic losses from 3-year civil war, public investment that was not productive, institutional and policy constraints, macro-economic volatility. The institutional and policy constraint contributed in limiting efficiency gains and more productivity private investments.

Capital contributions to economic growth made within the period came mostly from public investments during the oil boom years. Oil and gas related investments also contributed to the growth.

According to IMF country report, non-oil private investment between 1960 and 2000 averaged less than 7percent of GDP. This figure failed to keep pace with capital replacement costs as well as contributing negatively to non-oil GDP growth. It is also well below the 20 percent of the world's fasted growing economies average.

Governance in the Public Sector

The federal government's recent announcement of its plan to lay off thousands of its workforce and recruit fresh first class brains is part of the government's grand plan to strengthen governance and improve the quality of public institutions. Building strong institutions is critical to achieve higher sustainable growth and reducing poverty in the country.

Nigeria's weak growth over the years and ineffective public policies and marginally productive public spending are attributed to weak public sector institutions, poor governance principles, lack or transparency and accountability.

The 2004 Global Competitiveness Report ranked Nigeria 98 out of 120 countries studied within the period on the following issues: the rule of law, degree of corruption, and enforcement of contacts. Also Nigeria was ranked 5th among 102 countries assessed on such key issues necessary for good investment climate which include transparency and predictability of policies, enforcement of property rights, judicial independency, even-handed treatment of private sector, low level of corruption and crime, quality of infrastructure and efficient bureaucracy.

In the 1960s, the Nigeria public school system was ranked among the best in Africa, but today it is among the worst in Sub-Sahara Africa. in 2005, Nigeria was ranked 6th among the most corrupt countries of the world by transparency international. an improvement over 2004 ranking of global second.

a recent World Economic Forum's Executive Survey Opinion reported that businesses listed, as the 6th biggest cost factor; security, theft of equipment and inventory by employees and other related crimes. Companies who participated in the World Bank's RPED survey highlighted the issues of security of grave concern in Lagos area. This is because of the frequent arm robbery attack along main transportation routes. British American Tobacco Nigeria lost a number of employees to different robbery incidence in the past few years. So they take security of life of employees and property very seriously. But not without heavy financial cost though the issue of security and crime, according to some companies, make it more difficult to attract businesses even expatriate workers.

Physical Infrastructure
Compared to the rest of the world, Nigeria's physical infrastructure in terms quality is inferior. The 2004 Global Competitive Report ranked Nigeria 100th in overall quality of infrastructure.

Epileptic power supply by NEPA is about the biggest problem of businesses in Nigeria.
Nigeria, with a telephone density of 0.6 lines per capital is the lowest in Africa.
Nigeria has the most inefficient port system. It takes an average of 28days to clear shipments compared to 2days international norm.
The road density is the lowest in Africa. The road network is very poor as a result of inadequate

funding by the government for road construction and maintenance.

It is estimated that 70percent of rural dwellers and more than 50 percent of urban dwellers lack access to portable water.

The following have been attributed to the mismanagement of funds and insufficient infrastructure investments; corruption, weak procurement practices and lack of public accountability. Others include licensing, government pricing policies and other government restrictions. The government entry restrictions have been said to prevent private businesses from competiting with state monopoly in the provision of infrastructure in Nigeria.

Stiff Business Regulations

Administrative procedures and regulations are quite costly when doing business in Nigeria compared to other parts of the world. Coupled with these are excessive red tape and rent-seeking activities of public officials. These are what stifle operating or starting a business in Nigeria. According to a World Bank 2005 report on doing business, to start a new business in Nigeria the entrepreneur need to go through a minimum of 10 bureau Cratic procedures which will take a minimum of 44days. In OECD countries, it takes 27days and an average of 6 bureaucratic procedures. The report also stated that it takes an equivalent of 60 percent of per capita income to establish a limited liability company in Nigeria. Ordinary routine business applications are awfully show and this add to the cost of doing business in Nigeria.

The overlapping jurisdictions and procedures results

in companies being required to pay new, arbitrary local taxes and fees, submit additional documents to local government official and clarify plans. Foreign companies coming into Nigeria are required to go through additional steps of having to register with Nigerian investment promotion commission, which is renewable every year.

Private Sector-Led Growth Reforms
The present administration has embarked on a very ambitious economic reforms strategy. This reform is a broad based medium term strategy. The platform of this economic reform is NEEDS (National Economic Empowerment Development Strategy). It is paradoxical to see Nigerians living in abject poverty in the midst of abundant natural and human resources.

That's why the NEEDS program was designed to unleash Nigeria's great growth potential and to a large extent reduce the level of poverty that has bedeviled the country. NEEDS also aims to correct economic policies of the past, which created an environment that was hostile to the growth of the private sector.

To borrow from Stephen R. Covey who said; "if you want incremental improvement change attitudes, behavior, but if you want revolutionary improvement, change paradigms, world view or way of thinking." The NEEDS program of the present federal government is a break away from the past policy failures which also recognizes that fundamental changes and bold reforms are necessary conditions to getting Nigeria out of the present deep rooted structural and economic problem. Without these reforms, Nigeria will perpetually remain stuck in the trap of low productivity, low savings, and low investment.

NEEDS also aims to boost productivity growth and external competitiveness, diversify the economy away from oil, reduce role of the public sector in economic activity, and free the business sector from strangulating government controls, regulations and gross inefficiencies.

Key Objectives of the Government
The federal government in recent times has focused on few key economic objectives. One of such key objective is to restore agriculture as the leading sector in the economy. Agriculture, before the advent or discovery of oil, used to be a major foreign exchange earner in Nigeria. The government's plan is to enhance its contribution to export earnings and employment creation.

Another area where growth is expected is the manufacturing sector. Added to this is the solid minerals sector. The aim of the government is to raise growth in the non-oil economy to 7percent every year for the next 10years. Government believes that this high growth rate will reduce poverty by 50per cent, by the year 2015. Meanwhile, some experts believe that to reduce poverty to a reasonable level, a growth rate of about 15per cent is required for the same period. Even through this may seem very ambitious but it is achievable. To achieve the 7percent growth the government aims at, real investment would have to increase by at least 15 per cent in real terms. This also means that national savings must increase and total factor productivity growth have to average about 2 per cent every year for 10 consecutive years.

Goal Achievement Strategies

Some of the strategies the government intends to deploy to achieve the above stated goals include the following:

Create a stable and predictable macroeconomic framework
Privatize state-owned enterprises
Strengthen institutions and governance standards
Improve and develop infrastructure
Liberalize the trade regime
Reform the judicial system and enforce rule of law
Create competitive business regulations
Strengthen the financial sector
Fight corruption

Some of the actions taken by the government toward accomplishing these goals include the signing of the Extractive Industries Transparency Initiative (EITI) law. The EITI law requires oil companies to publish all oil and gas-related information. The second action is the establishment of Economy Financial Crimes Commission (EFCC). This commission was set up to fight corruption in the public sector and financial system.

Conclusion

My submission in the foregoing therefore is that the non-oil sector holds the key to Nigeria's economic growth and development. Government's continued dependence on oil is compounding Nigeria's economic woes. Research has shown that countries that are endowed with natural resources such as oil and gas under-perform countries without oil or other natural resources. Large natural resources tend to encourage waste and corruption. So, growing the non-oil sector in Nigeria is one strategy to create jobs. The government must focus on this always. The recent debt relief and debt rescheduling with Paris club and subsequent payment of $12billion will aid economic growth if the conditions are made lighter. Common sense finance tells us that when a company, just like a country, reduces its debt burden growth takes place because resources that would have been used to service the debt will be channeled to a more productive sector.

It is hoped with the debt burden removed, Nigeria's credit rating will improve internationally, and more Foreign Direct Investment (FDI) will be attracted. By increasing investment, the Millennium Development Goal (MDG) of reducing poverty by 50percent per annum will be achieved.

The issue of import tariff should be redressed. It is believed that Nigeria's high tariff is anti-export. Reduction of tariff from the current high to a manageable low level will attract foreign investment, and at the same time make Nigeria a hub for export to other parts of Africa.

Other factors that will drive economic growth in Nigeria are sound fiscal policy and discipline, good financial development, strong institutions, technology and agriculture. Sound fiscal policy will impact growth in three ways: when deficit is low, growth is positively affected. Fiscal consolidations that reduce reliance on domestic financing enhance growth. And the composition of fiscal spending effects growth. For example, a higher share of spending on education and health benefits growth. These benefits, on the other hand, could be reduced drastically by poor governance or unsound macroeconomic policies.

The financial sector needs to be further developed. The bank consolidation exercise, hopefully, will go a long way to doing that. Economies with best-developed financial sectors usually experience higher per capita growth rate than the average economies.

Strong institutions are the most Important determinant of long-term growth. Therefore, there is need to strengthen, improve and even develop institutions. Such institutional improvement includes the laws, rules and other practices that govern property rights, the freedom to do business and enforcement of contract.

CHAPTER
THIRTEEN

ECONOMIC TALIBANISM

T he history of Nigeria's checkered economic development is filled with missed growth opportunities and policy flip-flops. Economic growth and development have been adversely affected by prolonged economic recession occasioned by the collapse of the world oil market from the early 1980s and the attendant sharp fall in foreign exchange earnings. There has been also other plethora of problems that hampered the growth of the economy. These include dysfunctional social and economic infrastructure, excessive dependence on imports for consumption and capital goods, unprecedented fall in capacity utilization rate in industry, inconsistent macroeconomic policies, and neglect of the agricultural sector, etc.

High productivity is important in boosting economic growth and the standards of living of the people, and as such its measurement should therefore be of importance to both policy markers and researchers. Productivity measurement is used to evaluate the efficiency of an economy in relation to other factors. Also it is useful in ascertaining the relative efficiency of firms, sectors as well as sub-sectors of the economy. So, knowledge of the relative efficiency of industries and their profitability will assist or aid governments in planning their programs and policies.

This is so, especially in deciding on which industries should be given or accorded top priority. This in addition will help the government in deciding the wage level of workers as the input and output of labor will be well quantified. Determining the appropriate wage level has been a contentious issue in Nigeria for several decades. This has often resulted in labor disputes and strikes by workers. Productivity measurement, at the micro level, will aid sales and production planning, especially in checking costs - which includes wages, reduction of waste, and substitution of factors of production, among others.

Competitiveness

In his editorial in the October 2009 edition of African Business, Anver Versi commented on the recent World Economic Forum's African Competitiveness Report (ACR). This is a report jointly produced by the World Bank and African Development Bank, and also considered to be an important document for African economic planners, businesses, academics as well as NGOs. The document defines competitiveness as "The set of institutions, policies and factors that determine the level of productivity of a country. The level of productivity, in turn, sets the sustainable level of prosperity that can be earned by an economy. More competitive economies tend to be able to produce higher levels of income for their citizens. The productivity level also determines the rates of return on investment."

According to the report, the duty of government is basically to raise the living standard of the citizens. This, unfortunately, has not been the case in Nigeria. Therefore, it is not surprising that Nigeria was ranked 99th out of 134 countries in the global ranking and also occupies a one of the lower positions in the continental ranking. The continental ranking is out of 31 countries. This is despite the fact that Nigeria is a resource-rich country. The ranking was based on twelve pillars that are deemed to be essential for progress in development. Versi went ahead to list these pillars as: institutions; infrastructure; macroeconomic stability; health and primary education; higher education and training; goods market efficiency; technological readiness; market size; business sophistication; labor market efficiency; financial market sophistication; and innovation.

One major revelation of the ACR is Tunisia. Tunisia is ranked number 1 in Africa ahead of South Africa and 40th in the global ranking. While South Africa came second, countries like Botswana and Mauritius were ranked third and fourth respectively. Versi noted that the rankings did not take into account factors such as wars or the aftermath of the genocide and the rebuilding that has been required in places like Burundi, but they are the accurate reflection of the actual stage of affairs in each country.

What did Tunisia do right that Nigeria floundered? Tunisia scored highest in 8 out of the 12 pillars listed. It may be interesting to note that Tunisia more than 80% of the population of Tunisia falls within the middle class bracket. Also, its per capita GDP is the highest in Africa. Education is free and compulsory in Tunisia. It also leads the world in the amount of GDP allocated to education (estimated at 7.5%). Nigeria allocates about 1 % or less to education and it is not free, neither is it compulsory, except in some states like Lagos. Rather than encourage the citizens to be educated, the government policy toward education shows otherwise. The frequent strikes in the education sector due to government's insensitivity to the need to invest in education and improve the educational system.

Again Tunisia is ranked, with the exception of China, as being more competitive than the four emerging nation s of Brazil, Russia, India, and China (BRIC). Also, Tunisia and South Africa – from the report – are more competitive than some European countries like Poland, Italy, Turkey, Hungary, and others. Tunisia's main market is the European Union. And out of the 27 member-countries of the European Union, Tunisia is more competitive than 20 countries. A mention should be made of other African countries that ranked low, including complacent and resource rich countries like Nigeria, Cameroon, Chad, Zimbabwe, Mali, Mozambique, Burundi, Burkina Faso, and Mauritania.

Now hear this; the report listed, in order of ranking, Switzerland, USA, Singapore, Sweden, Denmark,

Finland, Germany, Japan, Canada and Netherlands. Among these top ranked countries, only USA and Canada have natural resources that are quite significant while Germany is endowed with strategic resources like coal and iron. What this report has shown is that economic growth and development do not depend on how much natural resources a country is endowed with. Versi concluded that "you do not need natural resources to deliver high incomes and living standards for your citizens – but what is indispensible is education. Invest in education and all else follows."

What manner of reforms?

When the Obasanjo administration assumed office in 1999 they embarked on series of economic and financial reforms to turn around and shift Nigeria's economy from mixed to market-led economy. Efforts were made to diversify the economy from oil dependence and develop the non-oil sector. The government of the day worked tirelessly to deregulate and open up or unbundle the telecommunication sector which was originally initiated by the late Sani Abacha's military regime. Then entered the Nigerian telecommunications market MTN, Econet (now Zain), Mtel (a subsidiary of Nigeria's national carrier NITEL), and Globacom to provide GSM and fixed wireless telephone services to the people.

As a follow up, the privatization exercise of the Federal government was fast tracked as if the government was a hurry to get out of business and allow businesses to be run by those who better know how to – the private sector. Few Nigerians like Aliko Dangote, Jimoh Ibrahim and Femi Otedola, and others benefited from the privatization exercise and bought over some these enterprises that were hitherto owned and run by the government. The international business community and governments applauded this new policy thrust and Nigeria was gradually being welcomed to the international community of nations.

Coupled with this was the appointment by the Obasanjo administration of Professor Charles Soludo, Nigeria's internationally respected and brainy macroeconomist who never had any banking experience as the Central Bank of Nigeria (CBN) governor. As a matter of fact, he was the first CBN governor that came from outside the banking sector. Soludo's appointment heralded the banking sector reform between 2004 and 2005 to produce mega Nigerian banks that will compete favorably in the global financial services market. Banks were required to beef up their capital base to N25 billion each. They were given 18 months to complete the recapitalization. Those that could muster to raise their capital to that amount survived while those that could not were encouraged to merge or be acquired by the stronger ones. At the end of the exercise only 25 banks were the last standing out of 89 banks.

Following the successful banking consolidation Soludo turned his focus to the insurance sector. That sector also was consolidated and the number of insurance companies reduced to less than half after the exercise. Being cash awash, the CBN encouraged the banks to take more risks by venturing outside the shores of Nigeria. The banks took advantage of the perceived opportunities and embarked on expanding their branch networks to Africa and global marketplace. Consumer finance that was hitherto non existent was introduced for middle class income earners that was at that time re-emerging. For a very long time Nigerians were denied consumer loans that have been available in Western nations and the US – such loans like overdrafts, mortgages, credit card, as well as car loans.

The banking reform and the introduction of new products and consumer financing fuelled the growth of the domestic stock market. Investors got margin loans to invest in the stock market and the market was thriving. The financial services sector and the overall economy thrives on confidence. If the people or investors perceive the economy to be doing well they will invest in the economy. If they think otherwise (i.e. if the confidence level is low), they will not invest. This confidence in the market attracted foreign investors such as hedge fund managers and private equity companies to invest in the market. At a point between 2005 and 2007 the Nigerian Stock market was more than 80 percent capitalized by the banks. And it constituted about 93 percent of the financial services sector. The economy generally grew by between 5.7 percent and 7.5 percent. The foreign reserve, occasioned by the rise in global oil prices rose to $63 billion.

August 14 "tsunami"

The end of Soludo era also seemed to have ended temporarily the little progress made in both bank and economic growths. During Soludo's era and after the consolidation, the CEOs that ran the 25 new mega banks which later became 24 due to some mergers of Stanbic and IBTC, received international awards.

The recent publication of African Business magazine (October 2009 edition) did annual ranking of Africa's Top 100 Banks (based on market capitalization, asset base, capital asset ratio, profits, return on equity, return on total assets deployed) and some Nigerian banks made it among the top 10. These are how they stand according to the ranking: Zenith Bank (6), First Bank (7), Oceanic Bank (10), Intercontinental Bank (12), UBA (15), Access Bank (16), Bank PHB (17), GTBank (18), Fidelity Bank (20), First City Monument Bank (22), Diamond Bank (24), Union Bank (28), Skye Bank (31), StanbicIBTC (33), Afribank (53), Sterling Bank (63), Ecobank Nigeria (67), Wema Bank (71), Finbank (81).

The above were the standing of the banks compared to their African counterpart until the "black Friday" August 14, 2009 when the newly appointed CBN governor, Sanusi Lamido Sanusi, let hell loose and descended on the first five bank CEOs and sacked them. Those affected by this "tsunami" include Cecilia Ibru of Oceanic Bank, Sebastian Adigwe of Afribank, Erastus Akingbola of Intercontinental Bank, Bartholomew Ebong of Union Bank, and Okey Nwosu of Finbank. Others that were sacked on October 2, 2009, include Francis Atuche of Bank PHB, Charles Ojo of Spring Bank, and Ike Oraekwuotu of Equitorial Trust Bank.

Sanusi accused the sacked CEOs of gross mismanagement of the banks. This is the reason Sanusi gave for sacking the CEOs: "The five banks are at the brink of collapse, due to poor corporate governance, credit administration processes, and lax credit administration practices." He further stated that "The Central Bank has a responsibility to act to protect all depositors and creditors and ensure that no one loses their money due to the failure of a bank.

The Central Bank also needs to move decisively to remove this principal cause of instability and restore confidence in the banking system." He further remarked: "Having read all the reports of the special examiners who continue to look into the banks' loan portfolios and other banking practices and the comments of the Central bank directors and deputy governors, I am satisfied that these five institutions are in a grave situation and that their management have acted in a manner detrimental to the interests of their depositors and creditors." On his visit to the Nigerian Stock Exchange on September 16, 2009, Sanusi was quoted as saying: "Regulators all over the world have looked at themselves and discovered that they messed up. At the Central Bank of Nigeria, we have looked at ourselves too and know that we messed up. And we expect everyone else who messed up to say so." Really?

The painful implications

The issue here is not a question of poor corporate governance or gross mismanagement, but the question is "could the CBN governor and his cronies have done this differently? Knowing that the banking sector is a very sensitive one and is also a critical sector of Nigeria's economy, the governor threw caution and decorum to the wind. They could have thought through the short and long term consequences of the decision before rushing to carry it out. This made some segment of the population to begin to wonder whether the governor was in a vindictive mission. How else does one explain it? These bank chiefs were his former colleagues whom he dined with for few months while he was the CEO of First Bank. Then suddenly these people are treated as if they were leprous. What could have been behind the CBN action? Was Sanusi sent to act out a script or he acted with genuine intension to sanitize a system he was part of in its creation, having been in the top echelon of some banks in the past?

Osasu Obayiuwana in the October 2009 edition of the New African magazine wrote: "As the financial sector reels from the crisis of confidence caused by Sanusi's public "execution" of the bank chiefs, opinions are sharply divided on the wisdom of the sudden dismissals. While many have hailed Sanusi's actions as timely and the tonic needed to instil a better lending culture in the banking industry, a bank vice president warned that the hard work done over the last eight years to make Nigeria attractive to international investors, could be ruined." This is partly the point being made here.

But before going any further, let us examine what other people also told Obayiuwana in an interview. "We are at the receiving end of criticism because half of the world believes bankers are making all the money. What about the people who were given these loans and refused to pay back, only for some people to turn around and say that no sound credit risk analysis was made? Do we think that these people (bankers on trial) were not normal? Why would anyone give out money and not expect it back? All I see is condemnation of the accused bankers without giving due recognition to what they have done positively for the economy. They grew an industry, which is the bedrock of any economy, without any government support."

Not withstanding what might have happened in the banking sector, no one should overlook the positive contributions they have made in growing this economy which has been mentioned earlier. From this very action, we have entered an era of "economic talibanism." Another grave consequence of Sanusi's action is that it has discouraged risk taking. Every nation or economy needs risk takers to make progress. These risk takers are majorly entrepreneurs who believe in their ideas and passionately work towards bringing those ideas to reality, thereby creating jobs and improving the quality of lives in the process.

Investors – both foreign and local investors - will be careful not to invest for long term. Most investments will be short-term because of the unpredictability of the government and its policies. Most of the banks in question were set up through entrepreneurial effort s. These were risk takers who, despite the environmental odds against them were able to establish these banks, provided employment and grew the banks to a level of national pride before the unfortunate axe that have fallen on them. This Sanusi reform has brought about loss of investors confidence which will take long time and effort to rebuild. Economies and businesses thrive on confidence. It has also killed, to an extent, the spirit of entrepreneurship. They (investors) will be apprehensive to commit to serious long term investment, feeling that if the government can turn around and sack entrepreneurs who set up businesses (banks especially), then they may likely one day nationalize their businesses without notice.

The case of how the former West Germany was able to develop more and faster than East Germany goes to show the importance of having risk takers in every society. Every society needs visionary and creative risk-takers. In explaining why the old West Germany outperformed their East German counterpart or neighbors when the German federation was split into West and East after WW11, the former Bundesbank president Karl Otto Pohl stated: "In every society there is the top 15 to 20 percent which includes the leaders, talented managers and, most importantly, the visionary risk-takers. In 1946, against British and American expectations, this talented group after the war brought about the first German economic miracle under Ludwig Erhard, minister of economy. The risk-takers had no other place to go, but today is different. The moment the Berlin Wall fell, that high-powered group in East German society immediately raced across the border, fully confident they could compete in the West and immediately earn ten to twenty times their current income. Left behind are the less talented, the more dependent, and the more fearful. These people lack the ability on their own to rebuild that economy."

CBN and bank ownership rights

The following was a mail from the editors of newsletter@proshareng.com (www.proshareng.com/blog). The editors posed very salient questions which are worth repeating here: What has happened to the Nigerian intelligensia - Why is no one asking or answering a fundamental question that goes to the heart of our nationhood: Where does ownership rights of firms/shareholders end and regulatory rights begin?

What is going on in this country?

These are landmark developments that define us as a people and a nation. Our economy and socio-political life is dependent on the resolution of this one question.

While we all acknowledge that things have gotten too bad and that action was needed to be taken, enter Sanusi Lamido Sanusi (SLS) and we expected that radical changes - much anticipated will occur to shake our banking foundations because it was rotten. He was a man whose value system indicated that he would not be moved by self interest or the very trappings of wealth that made others dizzy. He started controversially, but we could all live with that because we knew that achieving change in Nigeria was not going to be easy.

The developments - flip flops, actions and unclear basis of actions since then have all made us all to stop and wonder. What could be going on? This is no longer a case of those affected spinning issues - it is about rights and responsibilities, the very underpinning of this administration.

When the appointments of new ED's were released we saw some odd names there but most analyst decided to let it go because we felt we should cut him some slack – after all there cannot be a perfect being and in this endeavor we accepted that there would be a few missteps.

But the appointments he made today leave much room for concern. They concretise the legitimate fears of a decision process not designed to deliver the el dorado we seek as a people.

We should be asking questions from CBN, in the spirit of full disclosure. They should provide insight, explanations and information to the following:

1. What criteria were used in the appointments of CEO's and Executive Directors of these banks?

2. Did it consider the rule that said that former directors of a failed bank cannot be appointed into an executive position of another bank?

3. How do you situate the appointment of a CEO who was asked to resign from the management of a failed bank so many years ago from the position of a Treasurer based on incompetence to manage a bank?

4. What input did the new boards have in these appointments?

5. How do we deal with the new reality of customers choosing not to do business with any of the banks with such leadership challenges?

6. Why does the 'rush' to raise funds through issuance of corporate bonds by the banks cleared in the first wave of the SLS audit support the 'coincidence theory' of the action taken?

7. Why would a bank like Wema Bank Plc (with Tunde Lemo as former CEO now at CBN) explain the 2007 audit report by the NDIC that it never had the N25bn which was the basis of the bank licence to operate under the consolidation era especially with the 'mud' thrown out for which no concrete explanation was provided?

8. What does the CBN want the market

to take away from this exercise where the banks cleared in the first wave are not able to explain away their problems giving the revelation that some of them are now chasing debtors whom they had given uncollaterized loans and are calling same in with limited success?

9. What happens to investors who are now at the mercy of CEO's and ED'S who have no stake in the businesses?

10. Who does the new CEO'S report to?

11. Why would these individuals, who appear not to have succeeded in running or owning anything in their lives at a scale and magnitude they are now being asked to manage, take on this assignment? What is their motivation and who do they represent - regulators, depositors or/and shareholders?

12. Did the CEO's needed to have managed a bank before like in the first set or what was it the second set had and why the difference in criteria for appointments?

13. Were these people headhunted for the jobs and what is their brief or since when did they know of their job responsibilities?

14. What is the investment advice to shareholders, depositors or customers?

15. Are these CEO's going to be non-shareholders in the banks they run and how do we prevent the 'homogenization' of banking being put in place by Sanusi Lamido Sanusi inevitable?

The other issue that should be looked into is why should

CBN bail out Wema Bank and Unity Bank at a time when other banks were being accused of being at the brink of collapse? Does that mean that the CBN, who duty is to provide a level playing, is now practicing favouritism? The CEOs of these banks were not sacked; instead more money was given to them.

Reversal

On Thursday November 5, 2009 the Nigerian media – both electronic and print – were awash with the news of the CBN reversing itself. The report stated that Equitorial Trust Bank (ETB) was returned to Mike Adenuga, a telecommunication mogul and the owner of Globacom, Nigeria's second national telecommunication carrier. According to the CBN, no wrong doing was found on Mike Adenuga. In as much this reversal of decision is welcomed a new precedent has been set which others can latch on to make their case for a similar treatment to be meted on them.

This action also support the point made earlier that the CBN did not take time to think through its decision to sack the bank CEOs and the attendant consequences before carrying it out. The general public are beginning to understand this point and are therefore reacting differently. Some of the latter decisions of the CBN governor post August 14 have shown that the governor trying to correct some fault lines noted in its decision. In the case of ETB, it is a private company, though they have been mandated to go public and Adenuga has to dilute his shareholding in the bank.

Sanusi was too much in a hurry to score a cheap political point that he did not consider the colossal damage this would cause the economy if not well managed. The damage done to the image ETB, even though the bank has been cleared of any wrong doing by CBN, will take long to mend. The same goes for the other affected banks. It takes some one who has tried setting up a business no matter how small the enterprise may be to really appreciate what it takes to set up a bank and how it feels when you are sacked from or the business you suffered to establish and which took you so many years of sleepless nights to build is taken away from you by some group of people who never attempted setting up a corner shop business to provide services to their neighborhood.

The politicization of economic decision and the conspiracy theory

The political economy of any nation acknowledges the fact that politics influences economic activities, as well as economic development and underdevelopment. The economic and legal systems of any nation are shaped by the political system of that nation. No doubt Nigeria's economic development is a function of its economic and political system. But the challenge therefore is knowing where and when to draw the line between purely economic decision and the political counterpart. When economic decisions are politicized it brings about economic underdevelopment. This has been the case in Nigeria where politics always interferes with the location of economic activities and the distribution of wealth. Industries are supposed to be located, most times, closer to it resource base, but in the case of Nigeria it is often politicized with the various interest groups struggling to locate it in their constituency not minding the economics of it.

In the case of the recent bank reform being carried out by Sanusi Lamido Sanusi, some conspiracy theorists believe it was both politically, ethnically and religiously motivated. Is it a coincidence, they argued, that all the affected banks chiefs come from the south? They also believe that part of Sanusi's mission is to ensure the introduction of Islamic banking in Nigeria to further propagate the Islamic faith in Nigeria. They point to the background and the education of the CBN governor to support their argument. Let's deal with the issue of ethnicity and then later look at Islamic banking – what it means and how it will or will not work in Nigeria and how its introduction will impact the Nigerian economy.

In their October 15 article in BusinessDay newspaper titled "The North and a 'bank it can call its own' the authors (Ebere Onwudiwe and Okey C. Iheduru) cited paper presented by the CEO of Unity Bank, Falalu Bello, and titled "Nigeria, One Country, Four Economics" at a leadership seminar in Abuja organized by Leadership Newspaper and published in the Punch newspaper of March 5, 2008. In that presentation Falalu Bello was reported to have said that both the South West and South East controlled a large chunk of the Nigerian economy to the detriment of the North and other regions. The writers said that Bello warned that Nigeria would not know peace until there is a regional balance or the regional imbalance was corrected.

Olusegun Obasanjo, the former president, was blamed for the new economic structure that Bello said resulted in the two regions (South West and South East) controlling 94 per cent of the banking sector, 88 per cent of insurance assets and 90 per cent of industrial assets. He pointed out that the South West specifically controlled 60 per cent of Nigeria's industrial capacity, 44 per cent of banking assets, 67 per cent of insurance assets and also harbors three main ports – Apapa, Tin Can Island and Roro ports.

This leads to argument that every state and every region should be allowed to develop at its own pace. Bear in mind that different regions and states are endowed with different natural and human resources and do not necessarily have to develop at the same rate. Even in the United States of America there is no even development amongst all the federating states. Every state developed based on different factor endowments. New York, for instance harbors Wall Street and thus became the financial center. California on the other hand is known as the technology center because of Silicon Valley that is located there. The same goes for Lagos that harbors almost all the banks and other industries.

In the early 1960s there was a healthy competition amongst the three regions of East, West and North in development and industrialization. Let us reflect once again how the different regions developed and competed right from pre-independent days. "In the pre-independence era (1958-1959) the three regions in Nigeria had self Governments. The Eastern and Western regions had self government in 1958 and the Northern region in 1959. When Nigeria got her independence in 1960 from the British the regional Governments established what was then known as Development Corporations (DCs).

The Eastern region had Eastern Nigerian Development Corporation (ENDC), the Western region established the Western Nigerian development corporation (WNDC) and Northern region set up the Northern Nigeria Development Corporation (NNDC).

Before the advent of oil, the Eastern region was known for palm oil and coal. The Western region produced Cocoa and the Northern region, groundnut. With money from Cocoa, the WNDC established industrial estates in Ikeja, Lagos which harbors many local and multinational companies such as Dunlop Nig. Plc., Metal Box Nig. Ltd, Nigerian Textile Mill Limited, etc. WNDC also set up companies like the West African Portland Cement, Ewekoro and a Cocoa processing plant in Ikeja.

The Eastern region felt they should catch up with the Western region and started the industrialization of the region. ENDC set up palm oil mill, Nigeria Cement Company Ltd (NIGERCEM), Niger Steal Company, and a gas plant at Enugu. The NNDC in the Northern region established Northern Nigeria Investment Limited. It promoted the setting up of the Cement Company of Northern Nigerian among others.

The Development Corporations were used by the regional governments to promote various projects that added value to Nigeria's quest for sufficient raw materials for domestic use and for exports. Foreign investors were also encouraged to invest in the regions through these efforts.

When the former Head of State, General Yakubu Gowon, divided Nigeria into 12 administrative states during the Nigeria Civil War, 1966-1970, the ENDC collapsed because the administrative states in the Eastern region could not agree to work together. The WNDC was wound up and re-christened Odua Investment Company and the NNDC still remains.

Since the end of the Civil War, Industrial Policy making have moved from the regions to the Federal Government level. In 1963, the Federal Government introduced the pioneer status, an incentive to most of the industries. Payment of taxes was waived for Three to Five Years, and so were other permits required for setting up industries were facilitated for those identified as various investors. "

From the foregoing, it could be deduced that the different regions developed based on factor endowments and effective leadership that promoted healthy competition. Therefore, the government efforts should be directed at repeating the feat achieved by the founders of this nation and the leadership of the three old regions rather than the present day talibanistic tendencies of policy makers, if one should believe the arguments of conspiracy theorists.

Islamic Banking and Sharia Law

One of the earlier mentioned missions of the CBN governor (SLS) according to the conspiracy theorists is the promotion of Islamic banking in Nigeria. Based on is religious faith and education and training, it was widely believed by conspiracy theorists that Sanusi's tenure as CBN governor will accelerate the establishment of Islamic banking in Nigeria. Nigeria has the largest Muslim population in sub-Sahara Africa. The recent banking reform is tilting in favor of Islamic banking. Regulatory problems and the first round of banking reforms (Soludo's banking reform) prevented Islamic banking from taking off fully. This perceived problem is no longer there as the president, Musa Yar'Adua, seemed to have told the CEO of Islamic Development Bank (IDB) during a recent visit by the IDB team to the president.

Let us look at what Islamic banking means to Nigerians and the Nigerian economy. Islamic banking provides financial services that follow the tenets of Sharia law. The main difference between Islamic banking and the conventional banking is that the former does not charge interest on loans. Islamic banking emphasizes ethics and employment of capital solely as a factor of production rather than as a means of gain. The first Islamic bank was set up in Egypt in 1975. Today, there are over 300 Islamic financial institutions operating in about 75 countries and 300 Sharia compliant mutual funds. There has been an increase in deposits made in Islamic banks. The industry has grown at a rate of 15 to 20 per cent per annum in the last 10 years. In 2000, an estimated $140 billion was deposited in Islamic banks, mutual funds and insurance schemes and Islamic banking window at conventional banks. That figure has risen to $800billion and McKinsey & Co estimated that Islamic financial assets could reach $1 trillion by 2010.

The question is no longer whether or not Islamic banking will be established in Nigeria but how is it going to cope with enormous challenges it is will face. Currently some investors don't buy shares of companies that manufacture alcoholic drinks and tobacco for religious and other reasons. This is expected to also apply to Islamic banking. Another challenge is human capital – the ability to attract the right skilled and talented staffs who understands Islamic banking. Most of the skills will either have to be developed locally, which will take quite a bit of time to do, or be imported from outside or a combination of the two. Either way, training is important. The CBN document on Islamic banking states thus: Islamic banking is a "non-interest banking" to be undertaken by institutions "which transact banking business, engage in trading, investments and commercial activities, as well as the provision of financial products and services, in accordance with the principles and rules of Islamic commercial jurisprudence. Transactions and contracts under this type of banking are non-permissible if they involve interest; uncertainty or ambiguity relating to the terms or conditions; gambling; speculation; unjust enrichment; or exploitation/unfair trade practices."

Basically the position of Islamic banking depends largely on the position of Sharia law. This is a major challenge in Nigeria as Sharia law is being practiced only in few states. The non-Sharia states may not be impressed with whatever may be the derivable benefits. With these stringent terms and conditions in a secular society like Nigeria, one begins to wonder how many people will be interested in applying for such a banking license. Again let's wait and see what Sanusi has up his sleeves even as he seems to be wearing a moral toga round his neck. Let's hope he doesn't turn the banking environment to look more like Afghanistan or Pakistan. If he gets it right, the economy will begin to recover. But if not, the economic will sink deeper than it has already done since August 14.

This is the time for the media to start getting the other side of the story for us to have a balanced view of what happened actually. What we know now is what we have been told by the CBN and its agents. We need to hear from the victims – the bank CEOs themselves, or were they told not to speak or tell Nigerians their own side of the story. Those in the media are hereby challenged to tell Nigerians the true story of what happened.

CHAPTER FOURTEEN

IMPACT OF CORRUPTION ON NATIONAL DEVELOPMENT

A brief mention of what corruption actually means is important for a better understanding and appreciation of the subject. Corruption is defined and described as decay, rottenness; a changing or being changed for the worse; a making, becoming, or being corrupt; depravity; wickedness; perversion or deterioration of moral principles; loss of purity or integrity; bribery.

Broadly, corruption has been defined as a perversion or a change from good to bad. Sen (1999) stated that corruption or corrupt behavior involves the violation of established rules for personal gain and profit. Ipset & Lenz (2000) added that corruption is efforts to secure wealth or power through illegal means private gain at public expense; or a misuse of public power for private benefit. The UNDP policy paper described corruption

as the misuse of public power, office or authority for private benefit – through bribery, extortion, influence peddling, nepotism, fraud,
speed money or embezzlement.

Corruption is a universal menace. In the old English law "corruption of blood" designed the effect of an act of attainder of treason or felony, by which a person was disqualified from inheriting lands from an ancestor, and could neither retain those in his possession nor transmit them by descent to his heirs.

In today's modern world, corruption is found in: satisfying rules and obtaining licenses; access to publicly provided goods and services; decisions on the subject of public investment contracts; control over the application of tax fees; hiring within the public sector.

How and when it began in Nigeria

There is no recorded history of how or when corruption started in Nigeria or the world. It dates back to biblical times. It will not be out of place therefore to state that corruption has always been with mankind but in various degrees. The only clue or hint of the history of corruption in Nigeria, especially in the public sector, was the attempted reform of the civil service by the Murtala/Obasanjo regime.

The pre and post independence civil service was filled with seasoned technocrats, men and women who were more committed to their work and motherland and proven integrity. Not much was heard of corruption then until after the coup de tat of 1975 that ushered in the Murtala/Obasanjo regime

The reason given for the take over Gowon's administration by the coupists was too much corruption in the system. To prove their point to Nigerians, the new regime embarked on a massive sack of civil servants. They more or less destroyed that institution. Most of those sacked had no assets to their names. Some died few months after the sack as a result of the shock. A case in point was Dr. Emmanuel Manuwa the then head of service who died shortly after hearing of his sack in the news. He too had nothing, just like some others affected. It was only natural that those civil servants who survived the purge had to start preparing for their retirement by lining their pockets so that they would not experience the kind of financial stress their predecessor experienced.

The Nature and Characteristics of Corruption

Corruption can be in any of the following forms:

i) Political

ii) Bureaucratic

iii) Electoral

Political corruption: is the misuse by government officials of their governmental powers for illegitimate, usually secret, private enrichment. It takes place at the highest levels of political authority. It occurs when the politicians and political decision-makers, who are entitled to formulate, establish and implement the laws in the name of the people, are themselves corrupt. It also takes place when policy formulation and legislation is tailored to benefit politicians and legislators. Political corruption is sometimes seen as similar to corruption of greed as it affects the manner in which decisions are made, as it manipulates political institutions, rules of procedure, and distorts the institutions of government (*NORAD,* ch.4, Jan. 2000; *The Encyclopedia Americana, 1999*).

All forms of government are susceptible to political corruption. Forms of corruption vary, but include bribery, extortion, cronyism, nepotism, patronage, graft, and embezzlement. While corruption may facilitate criminal enterprise such as drug trafficking, money laundering, and trafficking, it is not restricted to these organized crime activities. In some nations corruption is so common that it is expected when ordinary businesses or citizens interact with government officials. The end-point of political corruption is a kleptocracy, literally "rule by thieves".

What constitutes illegal corruption differs depending on the country or jurisdiction. Certain political funding practices that are legal in one place may be illegal in another. In some countries, government officials have broad or not well defined powers, and the line between what is legal and illegal can be difficult to draw.

Bureaucratic corruption: This occurs in the public administration or the implementation end of politics. This kind of corruption has been branded low level and street level. It is the kind of corruption the citizens encounter daily at places like the hospitals, schools, local licensing offices, police, taxing offices and on and on. Bureaucratic petty corruption, which is seen as similar to corruption of need, occurs when one obtains a business from the public sector through inappropriate procedure (see NORAD, ch.4, 2000).

Electoral corruption: It includes purchase of votes

with money, promises of office or special favors, coercion, intimidation, and interference with freedom of election. This practice is very common in Nigeria, where votes are bought, people are killed or maimed in the name of election, losers end up as the winners in elections, and votes turn up in areas where votes were not cast. Corruption in office involves sales of legislative votes, administrative, or judicial decision, or governmental appointment. Other forms of corruption include: bribery, fraud, embezzlement, extortion, favoritism, nepotism.

The Causes of Corruption

Why is corruption a viable enterprise in poor countries including Nigeria? The causes of corruption are myriad; and they have political and cultural variables. According to Lipset and Lenz, there is a strong evidence points to a link between corruption and social diversity, ethno-linguistic fractionalization, and the proportions of country's population adhering to different religious traditions. And studies note also that corruption is widespread in most non-democratic countries, and particularly, in countries that have been branded neo-patrimonial, kleptocratic and prebendal (NORAD 2000). Thus, the political system and the culture of a society could make the citizens more prone to corrupt activities. However, we shall focus on the fundamental factors that engender corrupt practices in less developed nations, including Nigeria. Some of the factors include:

1) Great inequality in distribution of wealth;
2) Political office as the primary means of gaining access to wealth;

3) Conflict between changing moral codes;

4) The weakness of social and governmental enforcement mechanisms; and

5) The absence of a strong sense of national community (Bryce, 1921).

The lack of ethical standards throughout the agencies of government and business organizations in Nigeria is a serious drawback. The issue of ethics in public sector and in private life encompasses a broad range, including a stress on obedience to authority, on the necessity of logic in moral reasoning, and on the necessity of putting moral judgment into practice (Bowman 1991

Other factors are poor reward system, greed, peer community and extended family pressures, and polygamous household. The influence of extended family system and pressure to meet family obligations are more in less developed societies. Bad rules and ineffective taxing system, which makes it difficult to track down peoples financial activities, weak institutions and cultural values breed corruption.

Effect of Corruption on the socio-economic development of a nation

Hope and Chikulo in their volume stated that although the incidence of corruption varies among African countries, ranging from rare (Botswana) to widespread (Ghana) and systemic (Nigeria), the majority of the countries are in the range of widespread to systemic.

Corruption in Africa has now reached cancerous proportions and today has a demonstrable negative impact on the development process in the region. The effective of corruption is the same in both public and private spheres. It results in the misuse of scarce resources that significantly affect an entire economy through multiplier effects.

Corruption is negatively associated with developmental objectives. Controlling or eradicating corruption, they believe, takes on even greater significance in the quest for development.

Africa has attracted the lowest rate of direct foreign investment in the world as a result of corruption. A recent study of corruption index showed that a two-fold increase in the level of corruption is equivalent to raising the marginal tax rate by over 20 per cent, and a one percentage point increase in the marginal tax rate reduced foreign direct investment by 5 per cent.

It is believed that those who pay and receive bribes, just as it is the case in Nigeria, can expropriate a nation's limited wealth. What this means therefore is that the private sector is forced to engage in rent-seeking activities, rather than competitive activities, to make and maximize profits. When this happens, neoptrimonialism which is a perverse system that awards economic and political benefits to politicians and their followers becomes pervasive.

In Africa, particularly in Nigeria, corruption flourishes as a result of distortions in the policy and regulatory regime and the weakness of institutions of restraint. Corruption affects the poor disproportionately, due to their powerlessness to change the status quo and inability to pay bribes, creating inequalities that violate their human rights.

Corruption hinders economic development, reduces social services, and diverts investments in infrastructure, institutions and social services. The World Bank5 distinguishes between two main forms of corruption: state capture and administrative corruption. State capture refers to the actions of individuals, groups or firms, both in the public and private sectors, who influence the formation of laws, regulations, decrees and other government policies to their advantage as a result of the illicit and nontransparent provisions of private benefits to public officials.

Administrative corruption refers to the intentional imposition of distortions in the prescribed implementation of existing laws, rules and regulations to provide advantages to either government or non-government actors as a result of the illicit and non-transparent provision of private gains to public officials. Investors will be reluctant to invest in development efforts in a country where there is state capture and administrative corruption. In addition, international donors would not lend to a country with high corruption affecting the human rights and right to development of poor people in that country.

Corruption can also be classified as petty (need based) and grand (greed based) corruption Petty corruption is found where public servants who may be grossly underpaid depend on small kickbacks from the public to feed their families and pay school fees. Grand corruption involves high officials who make decisions on large public contracts6. Here too, there is a negative impact on the poor as they cannot afford to provide any gains to public officials, or if they do, it constitutes a great part of their earnings which they could have otherwise used for their own subsistence or development.

Corruption no doubt negatively impacts economic growth and reduces public spending on education. The effect of corruption on education is well captured by Costello who said that Nigeria has enough money to tackle its poverty challenges. If the government can win its battle against corruption and mismanagement, the money will start to turn into functioning schools, health services and water supply, thus laying the foundation to eradicate poverty. The effect of corruption on education, according to Shleifer & Vishny, comes from the fact that the government spends relatively more on items to make room for graft. And corrupt government officials would shift government expenditures to areas in which they can collect bribes easily. Large and hard-to-manage projects, such as airports or highways, make fraud easy. Poverty and income inequalities are directly linked to corruption. It is important to mention here that development projects are often made unnecessarily complex in Nigeria to justify the corrupt and huge expense on it. A typical example is the new Abuja stadium which cost about N30 billion to complete.

Corruption wastes skills, as precious time is wasted to set committees to fight corruption, and monitor public projects that are often abandoned by unscrupulous politicians and contractors. It also reduces the quality of products and services offered to the public by some unscrupulous companies. Corruption brings about political instability. It can cause social revolution and military coups, as we have seen in some poor countries around the world, including Nigeria. Even in business transactions, bribery and corruption create the culture of late payment, and delays and refusal to pay for services already executed.

The image of a nation where corruption is prevalent is badly tarnished. Nigeria has been badly affected even more than most African countries and other societies due to an appalling international image created by its inability to deal with bribery and corruption. We canno forget so easily the 1996 Study of Corruption by the Transparency International and Goettingen University which ranked Nigeria as the most corrupt nation among the 54 nations on the study. Two years after another study by Transparency International Corruption Perception Index (CPI) survey of 85 countries, also ranked Nigeria 81. In the 2001 Corruption Perception Index (CPI) survey of 85 countries, the image of Nigeria did not improve. The Transparency International Corruption Index, 2001 ranked Nigeria 90 out of the 91 countries studied.

Corruption leads to slow flow of traffic, manholes on the roads and poor waste management. It leads also to political killings as we have witnessed in the past few months. Corruption could upturn ethnic balance and cause serious problems in the area of national integration. Corruption destroys government structures and capacities, and the legitimacy of that government. Above all, it makes governance ineffective cause brain drain.

Irina Peaucelle posits that some empirical studies

provide evidence that different corrupt regimes have different influence on investment rates. When corruption is predictable, the impact on investment is relatively small because corruption risk can be insured. Certainly, the level of corruption matters also. Consequently, the countries with high levels of corruption and low predictability have as a rule huge problem in attracting foreign direct investment. Governance issues in the modern globalizing economy include issues of foreign direct investment and transfer of new technology.

R&D activity is vulnerable where there is corruption because self-seeking government is not motivated by long-run returns and for this reason does not fund fundamental research. At length, the credibility of agreements concerning intellectual property rights in the process of technology transference from one country to another determines the process of accumulation and the sustainability of world development. Using the knowledge gaps between the societies, the corrupt acts of governments consist either advertising forbidden technologies or consenting to transfer technologies of lower quality than those negotiated. The amount of bribery may reach the value of innovation or the cost of discovery.

In more specific terms, grand corruption leads to:

- Over-priced contracts due to lack of genuine competition.
- Low quality construction and services due to
- inappropriate contractors,
- the inability of the 'bought' officials to

supervise properly, and

- the need to recover money spent in bribes resulting in high maintenance or replacement costs.

- Companies operating on an unethical basis, leaving them open to further erosion of standards and potential blackmail.

- The possibility that the contract should never have been undertaken at all.

However, at a national level, grand corruption has far reaching negative impacts, as it will:

- undermine both free and fair trade, which should be based on price, quality and service

- hinder national, international and multi-national companies from operating legally and ethically

- distort development priorities affecting equity and the distribution of resources and services, as decisions are based on benefits to officials rather than needs of the poor.

- and therefore hinder progress and economic development.

How the world is responding to corruption

Corruption is a global problem which requires a global solution. The recent military in Thailand where the democratically was overthrown for corrupt practices is a case in point. There is also heavy pressure on the Taiwanese president to resign over corruption charges. The former Italian Prime Minister was voted out office for inability to deal with the daunting economic and social issues as well as corruption.

What is to be done?

Corruption is a world-wide problem, dating back to Old Testament times or before. As globalization becomes an increasing reality, international corruption becomes our problem too, more than ever before. Corruption will not be eliminated while humans live, but must be effectively curbed and restrained if nations are going to prosper and poverty be reduced.

There is need to press for Nigerian companies to observe the highest standards of ethics, and to sanction those who do not. Curbing corruption in Nigeria requires developing a culture of openness, merit system, and strong leadership and political will.

Above all, ethics, accountability and entrenchment of the rule of law are important.

CHAPTER FIFTEEN

Emerging Economies
Environment Case Study

OWNERSHIP, PREBENDALISM,
THE RISE, FALL AND REBIRTH
OF IMB – Pat utomi

T he weight of history was on the back of Edwin Chinye, Managing Director and CEO of International Merchant Bank (IMB), as he gasped - "it has not been easy but our bank is back on track and looking ahead". He could clearly recall the rumors doing the rounds as systemic distress gripped the Nigerian banking system in 1994, claiming among its victims ICON Merchant Bank and Continental Merchant Bank, which along with I,MB dominated merchant banking during the 'golden' years of the 1970s and early 1980s. Everyone, it seemed, expected IMB to go the way of its fellow gladiators of old, all of whom had been recently privatized. IMB's image was obviously as weather-worn as the tarnished blue glass building of its once spectacular corporate head office under constant punishment from the salty breeze of the Atlantic. But Edwin Chinye's new management team seemed to know something most people did not know about IMB.

What they knew obviously was to quickly get into the stock market, enabling the bank to offer its shares through the capital markets at a time when banks were in retreat. The outcome was an over-subscription that calmed Chinye's nerves. IMB had offered investors stock of N150 million, but the demand received was for N189 million. Warehoused IMB shares also went to the market after the capital increase and were over-subscribed.

These bits of good news on the apparent resurrection of IMB notwithstanding, Chinye had to deal with a rapidly changing environment. A new policy directive from the 1997 budget policy package called for a mandatory increase of minimum equity of banks to N500 million. Compared with the previous minimum of N50 million for commercial banks and N40 million for merchant banks this was an average increase of 1025%. The additional challenge from this policy was the elimination of the difference in capital requirements for merchant and commercial banks. The competitive implications of this elimination of the contemplated, If this was the herald for universal banking, was 1MB ready to go against the Guarantee Trust Bank, Nigerian International Bank and the new United Bank for Africa, all of whom were investing significantly in developing new competences and skills in their people. How would the new competitive realities affect traditional merchant banking services of providing term loans after a prolonged period of blurring of the lines between merchant banking and commercial banks as everybody focused on the treasury function to increase the deposit base so as to play the foreign exchange market?

If the new team was going to stay in merchant banking, they would be late corners to a crowded commercial banking scene in which the older players had already made investments in spread of their branch networks. The bank also lacked the advantage of the second generation of successful commercial banks which had already benefited from the shortcomings of the spread of the old banks. The big question was what kinds of products would the new IMB team be looking at? Edwin Chinye had his job cut out for him.

The IMB story

It used to be the yardstick for measuring effectiveness and innovation in banking. Its rise, fall and current effort at renewal encapsulate the evolution of merchant banking. These swings of fortune are closely tied to corporate culture, personnel changes and the nature of government participation in business. The turn of events at the bank have also been closely tied to varying strategies for adapting to the political and economic environment in a way that saw a tight niche player transform into an omnibus merchant bank, with consequences for skills-strategy fit and organizational discipline.

The International Merchant Bank (IMB) began its corporate course as a branch of First National Bank of Chicago (FNBC). The entry of FNBC into Nigeria itself is a classic story of tracking opportunity. It began with recognition of the acute inadequacy of quality hotel rooms in the then Nigerian capital city of Lagos by a Nigerian businessman, Chief I. S. Adewale. This was in the period following the quadrupling of oil prices as a result of the Yom Kippur Arab-Israeli war of October 1973.

Nigeria was experiencing a boom and new self-confidence that meant travel to Nigeria by foreign businessmen would go up. Also on the horizon was Nigeria's commitment to host the 2nd World Festival of Black and African Arts and Culture (FESTAC 77). This meant that there would be tremendous pressure on the Federal Palace Hotel which was the only international standard hotel in Lagos. Adewale's interest in developing a hotel complex led him to a USAID official who introduced him to the Overseas Private Investment Corporation (OPIC) in the United States. The outcome of Adewale's prospecting was that the FNBC agreed to be syndicate manager for a loan to fund the building of a hotel in Lagos.

The conditions laid down by FNBC required that a multinational company participate in the venture. Occidental Petroleum came along with a N40,000 (forty thousand Naira) investment. The consortium of banks to make the N12 million loans soon came together. Construction of the Eko Hotel complex was hardly under way when it became clear the project would be a huge success. A small phase of the complex, the Kuramo Lodge, had been quickly completed and put into operation. Within 12 months of opening for business the Kuramo Lodge was generating enough to fund the working capital needs of the project. In the end only five of the N12 million were drawn down.

At this time Nigeria's foreign reserves had shot up to U.S. $29 billion. There was not much by way of treasury management skills at the Central Bank of Nigeria. FNBC was immediately interested in being portfolio managers for the Central Bank of Nigeria (CBN). To be able to offer that service, FNBC was told it had to have an office in Lagos. FNBC Nigeria thus came into being in August 1974. When it opened its doors for business with a staff of fifteen persons it was committed to a small shop that would essentially give it access to working for the CBN.

The start-up philosophy of FNBC (Nig) emphasized tight credit control. The culture was that of a close-knit family exemplified by the fact that on the birthdays of each of the officers a box of chocolate came all the way from the chairman limit whatever exposure it had to known multinational companies. In that first year the bank had an asset base of N7.2 million. It also declared a profit of N89, 000.

Due to the indigenization policy of the federal government in the 1970s the First Bank of Chicago had to divest 60 per cent of its interest in the bank to the federal government. It thus became a joint venture partner with the government. At this time the bank changed its name to International Merchant Bank and entered into a technical management services agreement with the First National Bank of Chicago. The terms of this agreement expired in 1982. The bank by 1987 had opened four other branches in Kano, Kaduna, Port Harcourt and Aba.

By 1977 IMB began to feel the influence of the government on the bank when it appointed the board of directors to represent its shareholding. The government, being a major shareholder in the bank, had a say in the appointment of the board of the bank and its CEO. Since the bank was doing extremely well, each successive government was interested in seeing their interest covered by a representative on both the board and the management of the bank. A situation arose whereby every change in government or its policies led to a change in the leadership of 1MB and its policies. This did not augur well for the bank as there was a lack of continuity and accountability. Each management team realized that their term was limited to the time for which the government that appointed them was in power. This was the position despite the fact that the bank had a foreign partner.

The Americans played a very active role in the affairs of the bank. As of 1986 the board of directors had three representatives from FNBC, one of whom was the Deputy Managing Director. However by 1991,the FNBC decided to divest entirely its interest in the bank through a sale of its 40 per cent equity holding in what it described as a global restructuring of its overseas operations. Of the 40 per cent shares owned by the Americans, 10 per cent was sold to staff and the remaining 30 per cent was warehoused by IMB Securities Plc.

In 1985, the bank moved to its present corporate headquarters, the IMB plaza, located at 1 Akin Adesola Street, along the famous Bar Beach in Victoria Island. IMB became the fore-runner of banks in Nigeria today that conduct their business from unique architectural structures. It was unique not only in the physical structure of its headquarters building but also in its product mix.

IMB offered standard banking products. But it also gave more than was generally available in the market at the time. In those products it offered like the other banks, it tried to make a difference with the quality of service it provided. In its domestic money market services, it provided such products as treasury bills, commercial papers and bankers acceptances. It also developed a unique scheme known as the Short Term Investment Management Scheme, whereby it acted as investment manager for funds deposited by investors. IMB was also a key player in the international fund management services with a portfolio in excess of $100 million. At the time these were innovative products.

The IMB mission statement in its 1986 annual report read "Our mission is to infuse professionalism into the Nigerian banking system by providing international standard banking services. We remain in the forefront of the industry in assisting our customers to meet the challenges of the economic adjustment process. Our extensive representation both in the domestic and international industrial and financial centers has positioned IMB to efficiently execute financial transactions around the world. We remain committed to complementing government's effort in realizing the tremendous economic potential of the country."

To a large extent the bank was able to achieve these goals. It took the lead in providing banking products for the various companies that required such facilities. For instance IMB was mandated by the Imo state government in 1985 to arrange a 27-month N20 million projects tied bridging facility to activate the International Glass Industry Limited, Aba and to provide advisory services to the state government. Also in 1985, the bank was appointed financial adviser to the Plateau state government and technical manager for the establishment and management of the Lion Bank of Nigeria Plc. It was also appointed the issuing house for the public offer of the bank's shares. This was quite a feat considering the fact that the bank state when setting up Gateway Bank, as well as in Anambra state for the setting up of Orient Bank.

It was recognized that the bank possessed an expertise and skills mix that was not matched by most in the industry then. This was especially so with its strong capital market group. It led many of the major syndications of the time such as the N100 million multi-instruments public issue of SCOA Nigeria Limited. Also when in 1986 the Nigerian Bottling Company needed to finance its Maize Products Division, it was IMB it turned to for a N25 million syndicated credit facility. The bank's reputation also allowed it to have technical services agreements with Intercity Bank Plc and Lion Bank for the provision of management services to the bank. IMB has spawned executives for several other banks. The list of chief executives of Nigerian banks reads like an IMB alumni association.

In 1992, IMB became a public liability company and in 1994, following privatization of government-controlled companies, the federal government's shareholding in the bank was sold to the general public and IMB became a publicly quoted company listed on the Nigerian Stock Exchange.

The Evolving Nigerian Financial System

The tone for the golden years of the evolution of the Nigerian financial system was set in the great cooperation between the Central Bank of Nigeria (CBN) and the ministry of finance in the period leading up to, and immediately following, the blue ribbon commission chaired by Dr. Pius Okigbo which reviewed the Nigerian financial system. While the Okigbo Commission was still at work on the Nigerian financial system the government decided that it was compulsorily acquiring a stake of 60% in all banks in which ownership was predominantly foreign. Where there was some private Nigerian holding the government was going to acquire whatever would bring the Nigerian stake to 60%. This policy initiative was adopted after the fact by the Okigbo committee and was implemented with military despatch in 1976.

The tops of the big banks were soon Nigerianised with Sam Asabia, Paul Ogwuma and Umaru Muttalab hoisting the flag in banking as chief executives of the First Bank, Union Bank and in UBA, the big three. At this time, UBA was the bank to watch. It would seem that back in the mid-1970s the French made a big bid to improve their position in the Nigerian economy to have a balance with their high profile in the economies of francophone West Africa. The impact of this on the Nigerian bank that led the French assault, UBA, was that it was seen as innovative and aggressive even though BCCI turned out to be the first bank to dazzle the industry with spectacular profit. Subsequent history may now provide insight into the source of this phenomenal profit performance by BCCI. Societe Generale, which was also a new entrant into an industry where a presence since 1893 had given First Bank the advantage of a wide branch network, also attracted attention as they played for a share of the market dominated for a long time by Standard Bank (later First Bank), Barclays Bank (later Union Bank) and UBA.

At the time of the inauguration of the Okigbo panel there were four active merchant banks with ICON as clear leader drawing strength from the Nigerian Industrial Development Bank (NIDB), its primary shareholders, and Morgan Guarantee and Trust Company, its technical partners and shareholder. Citibank was at this time winding up, as their reaction to government policy to participate in the ownership of the banks was to opt to exit the Nigerian market.

NAL Merchant Bank which pioneered merchant banking in Nigeria continued as a quiet niche player focused on relationship management with a limited portfolio. This was consistent with its conservative British antecedents, the bank having come about by the merger of Philip Hill Nigeria, which was founded in 1960, with the Nigerian Acceptances Ltd. Buying into NAL's major competitor, the Nigerian Merchant Bank, was to be UBA's signal of intent to alter the structure of the Nigerian banking industry. This happened when UBA acquired 40% of the, stock of Nigeria Merchant Bank, NMB.

By 1981, however, Chase Merchant Bank (CMB) and IMB had begun to assert their strengths and were soon the clear leaders in both asset size and market leadership.

The leadership of these banks in merchant banking was to be severely affected by two factors. These were the extreme politicization of Structural Adjustment Program (SAP) was being implemented. The lowering of barriers to entry during SAP was a response to the thesis that more players intensify competition which, along with the deregulation of interest rates and the pricing of foreign exchange, leads to greater efficiency and better service so as to win more customers. The end result should be that the capacity of the system to finance venture initiatives increases. This increased depth of the financial market, or financial deepening, was one of the primary goals of adjustment policies.

The Legacy of Government Participation in Ownership of Banks

There is near consensus on the fact that the regime of General Olusegun Obasanjo which implemented the nationalization of majority interests in the banking industry primarily wanted Nigeria to participate in the remarkable opportunities for profit in banking. There was relative stability on the executive side of the boards and the cost of corporate governance remained quite low. In IMB, for example, Alhaji Lateef jakande, who was the first government-appointed chairman, would not accept any official motor vehicle and remuneration for services. He also did not encourage board meetings outside the country. The board also kept away from issues that were the traditional exclusive domain of management.

This culture did not continue after the exit of the Obasanjo regime. Even though clear notice was available from the very beginning when NAL managing director, Gamaliel Onosode, had a run-in with ministry of finance officials when he insisted that the officials follow proper procedure in introducing their very first director to the board in 1976. It would take the collapse of discipline, after Obasanjo before the full effect of government participation in banking came into full view. Corporate governance became a major expense item for most banks. Board meetings were routinely held in Europe and North America and most non-executive directors had cars assigned for their exclusive use. Non-executive directors began to interfere with promotions, appointments, location of branch offices; and the setting up of pet departments.

Two dramatic incidents related to the appointment of directors at IMB illustrate the extent of the disorder that characterised government-appointed boards. In one instance two people showed up to take the same seat on the board. Two gentlemen both named Ibrahim Lawal had come as chairman of the board in response to the press publications of the appointment of an Ibrahim Lawal as chairman. The board meeting had to be postponed to seek clarification on which Ibrahim Lawal was on the board of IMB. On another occasion a gentleman who had apparently been named to the board was accosted by a friend who was surprised he had not been showing up at board meetings. It turned out the newspapers had mis-spelt his name and the appointing authorities had not written to inform him of the good fortune of his being appointed to the board of IMB.

In what was most probably a bid to satisfy so many constituencies anxious to serve on the apparently "lucrative" bank boards the rate of reshuffle of bank boards had become an annual affair. If the remarks of the outgoing World Bank resident representative in Nigeria in 1995, that he had dealt with six finance ministers in three years is anything to go by, it should not be surprising that some bank executive directors lasted only one year on the job. Most of the finance ministers coming in quick rotation wanted to appoint their cronies to make the best of the opportunity. The impact of this uncertainty of tenure on the loyalty of executive directors and their ethical disposition is best imagined.

There were sometimes grave disputes between the non-executive chairman and the CEO, as we shall see with IMB at the peak of the intrigue in the disputations between one of the later CEOs and the chairman. FNBC decided they had had enough and it was time for divesting.

The ease with which executives could be appointed and dropped was such that every day spent in office by many of the executives was opportunity for lobbying to stay on. The effect was that all manners of loans were approved for all kinds of soldiers and politicians who could claim to have influence. This made for a deep hole of bad and doubtful debts in the books of many banks.

There was also the impact of government participate on the quality of management. Merit suffered very much as a criterion for picking top managers. Affirmative action, referred to as ensuring federal character in Nigeria, was abused, with cronyism becoming a major yardstick of measuring position in organizational hierarchy.

The Political and Economic Environment

When modern banking came to Nigeria with the Bank of British West Africa in 1894, Nigeria had a colonial government and the economy was primarily a subsistence agriculture economy in transition to a cash crop economy with the harvesting for export of cash crops being introduced by European merchants who themselves got together to found a bank that was to begin the modern age of banking in Nigeria.

The colonial cash crop economy persisted with banks essentially supporting produce merchants until the 1950s. The pressures to allow for an indigenous merchant class resulted in the rapid expansion of the banking industry with the founding of many indigenous banks in the 1920s. Many collapsed an experience that was to repeat itself in the early 1950s.

The 1950s were the era of constitution-making, self-government and the first real attempt at regulating the banking industry. Self-government led to competitive communalism and this competition between the regions of the Nigerian federation produced the first fruits of industrialization in Nigeria. Industrialization generally followed the new tradition coming out of Latin America where Raul Prebisch as Executive Secretary of the Economic Commission for Latin America was making the Import Substitution Industrialization (ISI) strategy popular. Independence came to Nigeria in October of 1960 with a democratically elected government working to boost infrastructure and provide jobs through ISI enterprises many of which were wholly owned by government.

By 1966 the federal structure on which competitive communalism was founded and which sustained a growth rate of more than 3.5% had crumbled following a military coup which replaced many political market structures with hierarchies aligned to the command structure of the army. Soon the international prices of crude oil discovered in commercial quantities in 1956 in the Niger delta quadrupled following the Yom Kippur war between the Arabs and Israel in 1973.

The political culture was to shift from competitive communalism to an obsession with getting a piece of the so-called national cake, a culture described by American political scientist, Richard Joseph, as bureaucratic prebendalism. Oil prices collapsed after peaking with the Iranian revolution and the resultant Dutch disease as Nigeria struggled to control a Midget that had grown dramatically and was not well managed. The divergence of Nigeria's exchange rate from its purchasing power parity became an international scandal that was not dealt with until foreign banks began to freeze lines of credit extended to their Nigerian correspondent banks. In the end, Nigeria embarked on an economic adjustment program which had as a key platform financial liberalization.

Financial liberalization was by this time a key part of World Bank's adjustment program prescription. Drawing largely from the McKinon-Shaw hypothesis, the Bretton Woods institutions had come to rely much on recovery through interest rate deregulation, exchange rate liberalization and the lowering of entry barriers to free banking from monopoly practices. The SAP was pursued with different levels of commitment and intensity from 1986 until it was abandoned in 1994. The disastrous economic performance in 1994 led to a change of heart and effort to return to the path of economic reform as the military struggled with the promise of return to democracy.

The Leadership Challenge at IMB

The rise, fall and rebirth of IMB comes across clearly in the way its many CEOs have handled the assignment and the strategies they have pursued.

The Banigo Years

Ebitimi Banigo had a clear advantage over the other Nigerian CEOs of merchant banks. Of the big five merchant banks competing in 1981, only IMB with Banigo at the helm had a leader with a background that was grounded in merchant banking. He came to the job with distinct competences in syndications, debenture issues and money market instruments in general. Banigo had just come to IMB via Chase (Nigeria) from Citibank in the United Kingdom from where he was posted to Nigeria as an expatriate. His return to Nigeria had been largely at the instance of government officials who were embarrassed that they were paying so much money to Citibank for managing loan syndications only to find out that the job was being handled by a young Nigerian. He brought with him the goodwill of knowing the correspondent banks in the UK as many of the bankers were his former colleagues.

The bankers abroad who knew Banigo on first name basis were obviously quite disposed to providing IMB with confirming lines of credit they were reluctant to offer other banks in Nigeria. This would prove to be a major competitive advantage for IMB in a heavily import-dependent trading economy. Once government got active in ownership structure of banks Nigerian deputy CEOs were appointed for the hitherto foreign-owned banks. Banigo was one of the new deputy CEOs and arrived at IMB in that position. He quickly set about his bullish approach which called for a plan to grow merchant banking very quickly.

Banigo found very willing collaborators in a few IMB people like Arnold Ekpe, who went on in later years to Citibank, London, and then to the position of CEO of the West African regional transnational bank, Ecobank. 'Soon after Banigo began to establish his imprint at IMB, the Nigerian deputy CEOs took charge as managing directors in the banks in which government had acquired majority shareholding. Once Banigo took over as CEO the stage was set for conflict.

The conflict was to flow from the clash of cultures and strategy between the First Chicago tradition and Banigo's disposition shaped by his antecedents. First Chicago was very conservative. This orientation was so clear that policy required 'MB to report on a daily basis all credit exposure. In the books of the parent bank provisions would immediately be made for such exposure. First Chicago was obviously more interested in liability management when compared with the general European tradition that emphasized the asset side of the business. Banigo clearly disagreed with conservative growth projections.

First Chicago wanted a strategy that focused on servicing local subsidiaries of multinational companies but Banigo obviously wanted to build the biggest and best merchant bank in the region. Banigo believed that if a merchant bank was to be competitive it really had to be a global player. He placed a high premium on the information-gathering value of a global presence. This perspective was driven partly by his feeling that poor countries were paying too high a premium to get foreign banks to buy into the risks they were syndicating.

Conflict was also lurking in the fact that Banigo did not see First Chicago as a technical partner but rather as a foreign partner because they were a commercial bank in the United States. Most of the products that were to make IMB the toast of the Nigerian banking industry were developed locally.

In spite of these clashes of perspectives, Banigo built on a First Chicago policy of training its people by inaugurating a human resources strategy that required the hiring of the best and brightest, exposure of these young managers through delegating responsibility, and providing them leadership that helped build team spirit. In addition a tradition of local and international training programs infused confidence in the comparatively younger officers of the bank, many of whom were catapulted to very senior positions by the new management. At a time during the Banigo years the mystic of IMB was of a gathering of the best and brightest young talent in. the country. So widespread was the myth that many 'accused' Banigo of hiring only old boys from Kings College Lagos and the Harvard Business School, his alma mater.

With the civilian regime firmly entrenched, the

nature of the board changed, affecting Banigo's very professional style. Questionable loans to politicians began to mount, causing First Chicago to begin to fear the possibilities of a "financial meltdown". One Nigerian group head at the bank confessed that he stopped signing off on loans because he feared the consequences of a future investigation. He recalled several "weird" loan applications including the request by a gubernatorial aspirant for a loan to build a hall he would donate to his community in Benue state. Another customer collected in cash the sum of a loan meant, ostensibly, for a furniture factory.

He checked-in the cases of currency at the Lagos Airport, leaving it at the mercy of careless baggage handlers who dropped one of them, scattering nearly $400,000 worth of naira notes around the domestic terminal.

When the civilian regime was overthrown at the end of 1983 the new regime of Mohammadu Buhari provided the trigger that First Chicago needed to come in and say: "no more". This brought back the professional in Banigo. Soon there were internal controls and loan review systems. Innovation and aggressive marketing were, however, not sacrificed at the altar of tightening credit policy. The bank began to grow rapidly in the face of a few very lucrative real estate deals. The Chevron estate deal reportedly had turned in a sizeable profit with the rent advance, and five years' rent was still to come. IMB estates were then constructed in Victoria Island, Lagos and Port Harcourt as was the blue glass ocean-front headquarters office complex, IMB plaza that came to symbolize the virility of IMB.

Even though personnel tradition had been badly affected by board interference and the promotion of mainly candidates sponsored by board members, the new thrust in 1984 emphasized meeting targets. It was the practice then to request those unable to meet the targets set for them to submit their letters of resignation. These practices as well as the new controls helped give IMB a distinct competitive advantage.

Banigo was to learn from the public media a few months later, after yet another change of government, that he had been replaced as CEO of IMB.

The Kollere Years

Banigo was succeeded as chief executive at IMB by Mohammed Kollere in 1985. Kollere met a bank that was already bloated from pressures by directors to locate branches around their home towns. Among the more difficult to justify was the setting up of two branches with less than an hour's drive between them, in Aba and Port Harcourt. Unlike the habit in many parts of the world where new CEOs move in on lingering challenges to organizational effectiveness, Kollere seemed to take his time to focus on these problems.

The change in leadership style was very quickly obvious. The tradition of delegating responsibility to younger officers seemed to stop. Most foreign business travel was now prerogative of senior executives no matter the competence required for the assignment. This was not motivated necessarily by the desire to reduce costs as board meetings which hitherto took place in Nigeria now tended to be scheduled for locations outside the country, leading to a ballooning of the cost of corporate governance.

The immediate effect of the change in style was the perception on the part of many of the staff that the organization had become more bureaucratic, less innovative and less creative. The decision-making processes became more centralized under the new leadership, a point of some concern in view of the fact that Kollere was often out of town. The bank's new management also brought in many new hands into senior levels of the organization. Even though many of these new hands were thought to be quite competent compared to what happened in other banks as federal character affirmative action intensified, it nonetheless affected morale. As career prospects dimmed for young officers looking forward to promotion into positions, now filled from outside, sharp practices and truancy increased. The organization also continued down a top-heavy path with its many implications for organizational effectiveness and cost.

Others give Kollere credit for beginning the process of turning the bank around once he became sensitive to the approaching precipice, especially after the federal government began the process of financial liberalization and the lowering of entry barriers into banking. He brought in Arthur Andersen to work with management on a restructuring program and was quite committed to implementing the outcome of the Arthur Andersen study. At this time he was beginning to win the loyalty of traditional IMB people because of his administrative skills. He was noted to have a good capacity for reading people. One IMB veteran called him "a shrewd administrator" giving him credit for his skill at allocating resources and picking the right people for assignments. He had set in motion a big drive to recover many of the non-performing facilities while beginning the implementation of the IMB program when he was removed as managing director by the federal government in 1990.

The Lawal Transition

The exit of the Kollere management as the implementation of the restructuring was to get under way meant that a big challenge awaited the new team led by Lawal as managing director and Evelyn Brume as executive director. That challenge was to tear the new management team apart very quickly. It would seem that Brume supported the implementation of the Arthur Andersen proposed reforms but Lawal was more circumspect.

Brume's effervescent personality meant the disagreement between the two leaders of the bank would not be quiet boardroom matter. The disagreement was so intense it nearly ground operations to a halt. In the end government had to step in to separate the feuding executives. Lawal swapped places with John Oyetan at NAL and Brume was moved to First Bank.

The Oyetan Valley

There are many who think the difficulties at IMB reached their lowest levels shortly after John Oyetan took over from Lawal as managing director. This is subject to quite a bit of conjecture. Some say Oyetan had been a rival too long to put his heart into the job. Others attribute it to personal leadership style which favored concentration of power at the top, a fact that clashed with the tradition of leadership at the bank.

The new Managing Director was locked in battle on many fronts. On one front he seemed to feud endlessly with the chairman of the board, Effiong Essien. On other fronts he engaged staff who imagined themselves the last line of defence for the IMB tradition. First Chicago had decided by this time to withdraw from the partnership, giving as an excuse its own global restructuring and repositioning. The responsibility for implementing the exit of the foreign partners fell on the new management team. It was to become yet another source of disaffection between some staff and the board.

The IMB board worked out an arrangement to buy out First Chicago interests at a specific price in U.S. dollars. It was a deal many IMB staff felt was shortsighted. The bank was to warehouse the shares for selling off later. Four weeks after the deal, the exchange rate changed and about 50 per cent of the value of the shares was lost.

Oyetan was eventually replaced by Bashir Tukur. The personable Bashir Tukur arrived when decline was in full throttle. This was a time when the challenge was to grow volume business and neither Tukur nor any of his executive colleagues had the background for such marketing-driven operations. As the fifth board of directors for the bank in about seven years, a very short-term outlook was sure to dominate their approach so they surprised no one by coming up with hardly any initiative. Tukur put his father-figure image to work trying to correct perceived wrongs of the years before.

Privatization and Resurrection

When the privatization program of the Babangida regime began under SAP the banks were not listed for privatization. Even though financial liberalization was being implemented Later, almost at a whim that caught the market by surprise, thr= President decided to sell government interests in the banks. Several of the privatized banks were soon to become moribund following systemic distress. This was not to be the case with IMB. A group of shareholders, including a former executive director, Edwin Chinye, bought enough IMB shares to seek to give direction to the bank. Chinye, whose short one-year tenure at IMB had provided him insight into the strengths, weaknesses and potential of the bank, was named managing director by the board when Tukur resigned.

As soon as he: moved in, Chinye knew he had to quickly produce a restructuring program if the bank was to escape the fate that befell other leading merchant banks of yore. The new management team decided to take a 3-staged approach:
• Address outflow, i.e. the financial position of the bank;
• Recapitalize;
• Refocus.

IMB needed to realign and restructure the internal flow of work in order to enhance its efficiency. A retrenchment program was embarked on. This had to be handled with great skill to avoid loss of bank assets. A lot of assets were varying circumstances in the past. It was also discovered that an average number of members of staff spent at least 25 per cent of their time doing nothing. Many of the senior managers were seen by the new management as inefficient, and they felt the need to weed them out. There was a reduction of at least 40 per cent and an injection of about 5 per cent new staff.

The bank went through two stages of retrenchment but at the same time also undertook two recruitment exercises in order to replace and upgrade the staff quality.

In his report contained in the annual report of the bank for 1994/95, the Chief Executive Officer noted: The major problem imposed on the bank by the depressed economy is the predominance of non-performing loans. Many companies considered as good prospects with healthy financial ratings at the time of credit appraisal/approval could not honor their obligations on due dates... Our primary objectives were and still are to maximize recovery potential on all non-performing loans while taking proactive account management approach towards healthy ones to make sure they do not degenerate.

The imperative of building loan recovery capacity could not be questioned. The problem with the financial position of the bank was the fact that the inflow of revenue was very low but costs were increasing, with inadequate controls. The Managing Director decided to address the issue of cutting costs first. A policy was introduced whereby all expenditure above N100 must be passed through the Managing Director for approval. This took up much executive time but the management felt it was a measure that was needed at the time to send a signal on the importance of cost control. The management believes that this procedure reduced the abuses that had been going on. Furthermore the contract for N26 million that was already awarded for the repairs of the bad air-conditioning system in the IMB building was cancelled.

Another objective was to boost its fee-based activities from acting as an issuing house. To this end it created a registrar's department. The bank also made every effort to improve on its capacity to be a player in the capital markets, taking Inland Bank to the market. Those shares were over subscribed by about N1 million.

The bank also opened discussions with some foreign investors who expressed interest in the warehoused shares, three of which deposited $50,000 each as a demonstration of their interest in buying the shares. The bank successfully pursued the course of recapitalization by way of a public offer of shares for subscription in 1996. This was necessary in order to strengthen the capital base and to provide the much needed working capital support. The proceeds were also to be used in computerization of the bank as well as refurbishment of the existing structures. At the time of preparing for the share offer, Chinye spoke confidently in spite of the fact that such leading banks as First Bank had suddenly lost nearly half their market capitalization in reaction to the growing weariness with prospects in bank performance. By the time the recapitalization exercise was over, Edwin Chinye noted, "We would have enough resources available to help us re-focus." The offer turned out successful with a significant over-subscription.

The sale of some real estate owned by the bank was another means of raising capital for the bank. IMB had a housing estate which had been conceived as a means of encouraging senior staff to live near the office. The bank's welfare package for most senior cadres included free accommodation in fully furnished flats. IMB also provided electricity with a stand-by generator and phones in bank owned estates. The cost of providing this free service was weighing the bank down and the estate was offered for sale. Allowances were increased and the occupants of these flats were asked to move out. The company also had 100 vehicles which it encouraged staff to buy while only a few were retained. The Managing Director noted that "if the bank had not been privatized it would not have been able to carry out all these reforms." IMB was also reviewing its management information system with a view to enhancing efficiency by capturing transactions on a real time basis, and considering-a long-term plan of converting the status of the bank from a merchant bank to a commercial bank.

In the bank's prospectus for the offer of shares, the Chairman had the following to say about the future of the bank: IMB has complied with the Central Bank of Nigeria's December 1995 stood at over 95 per cent of non-performing accounts. The substantial size of loan loss provision is to enhance its ability to maintain the earning momentum of its basic business while reducing the portfolio of problem credits. This development has now enabled the bank to operate on a clean slate while rigorous and fruitful efforts are channeled towards loan recovery. Thus IMB is now in a better position to withstand increasing competition and lay emphasis on service delivery, while continuing to explore ways to reduce risk in the years ahead.

As at March 1997, these early initiatives of the Chinye era are still being closely watched by a market that appears to have given a positive nod to the reforms. The next challenge for the management team is meeting the capital increase requirements of the Central Bank of Nigeria which has given all the banks in the country up till the end of 1998 to raise their capital base to N500 million (five hundred million naira). The criteria for evaluation of performance will, however, be significantly different from the earlier years because banking was highly subsidized by policy until 1995.

The Environment, Leadership Style and Performance at IMB

When FNBC opened shop in Lagos its primary objective was to provide portfolio management services to the Central Bank of a country with rapidly growing reserves but with limited skills in managing the investment of its cash. At the time the making of portfolio management decisions at CBN was based on very little analysis; the responsibility was left with officers with hardly any experience. First Chicago, which came precisely to get a piece of the action of providing portfolio investment services to the government of Nigeria, was focused primarily on offering that service. The strategy of the bank in Lagos was thus very clear and required little leadership to provide direction for the bank in Nigeria. Lagos was on autopilot programmed in Chicago.

The relationship between leadership, strategy, and performance really became a subject of interest following the arrival of Ebitimi Banigo at the bank. Banigo was determined to show that there was no technical benefit accruing from the foreign shareholders, the 'NBC. Basing his premise on the fact that First Chicago was a commercial bank and IMB a merchant bank, he insisted FNBC did not have the necessary competences. To prove his point he aggressively pursued the brightest talent he could find and attracted them to the bank. In one typical example, he went on a visit to Chase Merchant Bank, his former bank, and found a young Certified Public Accountant (U.S. equivalent of the Chartered Accountant) who had just returned from the United States and was waiting to see the CEO. He put pressure on the young man assuring him that the real action was at IMB. He followed up with persistent calls at the home of the gentleman until he opted to come to IMB.

On the new recruit's first day on the job he was asked to represent the bank at a loan syndication meeting with authority to commit the bank if he thought it was a good deal. Not even equipped with a call card he set out with Banigo's card with authority to commit the bank using that card.

With such aggressiveness it was not hard to tell that Banigo was totally focused on making IMB the prime merchant bank in the land. The strategy on which the intent was predicated was in creating trade finance products and taking the perspective that a global presence was necessary if IMB was to serve its Nigerian customers well. The strategy also placed a premium on empowering very bright and well trained young men and women. It was easy to develop shared values on this as Banigo himself was only about thirty-five years old. A culture of camaraderie in which use of first names was the norm underlined the IMB difference. This was reflected in the rate of change of performance indicators.

Following Banigo's arrival, gross earnings went up by more than 142% in 1982 and then continued to rise by an average rate of more than 25% per annum until 1985 before tapering off in 1986, the year Banigo left. Similar trends can also be observed for pre-tax profits and deposits. Given outcome from application of available resources, those early years turned out to be IMB's finest. But not all the Banigo years reflect hard-core professionalism and an obsession with being nothing but the finest and the best.

The veterans of IMB sometimes refer to the Banigo I and Banigo 11 years. They refer to the second phase as the period during which certain events apparently made Banigo more sensitive to life after IMB. In this period more politically motivated decisions became obvious, as were favours designed to satisfy certain interests. It was the legacy of Banigo 1I that Mohammed Kollere met when he arrived to replace Ebitimi Banigo in 1986.

Kollere seemed to have come not so much with a purpose to change the strategic direction of IMB, as he had hardly any merchant banking background, as rather with a mandate to bring some discipline into this bank where they called each other by first names. A mandate for some affirmative action to bring in northerners, who were not well represented on the staff roll, was also discernible. Strategic concerns came much later to Kollere's tenure. It was motivated more by the lowering of entry barriers as people with access scrambled for banking licences so they could participate in the rents that flowed through the huge 'subsidy' to banks through a dual exchange rate that left much room for arbitrage.

The new positioning proposed under advice from Arthur Andersen took cognizance of the increasing cost of money in a market that was increasingly built on how much cash was available to play the foreign exchange market. It was to see the bank move directly or indirectly towards commercial banking where direct dealings with savers reduced the cost of capital.

Kollere did not stay long enough to realize the change of strategic direction. Speculations were that some of his northern colleagues that came into the bank through him were increasingly frustrated with the fact that he was hardly around and that he depended much on a power triangle with Bismark Rewane and Evelyn Brume at the base. With time they began to complain in the right places that he ran the bank from the aircraft. This seemed to coincide with the efforts of his ambitious deputy, Rasaq Lawal. Kollere was soon removed and Lawal named managing director. Mrs Brume was appointed an executive director with Lawal putting them on the war path over the implementation of the Arthur Andersen report. The acrimony was so loud they were both sent off to the boards of other banks.

It was with this reshuffle that John Oyetan arrived at IMB from NAL Merchant Bank to which Lawal was moved. The pattern obvious from his tenure was a perceived personalization of procedures. Customers ostensibly sat for hours in long queues to see the CEO, some of the responsible officers suggest, while they sat idle wondering what was going on. The many fractious disputes and discipline issues from this era affected thinking on strategy. The bank's chief of corporate development during these years, Okey Udezue, recalls there was hardly any discussion of where the bank was heading to during this period.

At this stage the bank became polarised and tense. Ethnic divisions which were absent during the Banigo years and very much under control in later years were thrust to the fore. People hardly spoke openly on any matter at this period, some of the managers recall.

By the end of 1992, Oyetan was removed and a new executive group led by Bashir Tukur came in. Tukur's main objective, it would seem, was to calm nerves. He brought a very human angle to management and often went the extra mile to ensure fairness to all parties. He was hardly the self-serving type and he set standards of discipline that obviously were too high for one of his colleagues in executive management. His calming of nerves may, however, have played a critical part in saving the bank. One of his executive directors, a former CBN official, brought to the party his contacts and goodwill with regulatory authorities. This was an asset badly needed at the time in the bank. On competitively positioning the bank, however, the three in the executive team, as one staff remarked, were way out of their depths.

The effect of these developments can be seen in the fact that profit before tax continued to decline, in percentage of total terms, from 1987. A computation of real growth rates for most performance indicators show a sea of negatives from 1988 to 1995; this in spite of the huge subsidies the foreign exchange market provided the banking industry. Usually these subsidies showed up in the bottomline or in the accounts of individuals who managed banks during this era. The Tukur team was still in a holding pattern when privatization resulted in a core group which brought in the Chinye management team.

Evolution of Industry Structure and Performance

Modern banking started in Nigeria to support trade finance needs of British merchants in the colonial era. The monopoly nature of the banking of the 1890s was first threatened by the violation of cartel arrangements when shipping agents who started the Bank for British West Africa were accused of incursions into trading. The founding of the rival Anglo-African bank was designed by the traders to get back at the shipping companies. The rivalry was short-lived as BBWA soon acquired its rival. When Barclays Bank came on the scene to compete with BBWA which was then a Standard Chartered subsidiary, the intensity of competition was low.

Foreign Partners and Industry Structure

The structure of the Nigerian banking industry did not begin to change in a significant way until the oil boom of the early 1970s, and the stability of government in Nigeria following the end of the Nigerian Civil War began to attract foreign banks. The impact of the participation of foreign banks in evolving industry structure and performance has been an important variable in gauging the intensity of rivalry, the barriers to entry for those who could not find attractive foreign partners and the power of both suppliers and buyers in the industry.

As such, foreign players as UBA's technical partners, Banque Nationale de Paris (BNP) and BCCI entered the market with new strategies that produced remarkable performance outcomes, the stakes went up in banking as the competitive response of others intensified rivalry. Foreign partnership also provided a competitive edge in terms of linkages to correspondence banks which provided credit lines for financing import license based international trade. Possibilities of building foreign assets from interests accruing from trade funds transferred before Letters of Credit were presented for payment, proved to be very significant for banks with a big confirming network and, therefore, a huge volume of transactions.

Foreign participation also made a difference in that the balance sheet of the bigger foreign shareholder could be at the disposal of the local bank depending on the nature of the alliance between the bank and its foreign partner. NIB clearly benefited from this in its being able to serve in a custodial role for the Nigerian Stock Exchange. In this case, Citibank which is already a global player in custodial services, not only provides the guarantee for its Nigerian subsidiary but, in fact, facilitated the development of the modernization of the Nigerian Stock Exchange through a grant and consultancy services.

Foreign partners can also attract customers to a local

subsidiary by pulling their home country customers who enter Nigeria to their local subsidiary. This can have the effect of influencing the cost of funds for the bank from the volume of deposits from big cash-awash customers. In the same manner the bargaining power of their customers can be high because they are primarily blue chip enterprises.

Manpower Policy and Competition

Pre-1970s banking was not a high skills industry attracting the best and brightest. With the construction boom that followed the surge in the value of crude petroleum, the industry that many of the very bright young men wanted to go to was architecture. The significant investment IMB made in developing skilled young men who quickly got authority and became role models changed all that. Other banks which had given lower priority to training recognized the differential advantage IMB was developing through investing in growing the know-how and know-why of banking in its people. The competitive response was swift. It soon became easy to tell the banks that were investing in their people from those that were not. The self-confidence of IMB managers returning from professional banking training in Europe and general management programs at the Harvard Business School set the standards for the industry.

When financial liberalization came and lowered entry barriers into banking, investment in manpower development banks were the ones investing the most in manpower development. The relationship between knowledge and productivity is seen in the patterns of absorption of information technology in the banking industry.

Regulations, Government Action and the Competition Goal Post

If foreign participation and manpower policies have been key variables that shaped industry in banking in Nigeria, government regulation of the industry has to qualify as the super variable. The 1997 notice of a 1025% increase, on average, in the minimum equity required for banks is a typical example. Banks are already differentiating along the lines of those who already have shareholders funds in excess of that amount, those who have a decent chance of making it before the deadline of December 1998 and those who will be struggling to improve the odds through mergers and takeovers.

Another example of the way government action has affected industry structure is the withdrawal of government agency funds from the commercial and merchant banks into the Central Bank in 1989. The dramatic effect on financial deepening in the country can be seen in the relationship between GDP and monetary aggregates, M1 and M2 in fig. 1. The policy hit, particularly hard, those banks that had developed a competitive edge in their access to parastatals for deposits used mainly in the servicing of the lucrative trading in government-provided foreign exchange.

The arbitrary choice of banks to designate for collection of government revenues in an era of high profile treasury activities shifted the competition goal post in favor of some players. Those banks favored by government invariably have more deposits they use to earn revenue in trade finance and the foreign exchange market.

CONCLUSION

The performance indicators and market response to IMB capital increase suggested a rebounding for IMB. Many challenges remained, however. Which strategic focus Chinye would consider was not so clear yet. The bank was still locked in numerous litigations with staff who were dismissed or retired many years before and even some from the Chinye restructuring. Beside the cost of these litigations and bank assets tied up in court injunctions resulting from these cases, they were pointers to a culture of troubled personnel practices and leadership that had not come to appreciate the impact of best practice in human resource management on the bottomline.

There also remains the challenge of what to do with, and about, the once imposing head office structure which the bank cannot afford to maintain. Among options that had been bandied around was to sell the building and move to more modest accommodation, lease out a part of the building and occupy only two or three floors out of the seven available floor areas, or to sell and remain a tenant in part of the building.

Also remaining as a clear challenge was how to trim the branch network and improve communication with the remaining branches. Even as a privatized enterprise the nature of the alignment of the core group suggested political considerations could not be ruled out in the final choices about branch location.

As Chinye contemplated the future he needed to see a way through all these problems, and then deal with how to build competences that could give the new IMB a distinct competitive advantage in a banking industry on the throes of a major shake-out. If IMB was to go the way of commercial banking he would have to consider the disadvantage in competing with many banks which had a branch network of some significance. Should wholesale commercial banking be more attractive, what would be the strength IMB could bring to an industry in which a few newer commercial banks have been migrating upwards to a wholesale niche in which very few played? Then again, perhaps the Banigo vision of a global merchant bank that opens access for the less favored, reducing the 'prohibitive' rates foreign banks charge Nigerian customers for transactions whose only additional risk is the name of the country, is far from being dated.

For surviving the challenge of 1997 in which indicators point to margins being suite slim for banks, as interest rates drop far below the rate of inflation, Chinye and his team had to come to terms with the problem of asset quality and weighted average cost of funds. The choice between lowering asset quality and charging an interest rate that allowed for a wider spread, with the consequence of bigger provisions to cover bad and doubtful loans and staying with loss-making quality assets, were among the short-term worries for IMB.

Culled from the book *"Managing Uncertainty"* by Prof. Pat Utomi

CHAPTER SIXTEEN

NATIONAL STRATEGY AND
THE EMERGENCE OF NEW
ECONOMIC CHALLENGES
IN THE 21ST CENTURY

Quite a few people, including this author, have for so many years advocated for a national strategy as regards key sectors of the Nigeria economic life as well as issues that affect and threaten its very existence, and its relationships with the different nations of the world. This write up is intended to look at critical political economy issues in the fast changing global competitive economy. There is no gainsaying the fact that economic relations and economic policy tools will definitely play major roles in defining how Nigeria competes in the global market place. In recent times, financial and technological integration have been influencing both the political and economic dynamics within different countries as well as between nations. It's believed that electronic commerce will further change international economic relations. New economic threats - corruption and information technology terrorism - will counterbalance the identified new opportunities in the world of technology and finance.

Nigeria's attempt in developing a seemingly national strategy was haphazard and uncoordinated. To compete, Nigeria needs to be deliberate, focused and strategic in intent and actions in formulating a national strategy. Such strategy should cover economic, business, national security, education, science and technology, telecommunication, financial services and markets, and politics and governance.

Information Technology (IT)

The world expects Nigeria to provide leadership in all fronts due to its size – both economically and population – especially within the African continent. Nigeria has leadership thrust at her but what is not clear is whether the leaders at various levels realize this and the implications of inaction on their part. It should be noted that the new knowledge economy, propelled by information technology (IT), has changed and will continue to change the way we live and work. The question is: how prepared is Nigeria to face these new international realities that is already shaping our future?

Some pundits like Dave McCurdy believe that in this knowledge economy, comparative roles of government and private sector are changing at a lightening speed. Now, be reminded that one of the characteristics of the knowledge economy is speed. In the past, it was mainly government that funded and launched and operated satellites in orbit. That too is changing fast. It was projected that within a decade (ending in 2010) the number of satellites in orbit will increase to more than 2, 000, and the commercial use, within the same period, will also increase by 300 percent. The interesting thing here is that for the first, more commercial money or private sector funding is being spent on space projects than government. Most of this projected increase will be funded and operated by commercial multinational consortia. Deregulation of the various sectors of national economies globally is creating more opportunities for both domestic and international businesses. The value of the space telecommunication business is put at more than $1 trillion. These satellites are expected to drive the growth of electronic commerce.

Commenting on the dynamic future of electronic commerce that knows no national boundaries and represents the new reality of globalization, McCurdy remarked:

> *Historically, government provided the impetus for economic dynamism through research and development (R&D) funding and demand for systems that supported remarkable technological innovation. Whether it was space assets, supercomputers, or the Internet, the government pushed progress in technology. The reality today, however, is that commercial innovation outstrips government, resulting in approximately eight technology cycles in the private sector for every one policy cycle . moreover, because of the competitive pressure in the private sector to maintain market*

share or stay ahead of the competition, twenty-first century business must have ever shorter development-to-product cycles creating additional stress on policymakers to remain relevant.

The truly successful ventures of the next generation will be nimbly reacting to changing markets as well as generating time-sensitive customer research to assist in the development of products and services. Government, on the other hand, will seem ever slower by comparison.

Nigeria's attempt in participating in the space business resulted in the launch of SAT 3 by the Chinese government firm and managed by the National Space Agency. Despite the wobbly start, it is a step in the right direction. What is required now is people with the right skills to run the operations and realize the commercial value of the venture. Nigeria stands the opportunity of providing services to other African countries, if commercialized, which could add to the revenue stream of the country, in addition to aiding the developmental process of telecommunication and other sectors. If well harnessed, Nigeria can compete favorably in the over $1 trillion global telecommunication space. What is needed is the right people with the right skills.

Nigeria is already blessed with natural and human endowments which could be converted to a source of power. What should be done urgently is to refocus our mindsets from mining these natural resources to mining the minds of the people. This could be achieved by deploying resources to developing a good science and technological base. This is where the future of the country lies. Other countries that are similarly endowed with oil and gas are divesting from that to science, engineering and technology, which they believe will grow and sustain their economies in the future. The Nigerian leadership should note that the new realities of the 21st century, according to McCurdy, are changing the way we look at the world and our understanding of the meaning of power. Power now lies in the hands of those nations that are able to efficiently and effectively mine the mind and hearts of the citizens and channel them towards technological innovations. Emphasis has shifted from oil in some of the OPEC member nations like UAE and Saudi Arabia to services sector and science and technology. In UAE for instance, oil contributes about 5 percent to the GDP. Their focus now is in real estate, hospitality industry, and tourism.

Another element of the new knowledge economy is network externalities. Gone are the days when knowledge was concentrated in few nations and individuals. Knowledge has now been democratized and a level playing field created so that nations and individual can compete in the global market place. As McCurdy pointed out, the world is headed toward a period in which social reality is defined by "networks" based on an individual's ability to exchange a new currency, in this case information, with selected communities. Furthermore, the ascendancy of these networks has undermined traditional hierarchical organizations by instant access to information and activities anytime, anywhere, and without regard to physical or political boundaries. This has been made possible due to technological innovation.

The current dispensation is the information age. While

Nigeria is just entering the service economy, other more economically advanced countries like the United States, whose economy is 70 percent to 80 percent services, is fast moving away from service economy to information-based economy. IT is creating rapid change in Nigeria and the world over. To buttress, in the early 1990s Nigeria had only 400 telephone lines serving over 150 million people. Today, after deregulation of the sector, there are about 40 million telephone lines – both GSM and other fixed and fixed wireless. The cost of computing has drastically reduced as it increases in power. Internet penetration has also increased to about 500 million Internet-connected users. This has led to the development of an array of telecommunication technologies linking most individuals in the world and making the movement of goods and services, capital, people, and ideas cheaper and easier.

Nigeria should focus on IT as a major strategy in this competitive global environment for the following reasons: Number one is that the proliferation of IT will be of immense benefit to the country. This will further enable the development and growth of the sourcing (in-sourcing and outsourcing), R&D, production, marketing, and transportation. In fact, IT will greatly improve Nigeria's productivity rate. Number two is that the development of IT will unleash further entrepreneurial spirit which will in turn drive innovation and wealth creation. Take the telecommunication sector for example. There has been an explosion of growth in that sector since deregulation. This has also affected other sectors such as electronic, computing, software, and services industries.

The rapid change in technology has democratized knowledge. Peter Drucker (as in DeSouza, 2000, pp 48-49) once remarked:

> The knowledge society will inevitably become far more competitive than any society we have yet known – for the simple reason that with knowledge being universally accessible, there will be no excuses for non-performance. There will be no "poor" countries. There will only be ignorant countries. And the same will be true for companies, industries, and organizations of all kinds. It will be true for individuals, too. In fact, developed societies have already become infinitely more competitive for individuals than were the societies of the beginning of this century, let alone earlier ones.

Outsourcing in services such as Business Process Outsourcing and Information Technology Outsourcing could give Nigeria a competitive advantage if well harnessed. The federal government have recognized the outsourcing potential which led to the launch of outsourcing policy guidelines in 2007. The National Information Technology Development Agency (NITDA) was established by the federal government and saddled with the responsibility of development BPO/ITO outsourcing in Nigeria.

At the 2008 Africa outsourcing summit held in Abuja was aimed further creating the awareness of BPO/ ITO outsourcing and highlighting the potential in the economic development of the country. Prof. Cleopas O. Angaye, Director General / CEO, National Information Technology Development Agency (NITDA) in his speech enumerated the policy thrust of the government and the role of his agency thus:

The key thrusts of the policy are:

- *To promote an outstanding orientation starting with onshore outsourcing and progressing through nearshore to offshore outsourcing by encouraging stakeholders involvement in developing a vibrant outsourcing sub-sector;*
- *To grow Nigeria's image internationally as the preferred outsourcing destination and ICT business hub by developing a global competitive Information Technology enabled services sector; and*
- *To facilitate the development of appropriate ICT infrastructure to support capacity building for quality service delivery in the outsourcing sector.*

The Policy Objectives

- *The overall policy objective is the promotion of an enabling institutional, legal, regulatory, technological, and infrastructural environment for the sustainable development of the outsourcing sector in Nigeria. Some of the specific objectives are:*
- *Actualization of the goals of the NEEDS policy of Government in the area of Information Technology Development;*
- *Developing a globally Competitive Information Technology Enabled Services (ITES);*
- *Promoting local and foreign*

Direct Investment in Outsourcing Infrastructure development;

- *Developing an Export-Oriented ICT Product and Service delivery industry;*
- *Accelerated Human Resource and ICT infrastructure development to support growth in the outsourcing sector; and*
- *Facilitate rapid deployment of ICT and enabling and physical infrastructure.*

Policy Targets

Based on the objectives list, the targets of the policy are to:

- *Facilitate the creation of jobs to enhance the overall economy;*
- *Initiate the development of adequate capacity through providing relevant outsourcing Data Centres and Model Call Centres to set benchmarks for service delivery in the outsourcing sector;*
- *Enhance by 100% the contribution of the outsourcing sector to the national GDP within two years of launching the outsourcing policy; and*
- *Develop a national outsourcing orientation and information data bank on businesses involved in outsourcing.*

Creating a Competitive Environment for Outsourcing Sector

An important ingredient for the rapid development of the outsourcing sector in Nigeria is the institutionalisation of a competitive environment which would foster healthy competition amongst service providers and thus enhance the general service quality of service in the country. Government proposes to support the evolution of healthy competition in the outsourcing market with emphasis on specialisation.

Scope of IT Enabled Outsourcing

- *IT-Enabled outsourcing services include the following:*
- *Software Development*
- *Website/ ecommerce*
- *Hosted Applications*
- *Disaster Recovery Services*
- *Network Operations*
- *Desktop support*
- *Data Centre Support*
- *Banking and insurance services*
- *Help Desk*

Public-Private Partnership

Government will encourage public-private sector partnership especially with indigenous businesses and trade associations in the development of appropriate ICT infrastructure especially software parks as well as investor support through various parks as well as investor support through various forms of incentives in addition to those approved under the Nigerian investment promotions council.

Funding of the National Outsourcing Programme

Government proposes to create a funding arrangement that is safe, conducive and investor friendly. Government incentives to banks to allocate a greater proportion of SMIEIS fund to funding entrepreneurs in this sector. The creation of a National Outsourcing Development Fund, application of part of the Universal Service

Provision Fund (USPF) and using the Digital Solidarity fund towards the development of ICT infrastructure would facilitate the development of the outsourcing sector.

Role of NITDA

NITDA as an IT Agency is to develop and provide enabling ICT infrastructure that will bring about outsourcing businesses e.g. call centre communication and reliable high speed internet connectivity. To immediately develop a database of companies engaged in IT Enabled outsourcing business in Nigeria.

NITDA is also to register and accredit outsourcing companies for certification to stipulate minimum standards in conformity with the new policy guidelines and international best practices. To establish a special outsourcing Development Fund through the National Information Technology Development Fund.

Policy Implementation

An essential aspect of the development of the sector is the graduated approach towards realising the objectives of policy. Government will therefore undertake the implementation of policy in phases, focusing simultaneously on the legislative, infrastructural, funding and human capacity issues.

The development of the outsourcing market is focused first on onshore markets, near-shore markets and global offshore market.

Policy implemented so far

NITDA is also working on software testing centres first in Kano and some in other parts of the country. Software incubation centres is also planned for each of the six geopolitical zones. The multipurpose rural internet centres is on-going.

A full fledge Outsourcing Department is establishment in NITDA. This is being followed up with the recruitment and development of the requisite Human Resource to manage the department.

Another major area where work is ongoing is the development of Legal, institutional and Supervisory Framework that would attract IT Enabled Outsourcing in Nigeria. A committee is already working on a draft e-commerce Bill to be presented to the National Assembly for passage in order to build confidence and improve Nigeria's potential to attract outsourcing business. This is part of the attempts being made towards strengthening regulatory processes that would ensure that our environment is conducive for outsourcing business to thrive.

The Federal Government of Nigeria and Microsoft software agreement in 2003 also provides the establishment of nine digital villages in the country which will enhance the Business Processing and Information Technology Outsourcing Sector.

On-going Projects

- *Microsoft and Cisco Academy trainings;*
- *Collating IT enabled service providers in outsourcing businesses;*

- *In house training on eAssessment, eApproval, help desk management system;*
- *Collaboration with all states and local governments in Human Capacity Building.*

This is quite laudable and it is hoped that government will fast track the slow pace and encourage the private sector to get in the groove and drive this process. IT is a very important tool for economic development wealth creation. According to McCurdy, "it is important to harness IT as a positive force and, therefore, the next generation Internet capabilities should be ubiquitous and not burdened by regulation and taxes (some people were advocating in the U.S that tax should be imposed). Recent efforts by state and local governments to subject the Internet to new taxes have the potential to burden the one vehicle that, if used wisely, has the potential to link the world. The focus should be on using this tool to improve education and training, thus increasing economic opportunities and growth. Productivity, competitiveness, and innovation of a country its people will be important. By enlarging the economic pie and communicating common approaches, people will have some incentive to band together for productive ends."

CHAPTER SEVENTEEN

THE EFFECTIVE MANAGEMENT
OF THE AFFAIRS OF THE STATE

R ecently the Patito's Gang crew and members (I am also a member of Patito's Gang) led by Profssor Pat Utomi took a trip to Anambra state as part of the Moving Gang program to states to promote vertical accountability and good governance. Accountability involves an agreed process for both giving an account of your actions and being held to account; a systematic approach to put that process into operation, and a focus on explicit results or outcomes. This is basically the focus of the Moving Gang.

In 2008 the first Moving Gang was in Ogun state as the guest of His Excellency, Otunba Gbenga Daniel, the Executive Governor of Ogun State. At that live television program the members of the Gang took the governor to task on the issue of governance, accountability and other issues that the people wanted him to comment on. There was also a segment where some members of the public who indicated interest to be part of the parliament segment of the program were allowed to ask the governor questions of clarity on some of his government's policy both on the economy and workers' welfare and the general welfare of the citizens. It was a town hall meeting of some sort.

The next stop of the Moving Gang was in Owerri, the Imo state capital as guests to the visionary governor, Chief Ikedi Ohakim. We took him also to task on the dividends of his administration to the people of the state so far. When he started reeling out his vision and program it was quite clear he knew what the people expect from his administration. What weighed him down just a bit was all the legal battles he had to fight to gain legitimacy. Making Imo state a modern model state became his focus and passion.

As part of Chief Ohakim's desire to have a knowledgeable civil service, he reached out to Imo State indigenes in diaspora as well as embarked on massive training and retraining of the entire workforce (civil servants). He sat in several of the training workshops and retreats to further sell the Imo vision or as it fondly called the new face of Imo. Quite a few of the diaspora people from the state are commissioner, special advisers, and members of governing boards of the state parastatals and commissions. By the time he has served his term he would have laid a solid foundation for the successor to further consolidate on, all things being equal. If that happens, Imo state would be a good example of an effectively run government, and Chief Ohakim would have succeeded as a good leader.

In September, 2009, the Moving Gang called on His Excellency, Peter Obi the executive governor of Anambra State. Anambra has been known for many years for its political volatility and intolerance. A state where "god fatherism" was the order of the day before Obi assumed office after a hard won victory at the election tribunal and Supreme Court. The way and manner he came to be governor worked out well for the people of the state because the issue of "god fatherism" that made Anambra almost ungovernable and which also denied the citizen of the state not to enjoy the dividends of democracy was almost nonexistent. After the initial hiccups, as was expected especially in the circumstance where about 99percent of the members of state house of assembly came from one political party, Obi swung to action to provide effective governance and to deliver on the election promises to the people.

Good governance, according to *The Independent Commission for Good Governance in Public Services*, means focusing on the organization's purpose and on outcomes for citizens and service users. To buttress and also for better understanding, the free encyclopaedia, otherwise known as Wikipedia has this to say about governance and good governance:

> "The terms governance and good governance are being increasingly used in development literature. Governance describes the process of decision-making and the process by which decisions are implemented (or not implemented). Hereby, public institutions conduct public affairs, manage public resources,

and guarantee the realization of human rights. Good governance accomplishes this in a manner essentially free of abuse and corruption, and with due regard for the rule of law.

Good governance defines an ideal which is difficult to achieve in its totality. However, to ensure sustainable human development, actions must be taken to work towards this ideal. Major donors and international financial institutions, like the IMF or World Bank, are increasingly basing their aid and loans on the condition that reforms ensuring good governance are undertaken."

Fulfilling organizational purpose, achieving intended outcomes for citizens and service users, and operating in an effective, efficient and ethical manner are the functions of good governance. It will not be out of place to say that the hallmark of good governance is actually having clearly understood sets of organizational objectives and purpose. What you find in most cases is that people get into power through questionable means and don't ever know why they are there. There is no purpose and no objectives. They are just there coasting along or like a sitting dock.

It is important to keep in mind that governance is all about service to the people. The scriptural injunction is that if must lead, you have to first service. Power is derived from service to the citizens. Good governance is also about the relationship between the governed and the governors. In some cases there exists a huge gap between the governors and the governed – some sort of "them versus us." Do the citizens feel the impact of the government in power? Are their voices heard? Do they have a sense of belonging? Are they allowed to make quality contributions, directly or indirectly to the economic and political growth and development of the state? Are the available resources in the state used judiciously to improve the quality of life of the citizens? This brings us to the issue of social capital.

Basically, "social capital is the feeling of belonging and unity in a country, a sharing of values and low incidence of inequality." Economically speaking, the higher a country moves toward the maximum level of social capital, the richer the nation becomes, and on the other hand, the lower the level of social capital the more the country tends towards poverty. This is pure common sense. This is what makes a nation. The higher the social capital the more prosperous a nation becomes and the quality of life as well as the standard of living of the people are bettered.

Has Nigerian experienced high social capital since independence in 1960? The answer is obvious. What about Anambra state? The same goes. But good governance can help achieve the above state - to produce high social capital. The major challenge in Anambra is that governance or political power is considered an extension of business. In fact, it is seen as pure business. That's why you have 100 candidates struggling for the soul of the state in the 2010 governorship election in the state. More than half of them are members of one political party. For as long as political aspirants see political office as business, they can never deliver good governance to the citizens.

The management of the affairs of the state should

be purely service. Providing quality services demand sacrifice on the part of both the providers and the stakeholders – in this case, the governors and the governed. For effective management of the state the governors or leaders must abide by the principle of good governance with its characteristics such as participation by all citizens irrespective of gender and religious leaning. Rule of law and transparency must be the watch word and must guild the actions and behaviors of booth the governed and the governors. The government must be responsive to the needs and yearning of the citizens through building of strong institutions and processes.

Equity and inclusiveness must be practiced. That is, ensuring that all members of society feel that they have a stake in it and do not feel excluded from the mainstream. This requires all groups, and especially the most vulnerable to have opportunities to maintain or improve their well being. The bottom line is that generality of the people must be catered for in all policies and actions of the government. Anything less is tantamount to failure.

CHAPTER EIGHTEEN

Book Review

THE INCUBUS: THE STORY OF PUBLIC ENTERPRISE IN NIGERIA

By Emeka Iheme

T he background to direct state participation in enterprises in Nigeria cannot be fully portrayed without recourse to the colonial beginnings of the Nigerian State. A the turn of 20th Century, after a series of treaties with and conquest of the various native principalities and people, British colonial authority in Nigeria had been affirmed. The territorial boundaries with the neighbors - French colonies and the then Germany colony of Cameroon - have been delimited.

Yet the country's huge expanse of territory has not

been fully explored and made easily accessible, and functional colonial administrative machinery had not been put in place. All parties interested in the colonial enterprise appreciated that their purpose could not be attained if the country was not opened up and peace, order and good government assured. There was therefore a pressing need for the establishment of a modern postal system, telecommunications network, transportation system, etc.

No doubt, the mission of colonialism was to advancement of the interests of the imperial power – to secure for its industries a source of raw material and a market for finished products, to control strategic locations on the globe and generally to expand its sphere of influence. Surely, it was not a divine mission to gratuitously 'civilize' the colonial people.

The task of providing the required infrastructural facilities fell squarely on the colonial government, due to the absence of indigenous companies with the required capital as well as the inability or willingness of the foreign trading companies to embark on these capital intensive projects. This was a department from the experience in Britain itself (and even in the United State) where private companies were building and operating these facilities, including the railways. Thus, the government establish "Industrial department" within the civil service to build and run the required utilities.

The Case for Public Enterprises

Public enterprise are said to be necessary for number of reasons. Firstly, they would help create employment thus killing the "urge of employment" which had confronted Dr. Azikiwe and other pioneers. Secondly, in certain key industries which urgently demanded investment the required capital and expertise was lacking on the part of private investors and the intervention of the government became necessary. This factor had informed the decision of the colonial government to set up the railway, ports, telecommunications, etc. it also explains the decision of the government of an independent Nigerian to invest in industries like iron and steel and fertilizer. Such industries have a "multiplier effect" on the economy as they facilitate other economic activities. Therefore, it is argued, the need for them cannot be delayed or await the pleasure of private investors. This reasoning was encouraged by the theories of the Britain economist, John Maynard Keynes.

A third factor, closely related to the second, is the policy decision that the state ought to control strategic industries so that it can effectively control and direct the course of the economy. One difficulty that arises in this respect is that it is not easy to achieve a consensus on whether or not a particular industry is "strategic." Indeed, the question may be a relative one and the answer may change from time to time.

Fourthly, government investments are said to be a way of enlarging revenue base as returns on (i.e. profits accruing from) such investments will flow into the hands of private investors. From the treasury, goes the argument, such funds can then be employed to provide for public welfare and in so doing a more equitable distribution of wealth is achieved.

Poor Conceptualization

This is a corollary to the issue of ideology. In classical terms, the object of government is to deliver administrative efficiency, while the object of business is to a make profit. Whenever it is sought to combine these two functions in one outfit, problems arise not only because the function are often mutually exclusive but also because they require different orientations and methods. The Nigerian Airports Authority (NAA) was established by a decree in 1976 "to develop and maintain at airports all necessary services and a facilities for the dafe operation of aircraft excluding navigational telecommunications facilities and air traffic control services" and, among other, "to carry out at airports (either by itself or by an agent or in partnership with any other person)" such economic activities as are relevant to air transport.

The Privatization Program

Full Privatization and Partial Privatization of 111 enterprises slated for Privatization under the decree 68 were listed for "full privatization," 43 for partial privatization." Full privatization denote the relinquishing of the entire government holding in an enterprises while partial privation refers to the transfer of only a part of government's interest. Full privatization offers a direct and clean break. It is partial privatization that arises some questions. What is the rationale? For instance, in the case of oil marketing companies, National Oil & Chemical Company Plc and African Petroleum Plc, in which the government equity holding of 60% was to be reduced to 40%, it is probable that the decision was informed by a desire to continue to receive dividends from these profitably run companies-profitably run due to the influence of technical partners.

Future Role of Government in the Economy and the Future of the Privatization and Commercialization Program

"In respect of new role of government in direct investment in economic activities, three distinctive roles have been identified – macroeconomic management, planning and regulatory,"

(a) *Macroeconomic Management*
In its responsibility for macroeconomic management, the Federal Government will continue to design policies to create a favorable environment for growth and undertake strategic decision of long term importance such as influencing the overall rates of investment and saving, pace and pattern of technological development and the expansion of basic social and economic services.

(b) *Planning and Regulatory Role*
In its planning and regulatory roles, the Federal Government will seek to strike an appropriate balance between public control and private initiative on the other. In redefining planning and regulatory mechanism priority will be given to enhancement of economic efficiency, promotion of domestic competition, technological development and enhancing the ability of various sectors to complete and

size opportunities in both the domestic and international markets.

(c)   ***The State as an Entrepreneur***
The extent to which the state plays the role of an entrepreneur directly in productive enterprises will be influenced by our basic philosophy of mixed economy. The management capacity of the private sector agents/actors in the economy will also be taken into consideration. The imperatives which led to wide engagement of Government in entrepreneurial functions are understandable but the imperatives of the changing circumstances call for a redefining of that role in the direction of greater selectivity and efficiency in its engagement in such operations."

ON THE FUTURE
Quo Vadis? Whither goes' thou?

In the confusion and tribulation that befell the Apostle in Rome after the Ascension of Christ, those words were said; whether to St. Peter, or by him, is one of the less serious disputes in church history. With a still large and inefficient public sector which has cast a pall on the entire economy, with a privatization and commercialization program that is now in stormy waters, Nigeria, whither goest thou?

We have argued that commercialization has not succeeded. Even before the enactment of the Public Enterprises Regulatory Commission Decree, the Federal Government seemed to imply as much by proposing, since 1995, a new policy of leasing out the facilities of the commercialized enterprises – a measure not contemplated by, and indeed contradictory to, the TCPC – packaged commercialization program. As a public enterprise reform strategy, leasing has been undertaken by many state governments.

Perhaps it is only Cross River State that has pursued a comprehensive leasing program covering 16 pubic enterprises. The state government is expected to receive over ₦100 million in annual rentals. A very attractive feature of the leasing packages used in Cross River and Taraba State is the incorporation of an obligation on the part of the lessees to provide some infrastructural facilities and pay royalties to the host communities.

While there is much to recommend it, a major problem with leasing is that the arrangement generally facilities the runnings of existing plant and machinery and does not easily conduce to the making required for the improvement of plant and acquisition of new ones. Such investments are usually written off over a long period.

The incubus is a "demon in male form that seeks to have sexual intercourse with sleeping women; the corresponding spirit in female form is succubus. In medieval Europe, union with an Incubus was supposed by some to result in the birth of witches, demons and deformed human offspring" The relationship between our inefficient public utilities and the rest of the economy has been one long and tiresome mating with the incubus.

Until that deadweight is lifted and replaced by normal

and virile private partners, our economy will continue to beget unusual offspring. "

CHAPTER NINETEEN

WEALTH CREATION: THE HOPES AND ASPIRATIONS OF THE AFRICAN YOUTH IN INVESTMENT AND ECONOMIC DEVELOPMENT

"The National prosperity of nations," Michael Porter insists, "is created, not inherited. It does not grow out of the country's natural endowments, its labor pool, its interest rates, or its currency's value, as classical economists insist."

In the book, Enterprise Champions: Entrepreneurship in Ascent in Nigeria, which we authored (Prof. Pat Utomi and Dr Austin Nweze), we argued that Africa does not need foreign aids. What Africa needs to alleviate poverty is a systematic wealth generating program. Africa needs progressive leadership with foresight to grow the value chain of the abundance natural resources. Of great importance also is the development and skilling of underused human capital such as the young professionals.

In this new knowledge economy where more work is knowledge based and wealth generated through knowledge, Africa needs to be transformed into a knowledge society that will be provide better quality of life for its citizens.

Opportunities in the ICT

African leaders need to invest in ICT infrastructure. This is a vital element in transforming Africa into a knowledge society and a region that creates or generates knowledge. Sustainable capacity building will unleash the potentials of the African youths and economic growth in African communities and nations. Technology is critical for transforming raw materials into finished good, but yet Africans did not have access to technology advances of that critical nature for many decades.

Transforming Africa – Role of the ecosystem

Transforming Africa requires the collaboration of all the entities that make the ecosystem. This ecosystem consists of the private sector; regulators; policy makers; civil society; and customers or users of the products and services. Private and public partnerships are required improving higher educational institutions that will train and develop leaders that will work in government, industry and society.

The recent World Resource report tend to provide a leeway to the world's 2 billion rural poor escape the cycle of poverty and generate sustainable wealth in Africa by establishing nature-based enterprises..

The report stated that today, 2.6 billion people live on less than $2 a day. 75 percent of people at the bottom of the economic pyramid live in rural areas and are dependent on natural resources for some or all of their subsistence. The rural poor face even tougher challenges ahead, as climate change threatens to destroy the ecosystems and natural resources on which they depend.

The report further stated that well-designed, community-based sustainable enterprises can improve the way the rural poor draw from their area's natural resources. Ultimately, these programs can make their communities more resilient against climate change and the other economic, social, environmental challenges they will face.

The World Resource Institute report concludes that there are three common elements nature-based enterprises need to be successful:

- **Community ownership and self-interest:** Legitimate ownership of local resources and a sense of self-interest must be granted to the community.

- **Help from intermediary organizations:** Governments and development agencies need to provide the rural poor with the technical and business skills they need to become more resilient.

- **Formation of formal and informal networks:** Support networks among communities and the organizations working with them must be present for the rural poor to sustainably manage natural resources and generate income.

When these three elements are present, the report concludes, communities can begin to unlock the wealth potential of ecosystems in ways that actually reach the poor. In so doing, they can build a base of competencies that extends beyond nature-based enterprises and supports rural economic growth in general, including the gradual transition beyond reliance on natural resource income alone.

Youth Economic Empowerment

It was Jeffrey A. Timmons that said, "Thinking of money first is a big mistake. Money follows high potential opportunities conceived of and led by a strong management team." Youth economic empowerment therefore involves seeking to transform or improve the quality of life of the citizens or communities by engaging them in productive economic activities.

CHAPTER TWENTY

*AID, HUMAN SOLIDARITY
AND THE SCOURGE OF
POVERTY IN AFRICA*

Poverty is declining around the world. In Africa, however, the number of poor people has been on the rise, as Africa has been left out of much of the increased global trade flows sustaining growth in Asia and other parts of the world. The bad news from Africa, borne by the Human Development indicators, and other statistics, has not been lost on the wealthy nations who have continued to pledge more aid, as they did in Okinawa regarding the digital divide, and in Gleneagles, when G8 leaders met, with host Tony Blair of Britain trying to focus world attention on Africa but so little progress has come from foreign aid to Africa.

Critics of foreign aid traditions have since become legion. Some, like William Easterly, in his White Man's Burden, in fact sees aid, in Daniel Patrick Moynihan speak, as iatrogenic policy intervention in which the patient suffers more from the cure than the original ailment. In such circumstances, is smart aid possible? The hope that aid can bridge resource gaps in post colonial Africa and propel human material progress has received popular boost in celebrated musicians like Bob Geldof leading initiatives like the Live 8 concert, and by academics such as Jeffery Sachs writing books like The End of Poverty.

But much of the available evidence suggest the need for a rethink of the way aid is given if in fact Aid does indeed aid development. We suggest, in the following discussion, that while human solidarity makes aid an imperative of human interdependence, its effectiveness will depend on a more robust understanding of the factors that drive economic growth and an alignment of intervention to impact what Richard John Neuhaus describes as "the basic social, economic and political causes of poverty"(First Things. August/Sept 1992).It shall be proposed that the key variables that sustain human progress for which aid donors need to find creative ways of making interventions to stimulate local capacity to drive initiatives, are:

Policy choices that favor increased trade; the building of strong institutions that set the limits to human conduct, especially the ones that broaden democratic participation and accountability; investment in human capital and retaining professionals at home and perhaps turning extant condition from brain drain to brain gain; stimulating popular interest in entrepreneurship; inspiring values that shape progress; and building leadership development capacity.

We also contend that even as national interest and the promotion of a nation's values abroad, as Carol

Lancaster argues, should be the basis for aid in the 21st century, are respectable motives, smart aid will have to be driven by a 'Solidarity Humanism' in which the vision of a shared heritage in a global village makes a win-win abundance mentality the primary basis of assistance. In some ways this vision of the global order is similar to Senator Hilary Clinton's idea, at the US domestic level, of a 'shared prosperity'.

Responsibility here will rest significantly with African social entrepreneurs who get a boost from external stimulations and work to a global environment enabled for trade with Africa, and supportive of values that correspond to that of world peace and prosperity roughly equivalent to what Pope John Paul II calls a 'civilization of love'.

Why has Growth been so slow in Africa?

I have been part of a tribe that has made a living comparing the economic performance of African countries with that of Asian counterparts. With typical pairings as Ghana/Malaysia, Nigeria/Indonesia and South Korea/Cote D'voire Africa's spectacular failure to achieve the promise of the first development decade has made the question of why it grows so slowly a routine object of inquiry. A review of the literature shows a clustering of perspectives on the issue around policy choice and the so-called destiny argument.

The destiny school, whose logic is geographic determinism, essentially advances the notion that Africa is poor because factors associated with its geographic location diminish productivity as disease associated with the tropics such as Malaria affect human output negatively. Other thesis bunched into this group suggest that the spread of innovations was also hindered by dispersal of peoples on the continent and the poor nutrient structure of African soil which did not take on so well to the replenishing of micronutrients with fertilizer.10 Jeffrey Sachs, even if a little unfairly in some instances, is most identified with this school and the idea of foreign aid he advocates is a big push through massive transfers of capital to help Africa overcome these factors for which it cannot be blamed. He is therefore caricatured as an apologist for bad leadership in Africa. At the least, Sachs is seen as not trying hard enough to get Africa's leaders to be more accountable, in rushing to provide them alibis for poor performance.

The competing school essentially posits that Africa's poor performance is largely the result of poor economic policy choices by Africa's leaders. Paul Collier tends to be at the thick of this pack. In 1999 Collier and Gunning took the position that "exchange rate and trade policies which were atypically anti-export and accumulated large foreign debt" retarded growth in Africa.11 In our view, even though we have often taken the Collier side of the debate, neither perspective on its own fully captures the reason Africa grows so slowly. Drawing from both growth and stagnation experiences in Asia and Africa we have offered a framework for evaluating man's material advance.

The growth Driver's framework involves a set of interdependent variables that act together, in a dynamic way, to shape human progress. These are Policy Choices; Institutions; human Capital;

Entrepreneurship; Culture; and Leadership. In the 2006 book Why Nations are Poor I have provided a more detailed discussion of how these variables impact one anther and economic performance.12 Particularly of note in those discussions has been the tendency for those Easterly calls do-gooder planners to focus almost exclusively on changing economic policies and occasionally in transplanting institutions to support those policy choices.

The Structural Adjustment Programs, which most African countries began to subscribe to in the Mid 1980s, were typical of the reform interventions that depended almost exclusively on policy changes to bring about transformation of living conditions. The view that policy changes such as the shift from bureaucratic controls to market prices for the allocation of such scarce resources as Foreign Exchange were necessary but not sufficient conditions for sustained performance improvement.

One of the authors (Pat) found remarkable anecdote for how it left many frustrated in an amusing encounter at the World Economic Forum Southern Africa Summit in Durban, South Africa, in 2000. The Vice-President of Mozambique wanted to know when the promised investments would follow their religious adherence to prescriptions by the multilateral agencies and donors. He lamented that when he first raised the question he was told that a track record was required. They kept at it for long enough that the tracks and the records were literally visible from space but few investors were sighted. And they asked how much longer they would have to wait but were told they needed patience.

Now Patience was beginning to sound like their middle name but investors were still out of sight. This hilarious encounter, proximately captured here, shows how aid's failure on its promise generated frustration, after raised hopes based on the outsiders certainty about prescribed intervention. For the client result more modest than he made out becomes a betrayal which lowers trust and compounds the problem. In our evaluation if aid had supported not just getting policy right but also the other factors we have identified in this framework we would probably have had better chances of success. If aid is to become smarter, it seems that we have to ask how well it targets these key growth drivers and the vehicle it uses to ensure optimal return on effort and other resources. Let us then briefly examine the emphasis of aid effort with the growth drivers.

AID and Policy Choice

As already indicated, aid efforts were significantly skewed in the direction of policy choice. When exports began to tumble and balance of payments deficits forced African Central banks into crisis and a debt trap, the need to get out of structural challenges forced many African countries to seek IMF, and later, World Bank adjustment support. Some of those troubled economies were managed by men who had been influenced, as students in England, by the Harold Laski School and Fabian socialism. Some more had been inclined to the East in the Cold War competition for influence around the world. As a result some bilateral donors from the West were keen to reinforce the economic orthodoxy at the Breton Woods institutions inclined to neo-liberal preference for price-based prescriptions.

Support for Privatization initiatives, exchange rate liberalization and deregulation of many sectors of African economies became the mantra that supplanted help with infrastructure development that dominated the first development decade of the 1960s.Unlike an earlier aid candidate, South Korea, the African countries did not turn the bend down the path of export led industrialization that has put the East Asians in the currents of global trade flows and prosperity. Some, like Nigeria, were driven by adjustment policies down the path of de-industrialization with manufacturing dropping in its contribution to Gross Domestic Product (GDP) from about 14 per cent to less than 4 per cent.

A focus on policy alone would never be able to explain what happened until you look at the investment in human capital and how trends diverged in these two countries; how the institutions evolved differently; and the values in one supported a work ethic and entrepreneurship, while in the other, economic rent was favored by an elite that scorned hard work.

Policy options in aid to Africa very often did not involve enough work on the institutional underpinnings that would sustain new orientation for policy even when prescriptions of policy change, the so called reforms, dominated consideration for donor giving.

Foreign aid took a long time to recognize the importance of institutions even though some World Bank personnel had spent considerable time reflecting and writing on the role of institutions in development. Typical example was in the frustration with grants for infrastructure development.

Donor frustration with Tanzania's inability to maintain roads, built through donor   funding, with the evidence of the grants quickly washed up, seemed not able to stimulate support for erecting institutional foundations that would make Build Operate and Transfer (BOT) projects feasible. The Asians moved very quickly in that direction shifting roads which were generally considered the ultimate non-appropriability goods quickly unto the domain of private goods and of Public/Private partnerships.

In the main the failure of aid to connect with change elements in Africa who could drive policy down the road to expanding trade, which has been the engine of economic growth since World War II, and not considering other variables along policy interventions are key reasons growth is slow in Africa. Add to this the unwillingness by donors to open up agricultural produce markets, as many of them subsidize their farmers and protect certain industries, and the reason the original G7 countries have 100 times more trade than the poorest ones is evident. It is understandable; therefore, that some say what is required is trade and not aid.

AID and Human Capital

Almost in the same way as Hernando de Soto shows that the poor have assets but stay poor because representational systems deny them the opportunity to convert assets to capital, Africa has a fair amount of human capital but is unable to convert this into African Human Capital because, as Holman and Rugasira noted earlier there are more doctors from

Malawi in Birmingham than Malawi. If the mystery of capital is how representational systems makes assets more fungible the mystery of human capital must be about how to make skilled Africans make those skills available for Africa's development. While it is true that Africa requires massive new investment in education, reversing the flow of African professionals is an important first step. It is those leaving who should teach in those universities and primary schools, should more funding and better resources become available.

In the this age of the knowledge worker human capital is a critical factor in National competitiveness which affects decisions on investment and the place of a country in global trade flows. The two components of Human Capital, education and skills development; and health care or well being of the so educated, require substantial investment.

Traditional capacity for effective delivery of education and health care through faith based PDAs like the Missionary churches is evidence enough that the way to drive forward this important factor would be through cooperation between donors and these PDAs.

A good case would be the effect of support from the US government for the Jesuits in the erection of a high school in Nigeria. The Loyola Jesuit College in Abuja was soon to become one of the finest institutions for educating young men and women in Nigeria. In the same manner voluntary agency managed hospitals where they have the resources often mange hospitals and health care agencies much better than government hospitals with much more significant budgets.

At this time the Bill and Melinda Gates Foundation

and the US Government among others have committed significantly to combating the HIV/AIDS pandemic. UN reports read by Deputy Secretary-General Asha-Rose Migiro suggest that the Africa is still way off track in checking HIV/AIDS with the number of people dying from AIDS in Sub-Saharan Africa going up to 2 million in 2006. Creative effort on responsible sexual behavior, through education, and work to contain the threat to human capital, by Malaria, needs to be encouraged. Strong support for rural health initiatives should deliver the desired message, especially where they mobilize lots of young professionals either as volunteers, thus enhancing their civic consciousness, or as employees, taking them off the unemployment queue for a while, should be a smart approach.

For Aid to facilitate how human capital drives growth it needs to follow the linkages between the factors of the Growth Drivers framework and seek optimal outcomes in how the synergies are captured by intervention designs that also draw in and build up local social entrepreneurial talent.

While institutions reduce uncertainty and transaction costs they, essentially facilitate the environment in which the appropriate human capital transforms ideas into value that enhances the human material condition.

We shall indeed be showing how failure to invest appropriately in education and health care impacts on available human capital and affects the competitiveness of National economies.

Often, rich human capital, where institutional

arrangements are right, as Ragu Rajan and Luigi Zingales, richly show, in Saving Capitalism from the Capitalists, will produce a tradition of entrepreneurship.

The process of creative destruction embedded in venturing generates value that impact the quality of life, results in significant creation of new jobs and invariably on poverty reduction. To find illumination about why entrepreneurship is at such low ebb in poor countries one needs to see the close relationship between institutions, human capital, policy choice of governments and, very importantly, culture, on new venture prospects and inclination towards risk.

Culture does indeed matter. The work ethic, orientation towards perseverance and delayed gratification, attitude towards failure, all shape disposition towards venturing.

Entrepreneurship

The spirit of enterprise, that process of creative Destruction that Joseph Schumpeter found critical to economic growth, needs to be stimulated at the Bottom of the Pyramid if poverty is to be alleviated.19 Just as overcoming the mystery of capital, and ensuring property rights are very important areas for Aid intervention aimed at building institutions, democratizing entrepreneurship values is important for getting the poor out of poverty.

Support for micro credit and community venture capital; and entrepreneurship extension services offered by PDAs would more clearly facilitate the rapid reduction of the scourge of poverty in Africa.

If poverty alleviation programs, supported by Aid, have great flaws it is that many do not combine building capacity for creative venture action in the poorest of the poor with opening access to small amounts of capital and providing those institutions that solve the mystery of capital.

Culled from the book Enterprise Champions: Entrepreneurship in Ascent in Nigeria by Prof. Pat Utomi and Dr Austin Nweze

CHAPTER
TWENTY ONE

WINNING THE GENERATIONAL WAR: IDEAS FOR GOVERNING IN THE FUTURE

The Chinese went through a period of excitement-a period where the leadership had to make important decisions that could make China great in the community of nations or keep the country in perpetual poverty and a state of unrealized potential. In the 19th and 20th centuries, it seemed the Chinese leadership and policy makers got it all wrong in the various decisions they made in the political and economic areas. It was not until the late 1970s that the then leaders changed course and decided to gradually open up the economy and move away from the closed economy China was hitherto.

That singular decision taken by the Chinese leadership in the late 1970s was responsible for the growth of the Chinese economy at the annual rate of between 10%

and 13% for three decades. Today, China is fast taking its rightful place in world's affairs. Why not? With over a trillion dollars in foreign reserves and a hard working population, China has set out to buy the world. Chinese companies and investors are scattered all of over the world hungry for new acquisitions in countries where they would have not dreamed of investing in the past. Their aggressiveness and confidence levels have increased and when they talk the world leaders listen and take them seriously. These are all as a result of making the right policy choices.

Nigeria in its part could be said to be going through a similar period of excitement just like the Chinese. There seems to be a 'generational war' going on in Nigeria between the old block (or to borrow the words my children use for me from time to time, "old school") and the new block. The old block are represented by the conservatives and the new block represented by the progressives. This cold war has been on for sometime, but has become intense since the last decade or so. The existing major political parties are formed along that line. The old block is fighting hard to retain the status quo and frown at anyone or anything that will bring about change. It has been a ding-dong affair between the two camps. No real progress has been made so far, and like the proverbial elephants it is the masses that suffer or bear the brunt. The new school represented by the likes of Prof. Pat Utomi and his cohorts (including the late Gani Fawehinmi) want a change that will lead Nigeria to its destiny and be able to compete in the global arena, but they are facing serious resistance from the conservatives who want to remain in control for as long as it favors their selfish ends. But they will not give up without serious fight.

The middle class that supposed to help bring about this needed change for progress were long rendered impotent by the ruling class of the old order. What the conservatives did was to destroy the middle class by destroying or taking away their economic power. They therefore became impoverished. They lost in the process the spirit to fight. They lost in the process the spirit to fight. The new middle class that is emerging, unfortunately, have no clue what they want. They seem confused and not aware of the role they play in moving Nigeria forward. They seem, also, hypnotized or overwhelmed or even covered by the ruling class. It is important to note at this point that no nation can develop and grow economically and socially without a vibrant middle class. It is often said that when you build a vibrant and sustainable middle class, you build a successful or progressive nation. Therefore, the middle class holds the key to Nigeria's economic growth and hence political advancement.

Having floundered for several years, the search should on now for ways to make traditional politics work in this age of transition. Yes! Nigeria is still going through a transition period. The leadership need to urgently gain a better philosophical understanding of where we are headed in the world. Policy makers need to engage the rest of us in debating Nigeria's future. We have to debate the need for limited government and free markets. We need to organize a policy and an economy that will make Nigeria competitive and to take its rightful place in the community of nations.
For us to get it right as a nation we need to get

our politics right, then the policies (both politically and economically) will be right and the ultimate beneficiaries of government programs- the Nigerian citizens-will feel the impact. Gary Hart, a foreign U.S presidential candidate once said:

> *"Programs derive from policies and policies derive from political belief systems called ideologies. Therefore, programs and policies debated at the end of the twentieth century are the products, directly or indirectly, of traditional conservation, liberation, or some faint reflection of very moderate democratic socialism-all belief systems derived from the Age of Enlightenment or from political reactions of it.*
>
> *Politics in democracies works only to the extent that there is congruence between ideas it produces and the realities experienced by individual citizen. Most of the liberal programs of the rapidly disappearing twentieth century, and the laisez faire alternatives to them, are not conceptually designed to address the new realities of the emerging twenty-first."*

A new political thinking is required in this knowledge economy. This is just the new reality, the new reality is that IT is the major driver of economic growth in this new economy. According to Gary Hart technologies have disintegrated old networks and integrated new ones. The new networks being integrated include new systems of communication, international financial networks, and cross-border transactions, and they are also creating a new class of transactional elites.

The second new reality is that "international markets are driven by systems of capital supply and demand that know no national laws or interest capital recognizes no political (or even moral) imperative. It recognizes no citizenship or special national obligation. It seeks only to maximize its own return."

The third new reality is that "as capital and finance are becoming international, policies is becoming more local. As individual citizens despair of participating in the public policy decisions affecting international finance, they revert to demanding greater control of their neighborhood lives."

The fourth new reality, according to Gary Hart, is that human conflict in the form of tradition wars between nation-states declines even as low-intensity, largely urban conflict between among tribes, clans, and gangs mushrooms in the post-cold war non-polar problem persists. Tribal or ethnic interest more often than not always takes precedent over national interest. It is only when a nation has less or even internal conflicts resulting from having a benign political system that it can focus on fighting external wars. Nigeria cannot afford to fight off external aggressive because of it is currently burdened with ethnic or tribal conflict. Ethnic and tribal conflicts are expected by experts to grow without abating in the future.

The fifth new reality has to do with the spiritual. Gary Hart noted that there is a rising sense of the spiritual limits if the scientific methods and the beginning of the end of the Age of Enlightenment.

The point being made above is that times have changed. The old systems of thinking or doing things have really changed. We need a new set of thinking to gorvern and make policies that will improve the quality of lives of citizens. We need to truly reform our political systems to fit and meet the new challenges. A new framework is urgently needed to be in sync.

In reflecting on the new political framework, it will do a lot of good to look at yet again, Gary Hart's four fundamental principles that can form the framework of a new political ideology. The first principle has to do with civic virtue-a classical republican theory-which simply is the citizen whose duties and responsibilities require participation in the public issues of the day. The second principle

According to Hart, there urgent need for the restoration of the ideal of civic virtue – civic duty and citizen participation – from classical theory established 2500 years ago as the centrepiece of republican government. Nigeria became a republic in 1963 and has now transformed to democratic republic. This evident in the electoral process where many people elect a few people to represent them. The citizens have a very important obligations, responsibility, civic duties and civic virtue. These are very critical to the right functioning of the form of government Nigeria has adopted.

The second principle elucidated by Hart is from radical democratic principle, the ideal of the ward republic, the immediate government in which all citizens can participate to achieve social progress and inclusiveness. This a radical notion "that all men and women are created equal, that they are endowed by their Creator with certain unalienable Rights, that among these are Life, Liberty and the pursuit of Happiness." The third also is from the radical principle, the Jeffersonian concept of "generational Accountability." This simply means that each generation has to give account of its stewardship or actions/inactions. Hart argues that "if the idea of generational accountability is joined with the notion of the ward republic and active local government, then there is little justification for the failure of civic duty in the form of citizen participation." The fourth is from traditional conservatism, reinterpreted in light of the need for generational accountability, the notion of "intergenerational compact" – the moral imperative of leaving to the next generation a better society than the one inherited. This last principle is "especially important because it is the glue for a social compact that should form the standard for judging all proposed public policies.

CHAPTER TWENTY TWO

ALIGNING NATIONAL STRATEGY AND FOREIGN POLICY FOR ECONOMIC GROWTH

In dealing with national strategy and foreign policy issues the basic question to ask is: should national strategy be aligned with foreign policy of a nation or should they be separate from each other? This is pertinent question policymakers and economic planners and managers should contemplate. This situation has been a challenge in the Nigerian context. It seems both are divorced from each other instead of being complimentary. But should it be so? The answer is capital NO. Unfortunately that has not been the case with the nation.

Nigeria fought for the prevailing peace and stability in the once war zones of Liberia and Sierra Leon. Nigeria committed human, material, and financial resources to ensure the peace and stability being experienced in both countries. It was estimated that Nigeria spent about $4 billion to prosecute the war in Liberia. The Obasanjo administration ensured that Ellen Johnson Sir-Leaf was installed. What did Nigeria get in return for the investment s made in human, material and financial resources to fight the wars and bring peace and stability to Liberia and Sierra-Leon? Nothing! Instead, Nigerians who live and trade in Liberia and Sierra-Leon are constantly antagonized, harassed and in some cases given inhuman treatment by the citizens of these countries.

But do you blame them? The answer is no. Who should be held responsible? The government of the day that committed such huge investments without bringing economic value to Nigeria and Nigerians should be held responsible for what happened. Whether it was an oversight on the part of government not to consider Nigeria's political and more especially economic interest before investing such a huge sum of money in the Liberian civil war or ignorance one cannot tell. It is only those that decided to intervene in the war with the "big brother" attitude that will one day tell Nigerians what they were thinking or the reason why they denied Nigeria the opportunity of benefiting from the war that cost tax payers such a huge amount without anything to show for it.

Time has come to rethink Nigeria's foreign policy making process. There has to be a shift from the current philanthropic mentality to a more realistic national interest first system of even the developed countries like the United States and Europe. When the United States pulled down Iraq during the invasion, the world shouted to no avail. What was uppermost was American interest. And the government of the day did not hide it. After the war, reconstruction started. But who are those that won contract to reconstruct Iraq? American companies of course. The American government was business minded in their decision to invade Iraq. At the end of the day, it is Iraq's money being used to fight the war and reconstruct the country. The American government took along their businesses to Iraq. This was exactly what Nigeria did not do in Liberia and Sierra-Leon. What a big opportunity lost.

Those reaping the benefits today are Lebanese, Syrians and Indians who never contributed anything to securing the peace in those countries. They ran away to their various countries and only came back when Nigeria had brought peace back to the nations. The same happened in South Africa during the apartheid years. Again Nigeria was at the forefront of the dismantling of apartheid and contributed to the African National Congress (ANC) coffers for many decades. In fact at a point Nigeria's foreign policy thrust was centered on fighting apartheid regime in South Africa. Again the Nigerian leaders couldn't manage the success of their efforts when apartheid ended. Nigerians were once again denied the benefits. Instead, it is South African companies that have invaded Nigerian economy.

It has been predicted that South African companies will in the next decade or so control a larger chunk of Nigeria's economy. But shouldn't it have been the other way around? Nigeria has signed several bilateral and multilateral agreements with many countries, but as always, businesses were left out during negotiations. It seemed to be purely civil service affairs which shouldn't be so. Those assigned as commercial attachés in Nigerian embassies abroad seem not to know or understand jack about business. No market intelligences have ever been provided to Nigerian businessmen and women who do or want to do businesses in those countries. This is not the case with other countries. Sometimes one wonders whether the ministry of foreign affairs still exists. The minister act as if he is the minister of internal affairs because he spends most of the time he should have been abroad canvassing and promoting Nigeria's interests.

Nigerian citizens languish in many jails across the globe and the ministry that supposed to cater to give them protection on the behalf of the government is not even aware, and even when they get to know through the press, they play the ostrich and do nothing. A change in attitude is urgently needed. There is urgent need to align Nigerian foreign policy with the national strategy for economic growth and prosperity.

For some years now, it seems that government's capacity to make policy has waned. It started declining since the 1970s. This is quite evident in the policy flip flops witnessed in recent times. Several factors could be responsible for this decline. To aid our understanding, policy making, according to John Coles, is basically the formulation of a course of action (or sometimes a statement of attitude) to deal with a situation or problem.

The recent civil service reform has focused more on the

management side than policy. Civil servants are being trained these days to behave and act like the private sector. This is a good development. efforts though should be made to reskilled them for more effective policy making. Another factor is that the knowledge economy has made government a bit more complex. John Coles stated:

> *The sheer complexity of modern government, the speed of communications, the extraordinary growth of the quantity of available information, the increase work load imposed on ministers and officials by these and other developments, all tended to limit the time and resources available for policy analysis and formulation. Time spent on management, on presentation, on digesting information, on responding to the day-to-day and often unpredictable demands of government is time lost for policy-thinking, for planning, for the formulation and orderly pursuit of policy objectives.*

When one considers the way and manner Nigerians are treated abroad – both in the United States, Europe, Asia, the Middle East, and even i the African continent, one wonders or ponder the kind of relationships that exists between Nigeria and other nations. If there are any relationships, such relationships should be reviewed towards serving Nigeria's best interest. The current rebranding efforts of the ministry of information and communication could be a part of the strategy of positioning Nigeria well in the committee of nations. But this will only happen after some house cleaning has been done – not before then. The bottom line therefore is that policy-makers need quality time to think through and formulate policies with Nigeria's economic and political interests utmost in their minds.

Having been colonized by the British, Nigeria's national life has been partly patterned after the British. Policy-making system is no different. There is a big lacuna in the policy-making system of the government generally. The recently drafted Trade and Industrial Policy document being debated in different forums is a typical case in point. At a recent forum organized by the Abuja based National Association of Nigerian Traders (NANTS) in September, 2009 in Abuja to review the draft policy and have the private sector input, thi deficiency of document was very glaring. The quality of the draft document showed that not much deep thinking was not put in it. Not much consultation was done either. There was no innovation as the process of drafting the document was not much different from the process ones.

Nigeria is not alone in this foreign policy-making challenge. Developed countries like the UK and Canada face similar challenges. Both countries' foreign policy system have been criticized at some quarters that they needed to be more innovative. Coles remarked that:

> *The making of foreign policy in Canada has not escaped criticism. One scholar recently observed that the Federal Government's 1995 statement on "Canada and the world" displayed no attempt to define priorities amid shrinking resources. Policy tended to focus on "splashy agenda-setting" and "announceability" rather than substance. Increased activism in "declaratory" foreign policy had been accompanied by a slash-and-burn approach*

to the management of Canada's foreign policy instruments, with cuts in the defence, aid and foreign affairs budget, so that greater activism was combined with atrophy in capability... The major problems with Canada's foreign policy resulted from, among other things, its conceptual basis and the persisting ambiguity about where Canada fits in a post-Cold War structure of international politics.

Borrowing from John Coles comment above, Nigeria's policy-makers should be able to decide from the start where Nigeria fits in the international politics. And that should be accompanied by the economics of it. That is to say how Nigeria is going to benefit economically from the policy. There has to be a strategy on how to deal with each individual nation – especially China. Nigeria has no clear strategy on how to deal with China, which has the potential of becoming the next world's economic power. This anomaly should be corrected immediately.

CHAPTER TWENTY THREE

BRIDGING THE GAP
BETWEEN THE PUBLIC
AND PRIVATE SCHOOLS
ELEMENTARY SYSTEM

I t was Emmanuel Kant, a German philosopher, who said that we are born with apriori knowledge. The society shapes whatever knowledge we have. But educational psychologists, through research, have found that 80% of a child's faculty is fully developed at age 18 months. No wonder Maria Montessori said:

> *"The discovery that the child has a mind able to absorb on its own account produces a revolution in education. We can now understand easily why the first period in human development, in which character is formed, is the most important. At no other age has the child greater need of an intelligent help...We should help the child, therefore,*

no longer because we think of him as a creature, puny and weak, but because he is endowed with great creative energies....When...we realize that the mind of the child in infancy is different from ours, that we can not reach it by verbal instruction, nor intervene directly in the process of its passing from the unconscious to the conscious...Then the whole concept of education changes. This is the new path on which education has been put..."

The world we live in today is in conflict. Education to some school of thought is one of the best means of its future reconstruction. Education, though recognized as one of the ways to raising mankind, is still thought of as education of the mind – a mere transmission of knowledge rather than in bettering of the child's future or total development (spiritual, physical, intellectual, moral). This is where there seems to be a huge gap between the private and public schools. During the early years of a child, education must be seen and understood as helping in unfolding the child's inborn psychic. So, teaching method must go beyond just talking.

Since independence in 1960, education at all levels has been the primary responsibility of both federal and state governments. The only form of private participation was by churches, which was known then as mission schools, and few other individuals or groups such as corona schools.

It was after the civil war in 1970 that the government took over mission schools and became the sole provider. This was when the fallen standard started. In the early 1980s the fallen standard became more glaring and that led to the avalanche of private schools to provide alternative to the public school.

There was a mad rush to the private schools which had to succumb to the law of demand and supply. Those who could afford the high fees in private schools sent their wards there while the not so rich sent their wards to the public schools. Another attraction in the private sector was the state of the physical environment and infrastructure. While the private schools are well maintained, the public schools are in sorry state of dilapidation.

The government in the past had laudable education policies like the universal primary education (UPE) which is now re-christened Universal Basic Education. The reason for the policy failure of the government could be attributed to poor policy implementation, incompetence of staff, corruption and bad governance. If the status quo remains, Nigeria will likely miss the Millennium Development Goal on education.

Education according to Harold Osuagwu, is one of the most important activities of our time. It identifies talents, recognizes achievements and grants economic and social benefits to its scholars. In his address to the 89th Congress of the USA on the importance of education, President Lyndon Johnson declared (as in Osuagwu):

> "Nothing matters more to the future: not our military preparedness, for armed might is worthless if we lack the brain power to build a world of peace; not our productive economy for we cannot sustain growth without trained manpower, not our

democratic system of government – for freedom is fragile if citizens are ignorant. We must demand that our schools increase not only the quantity but quality of America's education...The three R's of our school system must be supported by the three T's. Teachers who are superior, Techniques of instruction that are modern and Thinking about education which places it first in our plans and hopes."

Curriculum Gap

There is a minimum standard set by the government on the curriculum for elementary school system, both public and private. The difference between the public and private schools is in the ability to meet and surpass this minimum standard. Let's briefly consider the concept of curriculum and what it is meant to achieve.

The term "Curriculum" according to Placid Njoku, refers to planned total experiences offered to a learner under the auspices of a school. The intention of the "experiences" is to achieve set goals based on the needs and aspirations of the individuals and the society.

A curriculum can also be defined as an educational plan that involves learning experiences (content and methods) to be offered and learned using methodologies that incorporate techniques which enable the learner to benefit maximally by acquiring desired knowledge, attitudes, skills and values.

Curriculum is the written document that

contains the goal, contents and didactic methods of study program. Consider the following as the core elements of curriculum;

- The goals: what does the teaching involving?
- The content: what is being taught? And
- The didactic methods used: how is this content taught?

Curriculum is therefore the sum total of all the courses of study offered by an educational institution.

So, bridging the existing gap requires the coming together of the Government, Educators (in both public and private schools), and parents to formulate curriculum. Until then, the gap will still exist.

What we find, therefore, is that the curriculum used by the private schools is richer than the public schools in terms of offering special varieties of courses such as sciences, fine arts, home economics, foreign languages, music, etc. This is due to competition among private schools.

The teacher/pupil ratio is another challenge, especially in public elementary schools in Nigeria. While the ratio is about ten (10) pupils per teacher in private schools, it is as high as thirty (30) pupils per teacher in public schools. This could even be higher in some public schools located in poor areas.

In private schools you find recreational facilities, laboratories and libraries, which are almost non-existent in public schools. As a matter

of fact, private school
pupils can assimilate better because of the good
learning environment.

High costs of living also contribute in deepening the
gap between public and private schools. Private schools
are more expensive than public schools because of the
availability of more facilities and the quality of trained
personnel.

In the present democratic dispensation, the
government at all levels have not paid special attention
to rehabilitating public schools to close the huge gap
that exists between public and private schools. Some
state governors have even lost faith in the public school
system to deliver quality education to the citizens of the
state. Rather than think of a solution and investing in
that solution, they set up parallel private schools with
tax-payer's money and put their cronies to run these
schools. These schools are well equipped with modern
educational materials and facilities to the neglect of the
public schools. The question therefore is why can't the
government invest such monies in rehabilitating public
schools rather than using it to set up their personal
private schools? This bothers on ethics, accountability
and good governance issues.

The Way Out

These challenges in the elementary educational
systems, which is a microcosm of what obtains in
the overall educational system in Nigeria, could be
addressed via encouraging and supporting private
initiatives programs like what City Profs Educational

Foundation (CPEF) is doing in ensuring that every child gets quality education no matter where he or she is located and the level of income of the parents. Such programs will compliment the government's UBE program.

In addition, it will discourage the mad rush by parents to send their wards to private schools to the negligence of the plight of the poor communities who are the actual beneficiaries of uncharted public schools.

Government should embark on the massive training and retraining of public school teachers. The Education Tax Fund carried out some training programs for public school teachers in secondary schools across the six geo-political zones in the country which I made several paper presentations in all the zones. What I found was that, that workshop was the first ever workshop some of the teachers attended in their ten to fifteen years in the teaching profession. Isn't that too appalling? The ETF should do more than they have done so far and put retraining of teachers in public schools in every year's budget.

A situation where elementary school pupils will have to sit on the floor to receive teaching instructions in this modern day and time of information technology is completely unacceptable. This was the case of a public school located in the Ikeja area of Lagos State, until a church located opposite the school decided to provide furniture and improve the physical infrastructure of the school to make the environment more conducive for learning. There is an urgent need to invest funds to improve the physical infrastructure of public schools.

To bridge the gap between the private and the public school teaching curriculum requires not just in the curriculum per se, but also includes motivating the public school teachers by providing them with more incentives that will compare with their private schools counterparts. It is when they are well motivated that they will be creative in their teaching styles and develop richer curriculum.

This is not to say that all private schools are better than public schools. There are some private schools that are far below acceptable standards, especially the ones located in the poor areas or communities. Government should also check on these quacks and ensure that they comply with the minimum acceptable curriculum standards.

Finally, most of the public schools are badly managed or administered. The administrators of some of these schools don't have what it takes to run a school. They are not trained to acquire management or administrative skills. An attempt was made by Education Tax Fund in this area of impacting some management skills to the teachers but it was not enough. It has to be a continuous exercise. When they are not well trained it leads to bad governance.

CHAPTER TWENTY FOUR

BUSINESS, POLITICS AND
THE UNCERTAINTIES OF
2009 AND BEYOND

We have seen and gone through an exciting and very challenging 2008, and have entered a very uncertain year, 2009. So many unimaginable things happened in 2008. When the year began a lot of people – government, businesses, and individuals – were full of hopes and aspirations. Some were accomplished and many were not. Time and space will fail me to begin to chronicle all the events that took place in 2008. But let me mention the very few ones I can remember.

Domestic Scene
The Niger Delta topped the major events in 2008. It was expected because the federal government voted over N400 billion to tackle the Niger Delta problem. The money was basically meant to acquire rams and

ammunitions to deal with the militant and provide a peaceful atmosphere for oil and gas exploration and exploitation. This did not solve the problem neither did the region know or experience any peace for one month. Rather it helped fuel the conflict some more. The Joint Task Force (JTF) soon found out the militants had more fire power than they initially estimated.

In a previous interview in one of the TV stations, I did mention that the idea of force was ill-conceived and it was not going to achieve the desired result. There are two types of element in the Niger Delta conflict. One is the group that is only using the crisis to meet their selfish interest through some tinge of criminality. These are people involved in the kidnapping and killing of innocent citizens going about their businesses. Part of this group are oil thieves who seize the occasion to bunker oil. This is the group the JTF should really go after and deal with as the law permits.

Then there is the second group that is genuinely fighting the cause of the underdevelopment and the inhuman condition of the people living in that region. This is the group that believe in the dream of the late statesman from the region – Adaka Boro – who sacrificed his life for the cause in the 1960s. This group is the genuine group who should be encouraged for their nonviolence approach to conflict resolution. The question therefore is this: Must the people of a particular part of Nigeria engage in arm conflict for the federal government to look to their plight? Is it not the job of the government to give good governance to the people of Nigeria? It is written in the Holy Book – Bible – that a man that cannot provide for his family is worse than an infidel. In order words, any man that cannot feed and take of his wife and children has failed as a man and should not be regarded in the society as a man.

The same applies to governance. Any government that cannot give good governance to its citizens has failed as a government, and has consequently failed as a state. That's why I mentioned in a previous writing that Nigeria has every sign of a failed state because of the ineptitude on the part of the government to protect and provide basic amenities for the citizens. The people of Nigeria are not asking for too much. All they want is good road to travel from one part of the country to another. A recent statistics showed that more people die on the road – road accidents – than they die of HIV/ AIDS. People want to feel they are safe to move about their businesses without being afraid of being attacked by armed robbers or any of their kind.

They want to know that government can protect their lives and properties wherever they live and do business in Nigeria and abroad. So many innocent citizens have died for no just cause but due to political and religiously motivated conflicts in some parts of the country - the recent incident being Jos, Plateau State, where innocent citizens were killed for selfish and politically motivated conflict. From the reports in the media, it seemed it was premeditated and there was even intelligence report that warned about the incident, but the government, in its characteristics manner did not act to prevent the incident from happening. In a more civilized society, the state government would have resigned – just like what happened in Mumbai, India where the governor and his deputy resigned when accused of not acting quickly to save the situation in that city when the terrorists attacked Tajmahal and Regency hotels and about 178 people died, according to official report.

When the Yar'Adua administration took over reins from the previous one, they promised to declare a state of emergency in the power sector. Rather than improve on the existing level of generation and distribution, we experienced a drop to below 1000 mw according to one estimate. Another estimate has it a little above that figure. The point is that two major tyre manufacturers – Michelin and Dunlop – had to close down their operations in Nigeria citing poor power supply, among others, as one of their reasons. The companies now manufacture in a more competitive environment and import finished products into Nigeria to sale. In the case of Dunlop the government was well aware of their plight but turned a blind eye on them, and so they had to take the only reasonable option to quit Nigeria. Yet the government is not bothered about the implications of that decision – especially the over 1000 people that lost their jobs afterwards. This is the height of government insensitivity to the plight of not only Dunlop but businesses generally.

I have often argued that we need a business-friendly government for businesses to prosper in this environment. How on earth can Nigeria be competitive when, to start a business and comply with licensing and permit requirements, it requires: 16 steps, 465 days, 2/3 of GNI per capita, according to World Bank, "Doing Business Report," 2006. One would have expected that the present administration would have continued with the reform program of the previous administration and making some changes where necessary rather than jettisoning the whole idea. The seven point agenda the Yar'Adua administration adopted instead is not necessary. It does not make him a lesser ruler if he continues with some of the programs of his predecessor. We have seen yet again how continuity is a bane of our national development.

The oil and gas sector was not speared from the government's inaction. For some years the government had not been able to their financial obligations to the JVs which stalled further explorations. There is this government's attitude of expecting that something will just grow out of nothing without investing toward achieving that growth. One would have expected that with the coming of the present administration some money would have been invested into the sector to be able to achieve the projected or expected production level. The global economic crisis has not abated which is quite evident in the low prices of oil in the international markets. This is the time the government should invest heavily in the oil and gas sector to develop and sustain productivity.

Government's lack of investment in the sector is already having its impact as the operators are scaling down exploration and their search for new oil. KBR, one of the multinational oil services companies operating in Nigeria has closed down their operations for lack of patronage. I expect more of such companies to close down in the new year if the government does not act quickly to restore confidence in that sector.

The down stream sector is not fairing any better as the refineries are not operating optimally and no serious plans to build new ones. Those benefiting from the status quo will not allow any serious investor to set up. The government has to show some serious commitment for any serious investor to invest his hard earned money to set up. People are willing and ready to set up refineries but that will only happen if they see serious commitment by the government.

There is a high level corruption in the sector that will continue to stunt the growth of the sector. The national assembly touted sometime ago their interest in investigating corruption in the oil and gas sector. They will meet a mighty brick wall unless they have the backing and commitment of the Presidency. There is so much mess in the sector and it requires urgent cleaning up.

The manufacturing was and still is the most hit by the government's neglect and inaction for several years now. The Yar'Adua administration came up with a seven point agenda and visions to be the twentieth biggest economy by the year 2020. This is a plausible dream if they get the fundamentals right. How can they achieve this without an effective and efficient and strong manufacturing as well as industrial base. In the past, the manufacturing sector was contributing over 13 percent to the GDP. Today, it is virtually in a comatose, contributing less than 4 percent to the GDP, with less than 45 percent capacity utilization.

Take Kano state for example. The state used to harbor about 4000 companies and over 150 textile companies. A recent report by one of the daily newspapers showed that most of those companies have shut down their operations, leaving only a couple of hundreds still struggling to survive. The textile companies are almost nonexistent. They could not cope with competitions coming from the cheap Chinese imports.

The Chinese seem to have been given free rein in most sectors of the Nigerian economy. I have argued severally that the government needs to come up with a strategy on how to deal with the Chinese. The Chinese are known all over the world to be hard ball players. They are the most beneficiary of the recent global offshoring and outsourcing trends due to their low costs and high productivity. Recently, there was a deliberate devaluation of the Chinese currency to make their products more competitive against the US imports into China. The US government cried foul but the Chinese government could not care a hoot.

The Nigerian state is not viable in a business sense and neither are the states that make up the country. It is only Lagos State and probably Rivers State that could survive without the federal government monthly subventions. Other states may need to "merge" with other states to be viable. For the states to be viable there is need to diversify and decentralize the economy. When the economy is decentralized the right environment is provided for business activities to take place in the villages, towns and communities across the country. It will reduce the movement of people to the towns and urban centers, which is growing at an alarming rate.

Moreover, the kind of healthy competition that existed in the sixties before oil became the main focus of the national government's main source of revenue should be welcomed back. States should look toward developing their competencies based on available skills. Each state should decide or discover what it is good at and develop and build their competencies around it. At recent outsourcing summit organized by the Nigerian Export Promotion Council in collaboration with International Trade Center, Geneva, the Kano State government put up a strong showing at the summit. The state decided to compete in the ICT sector and has therefore built an ICT cluster to attract investor and other businesses to the state. The state wants to be an ICT hub in Nigeria as well as an outsourcing destination for BPO and ITO. This is directly under the governor's portfolio with a senior adviser to the governor in charge.

The global trend is toward a 24-hour economy. If Nigeria is to go with the flow to compete in the international market place, the all levels of government must invest heavily in infrastructure – road, transportation, power and energy, social, human capital (education and health) – and security, as well as restructuring of the political system. No nation has developed or will ever develop without this basic infrastructure. Nigeria will not be an exception.

International Scene
A lot happened around the world in 2008. Among the major events that played out was the subprime crisis that started in the mortgage sector and spread to full scale financial and economic crisis. Within a twinkle of an eye, some major investment banks collapsed before our very own eyes. There was a great shaking of economies and governments. It was the first crisis that started in the US and spread across the globe. That's

probably why the impact is so severe.

The crisis helped destroy the image of the Bush administration in the US in it's last days. But the decisive action of the Gordon Brown, the British Prime Minister, to bail out banks in the UK or should I say "nationalize" helped revive his government which was at its lowest ebb. But his Belgium counterpart was not as lucky as he had to resign for poor handling of the situation. Africa was not directly affected as the economic fundamentals remained little bit strong.

The most remarkable thing that happened in 2008, apart from what has been mentioned above was the election of Barack Obama as the first African-American president of the United States of America. It marked the beginning of the total emancipation of the Black race. Some religious buffs believe that it has ushered in the beginning of the "last days." They argued that out of the three sons of Noah – Shem, Ham, and Japheth – only Ham (Africa) is yet to fulfill his destiny which God has reserved for this time. But beyond religion, the election of Obama as the US president is very significant in the world political scene.

Some people believe Obama is going to restore the battered image of the US. The young man has a big challenge before him but so far he has shown that he is capable of tackling the issues before him. Within days and weeks after his election as president, he already has his team ready to work. His team is a mix of old school and new – a blend required to effectively manage the economic downturn and put America and indeed the world back to the path of prosperity.

Still on the political scene, what happened in Thailand point the way to how most bad governance issues will be resolved, especially in the emerging and developing economies. The Thais, through a mass action forced their prime minister out of office. They seized or rather took over the two major airports in the country for days until the Supreme Court sacked the then prime minister and barred him and few others from holding any political office till further notice. What won it for the people of Thailand was their collective resolve to get rid of bad governance and choose a leader that will take them to their promised land. Nigeria – both the leaders at various levels and the led should learn a lesson or two from the Thai experience and experiment.

The restart of the war between Israel and Palestine has some element of politics embedded in it. Hamas played into the hands of the Israeli politicians who seized the moment of the provocation to score some political points, moreso as they get ready to face the electorate. Israel id determined to rout out the terrorist elements that Hamas symbolized. World leaders seemed to have turned their eyes the other way pretending not to know what's going on. Israel had to retaliate the Palestinian rocket attacks because they are not sure the kind of support they are going to receive from Obama administration. So they decided to act before the expiration of the Bush administration, who Israel throughout his eight years in office.

If you are a good student of history or a religious buff, you will understand that these two half brothers can never live together in peace. The moment they are able to do so, the end of the world has come. We also seen how the past Israeli prime ministers who tried to broker peace with Palestine ended their political careers, some even paid a supreme price with their lives. The most recent example is the Israeli former Prime Minister, Ariel Sharon.

I remember how he led the war in 1982 and resettled Israelis in the Gaza strip. I was a student in Canada visiting the US for the summer holiday. I could not understand how he (Ariel Sharon) could go the extent of "uprooting" Israelis to "plant" Palestinians. When I read about it in the media, I told some people that the end of his political career was in sight. I even predicted he could die in the process. Well, we know what happened to Sharon and how he ended up.

We need to pay attention to history and devote time to study history. History is important to predicting trends. It gives you inspiration and vision. Barack Obama can testify to this. Any nation or company or organization that is serious about making progress must pay attention to history. The tone of the event of tomorrow is set by the events of yesterday – history.

What to expect in 2009 and beyond
The year 2009 began with the carry over of some the 2008 unresolved issues and challenges. In Nigeria, it will be business as usual in the political scene and governance. Some of the gains made in the past to curb corruption will be eroded as some powerful forces in the corridors of power will strengthen their strangle hold on the dastardization of the nation's resources and wealth. The style of the this administration is the one type that will take Nigeria to the next level of competitiveness and prosperity. If anything Nigeria has

returned to Shagari era.

Some states will experience a remarkable improvement, but on the federal level, don't expect much – except if some extraordinary things happen. The 2008 budget was only 14 percent implemented by the federal government. The 2009 budget brought no cheer either. Two-thirds of the 2009 budget is for recurrent expenditure, which means not much is budgeted for new capital expenditure (investments). Capital expenditure will help create jobs, support businesses, especially SMEs. The projected GDP growth rate of 6.9 percent is not realistic considering that the global economic crisis will take about eighteen months to recover.

Single digit inflation will be hard to achieve. In a period of economic recession like this one, what will help recovery is tight fiscal discipline. Monetary policy will be found to be ineffective. Oil prices will not improve much and will hover around $25 - $40 per barrel. Some are predicting that it will go as low as $12 per barrel. Whatever be the case, the search for alternative sources of energy will intensify – solar and biofuel. Nigeria's production level will be lower for the obvious reasons – Niger Delta and low investment in the sector. Heavy investment need to be made by the government to increase the production level and meet up the project 2.29 barrels per day as stated in the 2009 budget. In December 2008, the CBN devalued the Naira because of the plummeting oil prices and weak dollar. The 2009 budget was based on $45 per barrel, and few days after the budget was presented to the national assembly the price of oil went down to below $40 per barrel.

Some companies will close down due to inconsistent government policies. The manufacturing sector will continue to be the state of coma with high capacity under utilization. Competition in the provision of professional services will increase – legal services, consulting, etc – as the WTO and globalization open up the market space for services. Outsourcing of services in BPO and ITO will increase as the awareness increases.

Unemployment will continue to be on the rise and will become a troubling issue for the government. Insecurity of life and property will continue to be a big issue as the ill equipped and under funded police force will have a hard time fight crimes and providing security. More private security firms will spring up to fill in the gap. Youth restiveness will take new dimensions, especially in the Niger Delta as the citizens become more aware of the rights and demand more accountability from their leaders.

A preview of what could be the trend occurred in Yenegoa, Bayelsa State just before Christmas. I was spending time with some friends over there when the incident happened. Some group of about 500 youths in the area gathered in the government house and beat up two advisers to the state governor and sent them on errand to tell the governor they were hungry. That day happened be the day they were sharing rice and other items to some privileged few in the government house. Earlier, some group of persons went to the home of another top government official and beat him to the state of near coma, and told him to tell the governor that they were hungry.

I sampled opinions of some people, both literate and not so literate, about governance issues in the state. They were in unison that the present government is not providing good governance for the people. They believe that with the amount of federal allocation the state government receives they should be able to open up the economy of the state and create jobs, but this has not happened. Instead, the state is hobnobbing with some "criminal godfathers" that ruined Anambra state before Ngige sanitized the state for Peter Obi, the present governor, to have some respite to govern. Some the biggest investments you will find in Bayelsa state are hotels and petrol stations, many of which are owned by both serving and retired or sacked government officials and politicians.

Leadership

The global financial and economic crisis of 2008 will change the nature of leadership in both organizations and nations around the world. The tight credit squeeze will continue way into 2010, though some governments have given out monies to encourage consumer lending to stem the economic recession. By the time the economic and financial crisis is over there will a new global monitoring system or body to monitor money and its movement across the globe. It's either that the role of World Bank or IMF is reformed to include strict monitoring of global finance or an entirely new body is set up to do the job.

Since finance is global, it therefore makes sense that the monitoring of supervision will be global. The supervision or monitoring of the financial system will not be left to each country's central banks alone.

Investors and businesses borrow money from any part of the world where it is available and cheap to carry out project in different countries of the world. A new global standard monitoring system will emerge and new members will join the G8 – likely China, Brazil, India, and Russia. As these new rookies come on board, they will demand to have a say in what happens within the group and of course the world economy. The structure of the global leadership will be altered to include new players.

The leadership of organizations will be altered too. To run successful organizations in this knowledge economy will require the business leader possessing more intellectual depth and common sense. Added to these two qualities is the issue of business ethics which will be brought further to the fore. Visionary leadership is good and visionary leaders are still needed to lead organizations and nations, but the shift in 2009 and beyond will be toward the ability to execute and manage money. Leaders with good money management skills will be in high demand.

The Nigerian leaders, just like I stated above, should possess more intellectual depth and common sense to be effective. In this new knowledge economy, you cannot solve problems or handle challenges with what I will like to call "brick and mortar" intellectual capacity. They require new brains and new thinking. They need intellectual deepening and common sense. Enough of these shallow minded types of leaders we have been saddled with over the years. Nigeria needs leaders who are not only consumers of ideas or knowledge but also creators of knowledge - those who can think, because you can not create new knowledge without possessing deep think capability.

For Nigeria to make progress, in addition to intellectual depth, common sense and ethics, there is need for a Cultural Revolution or reorientation. Growing the economy is good but not at the expense of the quality of life of the citizens. I have often said that the economy supposed to serve the people, but in Nigeria the way our leader are going about governing the affairs of the state shows that the citizens are serving the economy. So much attention is given to growing the GDP but growing the GDP without accompanying development is tantamount to negative growth.

So, our emphasis should not only be in growing the GDP; we need to focus on changing, or better still, improving or rowing our value system and spiritual rebirth. Values and spirituality are as important as the GDP. We need to place more value on the life of the Nigerian at home and abroad. There is so much wastages of both our human, financial, and material resources. We have what it takes to make Nigeria great, so why don't we make it great for ourselves and our children. If we don't act now, one day our children will demand to know why we did not do something within our powers to make Nigeria a better place for them. What excuse would you give your children?

CHAPTER
TWENTY FIVE

FACTOR ENDOWMENT AND
COMPETITIVE COMMUNALISM

Have you ever paused to think of why resource-rich countries have performed worse than countries that have absolutely no natural resources - in terms of development? This is a commonplace phenomenon around the world, especially in less developed countries. Africa is no exception. Most African countries are pretty rich in natural resource endowments but in spite of all these, they are among the poorest countries in the world. Nigeria is no exception, despite the fact that Nigeria is endowed with numerous natural resources. In fact, it is often estimated that Nigeria is endowed with one quarter (25 per cent) of all the natural resources in the world. Nigeria is also the sixth largest producer of oil, and yet 71 per cent of the citizens live below poverty line of less than $2 a day.

African countries have struggled and are still struggling on ways to develop and get their people out of poverty for many years and even centuries, yet there is no end of poverty in sight. Many writers and economists have proffered reasons for poverty or lack of development in the continent. Economists like Jeffrey Sachs in his 2005 volume *The End of Poverty: How we can make it happen in our lifetime* identified eight reasons or categories of problems or why countries fail to achieve economic growth or cause an economy to stagnate or decline. They include poverty trap, physical geography, fiscal trap, governance failures, cultural barriers, geopolitics, lack of innovation, and demographic trap. Let's briefly peep deeper into each of these for better understanding of Sachs' argument.

Poverty trap: Sachs argued that poverty itself could cause economic stagnation because extreme poverty makes it difficult for poor people to get out of poverty. He said: "consider the kind of poverty caused by a lack of capital per person. Poor rural villages lack trucks, paved roads, power generators, irrigation channels. Human capital is very low, with hungry disease-ridden and illiterate villagers struggling for survival. Natural capital is depleted: the trees have been cut down and the soil nutrients exhausted. In these conditions the need is for more capital – physical, human, natural – but that requires more savings. When people are poor, but not utterly destitute, they may be able to save. When they are utterly destitute, they need their entire income above survival that can be invested for the future."

Physical geography: Sachs made the point that natural endowments play important role in economic growth.

He cited the example of the United States that inherited a vast continent rich in natural resource. Sachs also emphasized how other landlocked countries like Ethiopia, Bolivia and Tibet are not so lucky to be endowed like the US and few other countries. One could argue that in as much as natural resources endowments are important to economic development, one important point not to be overlooked is that when not properly managed, natural resource endowment can be recursive. A typical example is Nigeria, endowed with an estimated 25 percent of the world's natural resources, yet 71 percent of the citizens live below poverty line due to the mismanagement of these resources.

There are also few other countries that are not lucky to be well located geographically but yet have made tremendous progress economically and socially. The ones that easily come to mind are Japan and Singapore. The geographical location of Japan is not one that could be said to be of any advantage. For instance, it is only one-third of Japan that is habitable. The other two-third is mountainous and very prone to natural disasters; yet, Japan has made tremendous progress economically and socially and has become the second richest country in the world. Singapore on the other hand has no other natural resource safe that it is surrounded by water. That water became "Moses rod" which they have used to develop the country and has become the eighth riches country in the world.

Fiscal Trap: This is one factor that Sachs believes may be responsible for the poverty of the poor. This has nothing to do with natural resource endowment but has a lot to do with the provision of public goods (infrastructural facilities). He opined:"Governments are critical to investing in public goods and services like primary healthcare, roads, power grids, ports, and the like. Government may lack the financial means to provide these public goods, however, for at least these reasons. First, the population itself may be impoverished, so taxation of the population is not feasible. Second, the government may be inept, corrupt, or incapacitated, and thereby unable to collect tax revenues. Third, the government may already be carrying a tremendous load of debt (for example, debt carried forward from an earlier decade), and must use its resources to service these debts rather than finance new investments." A little reminder here is that foreign investors might also look at the sovereign debt overhang of a country before investing in that country. This was one of the reasons Nigeria attracted some bit of foreign direct investment, especially when the Obasanjo administration took advantage of the debt forgiveness by the European creditors to reduce or get rid of the nation's debt overhang.

Government Failures: Sachs stressed that "economic development requires a government orientation towards development." What then is government's role? Certainly governments have roles to play in identifying and financing infrastructure that are of high priority. Government must also create conducive environment for investment by private businesses. In addition, government must provide the much needed social and infrastructure services to the entire population. When government fail to provide the afore mentioned roles, the economy fails. In other words, bad governance is a sure root to economic stagnation and economic failure.

Cultural Business" There is element of truth in Sachs' argument that when governments try to develop the country, culture could act as a barrier to development. Cultural, social, and religious norms such as denying women their right to quality education or making women have many children (baby factory) could act as a barrier to economic development. Lawrence Harrison and Samuel Huntington added their voice in the culture debate in their 2000 volume "Culture Matters: How values shape human progress" by comparing Ghana and South Korea in their early and later levels of developments based on available economic data in the 1960s. The data revealed that the two countries' economies were similar in the 1960s. Both had "comparable levels of per capita GNP, similar divisions of their individual economies – primary products, manufacturing, and services; and overwhelming primary products exports, with South Korea producing a few manufactured goods.

The authors further noted that Ghana and South Korea received comparable levels of economic aid from the international community. They stated that "thirty years later, South Korea had become an industrial giant being the fourteenth largest economy in the world, multinational corporations, major exports of automobiles, electronics equipment, and other sophisticated manufactures and a per capita income approximately that of Greece." Unfortunately, the same cannot be said about Ghana. Though the two countries were at similar levels in the 1960s, but Ghana's per capita GNP is one-fifteenth that of South Korea's. Though many factors were identified as responsible for this huge disparity but culture was fingered by Harrison and Huntington as one "large part of the explanation." South Korea's values of thrift, investment, hard work, education, organization, and discipline were responsible for the rapid growth experienced within three decades. Ghana on the other hand had completely different values.

Geopolitics: This has to do with the politics of trade. Most often rich and powerful countries of the West impose trade sanctions on countries whose regimes they abhor or do not accept or like – could be for reasons of human rights abuses or for any other reasons. This imposition of sanctions has tremendous impact on the economies of these poor countries.

Lack of Innovation: Though inventors in poor countries might come up with new inventions but the marketability of such research and development output or the possibility of recouping such investment is very thin due to market size and the low purchasing power of the people. Market size will definitely affect the success of such new inventions in the market place. It doesn't matter whether there exists legal system that protects the property rights of such inventions.

Large market size is a big incentive to innovation which the rich countries have and the poor countries don't have. Large market size, apart from increasing the incentive for innovation also brings new technologies to market, raises productivity and expands the size of the market, as well as creates new incentives for innovation. This kind of chain reaction according to

Sachs is what economists call endogenous growth. "Innovation raises the size of the market; a large market raises the incentives for innovation. Therefore, economic growth and innovation proceed in a mutually reinforcing process." Sachs argued that what stands at the core of economic growth for the rich countries of North America, Europe and East Asia is research and development, leading to the sales of patent protected products to a large market. Of great importance to note is that these rich countries invest about 2 percent of their GNP into research and development and sometimes over 3 percent of GDP.

While in poor countries the innovation process is non-existent. Research and development drive innovation while innovation is the key driver of the knowledge economy. In poor countries the incentive to invent is not there because investors are quite aware of the fact that they will not be able to recoup their investment. Listen to this: "Although today's low-income countries accounted for less than 1 percent of all the U.S.-registered patents taken out by investors in the year 2000. The top twenty countries in patenting, all high-income countries, account for 98 percent of all patents." We can see from the foregoing why the rich countries are rich largely due to their investments in innovation, and the poor countries are poor due to their lack of investment in innovation. So, competing in the knowledge economy requires heavy and deliberate investment in the innovation process – in other words, heavy investment in research and development (R & D).

Demographic Trap

This is a situation where poor families in poor countries choose to have many children. The resultant effect of this is disastrous and poses an obstacle to economic growth. Sachs believes that "when impoverished families have large numbers of children, the families cannot afford to invest in the nutrition, health, and education of each child. They might only afford the education of one child, and may send only one son to school. High fertility rates in one generation, therefore, tend to lead to impoverishment of the children and to high fertility rates in the following generation as well. Rapid population growth also puts enormous stresses on farm sizes and environmental resources, thereby exacerbating the poverty." The bottom line, Sachs concludes, is that "high population growth leads to deeper poverty, and deeper poverty contributes to higher fertility rates."

Professor Pat Utomi's economic growth drivers' framework

Professor Pat Utomi responded to the foregoing Jeffery Sachs' argument in his own 2006 volume *"Why Nations are Poor."* Utomi argued that though Sachs eight reasons or categories of problems or why countries fail to achieve economic growth or cause an economy to stagnate or decline are relevant points but beyond all that are other reasons such as his growth drivers framework.

Economic growth in the work of Prof. Pat Utomi is a function of six variables which he described as the growth driven framework. These variables tend to explain why some nations stagnated while others have continued to grow their way out of poverty. There are also six sets of interdependent variables which intersect with one another and shape the environment of business, determining thereby the strategy choices of firms and performance outcomes that make up the wealth of nations. These variables are Policy Choices, Institutions, Human Capital, Entrepreneurship, Culture and Leadership.

Policy Choices

"Paul Collier and the group of academics who see the statistics orientation of African leaders as the source of policies that have taken away individual incentives and produced slow growth, if not stagnation. The intellectual view that dominated the early years of Nigerian independence was the mixed economy model. This model is that in which the state was active in commercial sectors and in "facilitating" the import substitution industrialization strategy and indigenization of the economy.

The military that had taken over the reign of power in Nigeria by January 1996 had little time for the intellectual left. Policy therefore began to withdraw from the broad open intellectual engagement, except for these academics sucked in by the corporatist state and very often destroyed by it. Then there were the urban biased elite-centered set of policies that saw marketing boards redistributes wealth from cash crops of the rural areas to administrative elite. This was worsened by dramatic leap in oil prices in 1973 following the Yom Kippur Arab – Israeli war. Just as oil was becoming very significant revenue source in Nigeria.

Policies became more statist and significantly insensitive to the impact of appreciating exchange rates for the performance of other sectors. The farmers, unable to survive on Naira value of the exports abandoned their farms. Nigeria was soon to become a monoculture economy. The other trouble with oil was made manifest as oil prices were noteworthy unstable and external shocks from oil prices savings would soon be a dominant feature of Nigeria's economy. Dutch disease would therefore enter the lexicon of everyday Nigeria as governments saw budgets balloon in the face of high oil prices today and crash tomorrow. This led the Nigerian economy to a structural logjam and needed reforms.

Policy reforms have, however, failed to bring the promised investment and growth. This is clear because experience from elsewhere shows that policy choice is necessary but not sufficient for economic growth. Institutions, Human Capital, Entrepreneurship, Culture and Leadership need be considered also. Structural adjustment program (SAP) was introduced, but these policy changes have not moved the people away from poverty on the extreme poor-high networth continuum.

Even though agriculture hosts a majority of the population as a place of employment, its contribution to GDP was only 34 percent in 2005. Tinkering with policies that abolished the Marketing Boards that had symbolized the extraction of profit with little invested back was a major plank of the reform initiative at the time of SAP. Exchange rate policy shift from the fixed to a two tier market determined rates was part of the package to return agriculture to a path of reckoning.

The new exchange rate mechanism, a precursor to the goal of free market determined exchange rate involved significant devaluation of the Nigerian currency, the Naira. The immediate effect of this is that it made the export of agricultural produce, which overvalued exchange rates had made unappealing in the past years, more attractive and this resulted to the abandonment of cocoa farm.

The policy choice process offered Nigeria a two tier foreign exchange market at the outset. With weak monitoring capacity, there was a wide side arbitrage and a mad rush of people with excess money to obtain banking licenses which were equivalent to license to print money for the unscrupulous. The basic law of demand and supply meant that the value of the Naira continued to be south bound.

In order to stop the tide of the depreciating Naira, the government introduced other policies like Central Bank requiring commercial banks to acquire stabilization securities which forced money out of the banking system without notice in order to bring down money supply and make Naira chasing foreign currencies scarce. Policy choice does matter but it matters in context of other variables. Failure to pay enough attention to that will only produce recursive outcomes. Institutions

Institutions are about containing uncertainty and bringing predictability to action. They are the guardians of the will of society to place limits to acceptable behavior. By putting cost to behavior that society has come to accept, either because the powerful have convinced others it is in their best interest or because practice and convention have led society to a consensus that the object behavior is in the common interest, institutions reinforce the consensus.

In many developing countries the institutions are weak and under them because many rules have not become settled habits. Rules related to modern economic transactions have not become settled habits in many transition economies because these rules are often new and alien as most new economic practices are imported as part of the race for modernity. Since these new ways hardly build on traditional habits for similar activities, the tendency is for deflection from these new norms in places where capacity of the new institutions for enforcement of the new rules is quite low. Institutions are critical to investments on which growth depends. Institutional weakness, on the other hand, is also a bane of development. Institutions can also be a source of threats and opportunities and competitive strategy demands an alignment of the strengths and weaknesses of the organization with trends in the evolution of institutions to protect it's weakness from being vulnerable to the institutions and to use its strength to make institutions work in favor of the firm.

As the effectiveness of institutions can affect most of the five forces of industry structure analysis, like the other environment mega factors, government and business associations, environment analysis would be incomplete without thinking of institutions.

How did the West grow rich and what are the lessons from how institutions evolve, how capital became available for building the wealth of nations? Hernando de Soto demonstrated that the major stumbling block that keeps the rest of the world from benefiting from capitalism is its inability to produce capital. Capital is the force that raises the productivity of labor and creates the wealth of nations.

Human Capital

Human Capital development is concerned with the skills, know – how, and know – why of persons, their managed capacity and their state of health so they can give enough to increase productivity. Unfortunately, contemporary Nigerian experience has witnessed a combination of decline in the quality of education through poor funding and not well thought – through egalitarian policies regarding contribution of beneficiaries to funding higher educations, declining enrolment in schools; and declining health care.

With HIV/AIDS pandemic and the stranglehold malaria still has on quality of life, especially with its toll on infant mortality, the challenge of human capital needs to be tackled in a more committed way to make progress. The challenge of human capital development in poor nations has been a major source of reduced competitiveness in a global economy in which countries position themselves to attract a share of investment flows, tourism and technology. In countries like Nigeria the rot in both tertiary education and healthcare has attracted some very provocative and some quite sober statements.

Human Capital is at the heart of the modern competitiveness economy and that the path of building a stock of human capital to out-perform others in both the investment in education and healthcare, and how a country manages the development of those investments. Many nations are poor either because they invest inadequately, or manage poorly that which is invested.

The UNDP Human Development Index provides a fair sense of the relationship between provision for healthcare and human material progress. Where it is possible for some countries that have a marginally higher per person index, it is the norm that most countries that invest significantly in the well – being and education of their people tend to be the more prosperous countries.

The National Health Plan document released by Nigeria's Federal Ministry of Health proposed that: "the goal of the National Health Policy shall be to establish a comprehensive healthcare system based on primary healthcare that is promotive of protective, preventive, restorative and rehabilitative, to every citizen of the country within the available resources so that individuals and communities are assured of productivity, social well – being and enjoyment of living." Unfortunately, the current situation is worse than when that statement was made about 20 years earlier.

The failure of education and absence of commitment to better healthcare management can be a major reason for poverty of nations because it translates to low human capital in the age of the knowledge worker when competitive advantage of nations derive significantly from the state of their human capital.

Entrepreneurship

Entrepreneurship can be described as that process of creating value where non existed and thereby reducing the gap between the level of satisfaction men enjoy with their lives and where they desire to be. Entrepreneurship is a master key to economic growth and development and reduction of poverty in the poor countries of the world, as it is about an understanding of how forces within and outside the narrow economic system produce a dynamic in which creative ideas in builders of enterprise sometime with access to capital, to yield a quantum leap in value creation.

Entrepreneurship is about creating value that did not exist, which bridges the dissatisfaction gap that exist between where people are in their needs state and where they desire to be on the hierarchy of needs. Understanding the phenomenon that enterprise is essentially the soul of human material progress, and how it is impacted by policy choices, institutional arrangements, human capital availability and the dominant values (culture) which are shaped significantly by leadership, is really understanding why nations are poor.

Why is high value enterprise opportunity not so easily pursued by a lot of people who want to make a lot of money? Outcomes are so had to predict in ideas that lead to big discontinuous changes that advance value to the customer that many walk past the opportunity without seeing it. A good measure for value is, therefore, the amount of uncertainty in the possibilities of commercialization of the new enterprise that shifts satisfaction. It is the quantum of value creation that distinguishes the businessman from the entrepreneur. Nigeria is a country of many businessmen but few entrepreneurs.

Between the businessmen and the entrepreneurs is a continuum from risk at one end (the businessman) to uncertainty at the other end (the entrepreneur). The policy choice, institutional arrangement, etc. tend to indicate which end people locate. The question why are these few entrepreneurs in countries that need more of them so that discontinuous change that yield value innovations will come in quick enough bursts to alter the welfare profiles of a broad part of the population? To answer this requires a little exploration of the evidence how the West grew rich, how Asia catching up, and what role entrepreneurship has played in the diverging performance of these economies.

A reason for the growth of the West, which comes from sociology, and the values of society, is the ethic that supported hard work and innovations. In the case of South East Asia it is the emigrant economistic ethic. The emigrant population, not distracted by politics and competing sources of prestige, enhances his personal welfare very quickly and contributes to the economic growth of the society.

The entrepreneurial process: The discipline to actualize the entrepreneurial process thereby creating value where none existed, in a manner that would be sustained for a significant period of time is subject to the effect and trends in society. The process usually involves opportunity conception, commercialization of the venture and institutionalization of the ventures.

Opportunity conception involves visioning the world affected by the venture idea and constructing backwards, a sense of execution that will accomplish the envisioned. This visioning for the opportunity that creates value is driven by the entrepreneur's view of identifying how change will take place and profiting from it. Peter Drucker put it this way in his book on innovation and entrepreneurship: "Entrepreneurs see change as the norm and as healthy. Usually they do not bring about the change themselves. But the entrepreneur always reaches for change, responds to it and exploits it as an opportunity."

Drucker further offered seven services of innovative opportunity which include: the unexpected, incongruities, process need, industry and market structure, demographics, changes in perception and new knowledge.

When the vision is validated by being written down, and reviewed, or thought through where the process is not formalized, the next phase of the process will involve commercialization of the venture. From evaluating the idea to developing a formal business plan and assembling the resources; financial, human, technological, etc, that is required to actualize the value proposition, the process of commercializing of a venture requires vigor and perseverance. When deferred gratification is not much rooted in the culture, the tendency will be for people to detect venture types that require commitment and much patience in favor of the quick economic rent that is expropriated for wasteful communication, usually of products not produced in the country, thus taking away the many multiplier effects of the economy of the derived rent.

The commercialized venture would, if it is to be sustained, be institutionalized. The process of transition from the hub – wheel – spoke kind of structure centered around the entrepreneur to a hierarchy of standard operating procedures is also much affected by common forms of organization and state of the management philosophy as it is by culture. Many entrepreneurs in poor countries do not professionalize and institutionalize early enough. The effect is that when the entrepreneur has a cold, the business sneezes.

Value created by these ventures tend to be lost to society on their demise by this failure to institutionalize the venture, and develop the value chain for new ladders of opportunity that allows the venture either to make incremental continuous changes as in circular flow of income or indeed to make discontinuous leaps in value creation.

Culture

Values affect risk – taking behavior, how people are managed, the context of trust and the cost of doing business and the work ethic. The relevance of culture in economic growth was best captured by Lawrence E. Harrison and Samuel P. Huntington in their volume "Culture Matters". In Nigeria, attitude toward venturing vary across a spectrum from fatalistic disposition in which all is literally left in God's hand, in fundamentalist Islam, to prosperity – preaching Pentecostals. Of greater significance for the effect of culture on economic performance are issues of corruption and rent – seeking behavior in patrimonial state and orientations toward the dignity of the human person. There is also the cultural dimension of reverence for age which invariably calls on the more competent to yield to the older in leadership situations with obvious consequences for performance. These values no doubt affect how policy choices are made. The female child, for example, is educated, and institutions respected, and new venture opportunities captured.

What is of great value here is that the recognition of culture's place in development has grown. But in Nigeria, unfortunately, the importance of culture for development tended to be overlooked. Daniel Patrick Moynihan puts it succinctly. "The central conservative truth is that it is culture, not politics that determines the success of a society. The central liberal truth is that politics can change culture and save it from itself". There are some aspects of culture that affect performance but which formal rules may not necessarily influence. Whereas the work ethic may be so strongly rooted in the sense of self worth of a group, another may actually believe that to try and get more credit than your neighbor is a sign of ill will. In many ways, our notion of culture is an application of ideas of corporate culture as shared values at the level of the nation – state.

Leadership

Leadership is the core of the of the growth drivers

from work. In many ways it can be a subject of culture because the key role of leaders is to transform culture in a way that ensures the progress of the society. Transforming leadership, the quality required to change the way of a culture, is not a leadership orientation most people who have captured power in countries like Nigeria are gifted with. According to John Maxwell, leadership is influence. How do some people influence others such that all are willing to pool energies and work together in a goal – directed manner in which out-comes far exceeds the sum total of their individual capabilities?

Influencing others in a goal – directed way usually comes either from naked exercise of power or through a quest to accomplish shared goals in trusting relationships in which the needs of the followership drive the visionary who direct society's energy to change, or overcome consequences of change. James Macgregor Burns in his book "Leadership" captured the characteristics of leadership in his definition thus:

> *Leadership over human beings is exercised when persons with certain motives and purposes mobilize, in competition or conflict with others, institutional, political, psychological and other resources so as to arouse, engage and satisfy the motive of followers. This is done in order to realize goals mutually held by both leaders and followers.*

There are, in essence, three factors that determine leadership effectiveness in the kind of challenges posed by the need to transform culture to a level of higher productivity, output increase, and consequently improved quality of life for the citizen. Where leadership object is dominated in the form of transactions between leaders and the led; trading off support, for example, with the promise of improved provision of pipe borne water, we have transactional leadership. The point about transactional leadership is that the parties, or bargainers, have no enduring purpose. Often power becomes, unwittingly, a substitute for purpose.

Transformational leadership in contrast has to do with a shared purpose and grand vision which unites the leaders and followers so that they become mutual support for a common purpose. The leadership process includes preparation, visioning, and execution."

Industrial policy and Nigeria's external competitiveness

At this point a peep at the nation's industrial policy is relevant to the foregoing discourse. Industrial policy is defined as "the policies implemented for raising the welfare level of a given economy when the defects of a competitive market system – market failure – create problems for resource allocation and income distribution" (Itoh, Kiyono, Otuno – Fujiwara, and Suzumura, 1991:8 as in Miyajima et al, 1999).

In the standard economics framework, it is theoretically recognized that Government can play a positive role in the optimization of collective economic welfare (or the achievement of "a Pareto-efficient" allocation of resources) when Government corrects a "market failure" in which the free competitive forces of a market economy fail to prevent outcomes that are not optimal for the economy in general (Miyayjima, Kikkawa, Kikino, 1999).

The Nigerian industrial policy could be traced back to the pre and post independence eras. In the pre-independence era (1958-1959) the three regions in Nigeria had self Governments. The Eastern and Western regions had self government in 1958 and the Northern region in 1959. When Nigeria got her independence in 1960 from the British the regional Governments established what was then known as Development Corporations (DCs).

The Eastern region had Eastern Nigerian Development Corporation (ENDC), the Western region established the Western Nigerian development corporation (WNDC) and Northern region set up the Northern Nigeria Development Corporation (NNDC).

Before the advent of oil, the Eastern region was known for palm oil and coal. The Western region produced Cocoa and the Northern region, groundnut. With money from Cocoa, the WNDC established industrial estates in Ikeja, Lagos which harbors many local and multinational companies such as Dunlop Nig. Plc., Metal Box Nig. Ltd, Nigerian Textile Mill Limited, etc. WNDC also set up companies like the West African Portland Cement, Ewekoro and a Cocoa processing plant in Ikeja.

The Eastern region felt they should catch up with the Western region and started the industrialization of the region. ENDC set up palm oil mill, Nigeria Cement Company Ltd (NIGERCEM), Niger Steal Company, and a gas plant at Enugu. The NNDC in the Northern region established Northern Nigeria Investment Limited. It promoted the setting up of the Cement Company of Northern Nigerian among others.

The Development Corporations were used by the regional governments to promote various projects that added value to Nigeria's quest for sufficient raw materials for domestic use and for exports. Foreign investors were also encouraged to invest in the regions through these efforts.

When the former Head of State, General Yakubu Gowon, divided Nigeria into 12 administrative states during the Nigeria Civil War, 1966-1970, the ENDC collapsed because the administrative states in the Eastern region could not agree to work together. The WNDC was wound up and re-christened Odua Investment Company and the NNDC still remains.

Since the end of the Civil War Industrial Policy making have moved from the regions to the Federal Government level. In 1963, the Federal Government introduced the pioneer status, an incentive to most of the industries. Payment of taxes was waived for Three to Five Years, and so were other permits required for setting up industries were facilitated for those identified as various investors.

The modern concept of competitiveness evolved from a long history of economic thinking rooted in the works of classical economists, including Adam Smith in 1776, David Ricardo in 1776 and Michael Porter in 1990. Competitiveness, as defined by the World Economic Forum (WEF) is the set of factors, policies and institutions that determine the level of productivity of a country.

Competitiveness depicts the ability of a country to achieve sustained high rates of growth in GDP per capita. A more competitive economy is one which is likely to grow faster in the medium to long-term. The Global Competitive Index, developed by Jeffery Sachs and John MacArthur and modified by Professor Xavier Salai-Martin provides a holistic overview of the factors that are critical to driving productivity and competitiveness. Accordingly, these factors are defined in terms of nine broad mutually complementary pillars of competitiveness: institutions, infrastructure, macroeconomy, health and primary education, higher education and training, market efficiency, technological readiness, business sophistication and innovation (BGL Financial Monitor, April-June, 2007, P21).

From the foregoing, the researchers set out to investigate, through this research, the obstacles to Nigeria's industrialization, reasons for industrials policy failure, how the government intervention program has worked, the impacts of technology and human resources, the competitiveness of Nigerian made products in the international markets, what should be done to improve Nigeria's major competitive advantages, why Nigerians are not thinking of establishing local industries, examine Nigeria's past experiences with industrial policy, articulate the specific economic conditions under which industrial policy did actually contribute to the efficiency and effectiveness of individual Nigeria's industries, as regards their international competitiveness.

Based on the above, industrial policy can therefore be defined as the supply-side microeconomics policy directly related to the competitiveness of targeted industries.

Nigeria's experiences in industrial policy pose challenging questions: why did the extent of government intervention differ among industries that clearly share similar developmental phases and characteristics? Do enterprises in the same industries react to policies in different ways?

In the standard economics frameworks, it is theoretically recognized that Government can play a positive role in the optimization of collective economics welfare (or the achievement of 'a Pareto-efficient' allocation of resources) when government corrects a 'market failure', in which the free competitive forces of a market economy fail to prevent outcomes that are not optimal for the economy in general (Miyajima, Kikkawa, and Hikino, 1999, P20).

The market failure approach has two weaknesses: first, Nigeria's industrial policy contained many policy objectives and measures that did not fit neatly into the neoclassical framework. Second, the market failure approach does not necessarily provide the ex ante instrumental guidelines for concrete policy-making.

The Nigerian Government operated a mixed economy. The role of the private sector is equally recognized. The Nigerian Enterprises promotion Decree (NEPD) was promulgated in 1972 to enable Nigerians participate more in the economic activities of the country. For this purpose, the government divided the economy into four sections:

1. Schedule I of NEPD was reserved for only Nigerians
2. Schedule II and III covered the sections which was open for partnerships between Nigerians and their foreign counterparts.
3. There was the sector that was exclusively reserved for the government. These included defence industries, security printing, public utilities as well as heavy strategic industries.
4. The oil and gas sector is where the government insists on having majority interest and it was reserved for partnership with foreign investors.

Most of the industrial policies of the government were usually contained in the National Development Plans and lately the NEEDS (National Economic Empowerment Development Strategy) documents. In 1999 the new dispensation of democratic government decided to operate a private sector led economy or free market economy. The government needed to reform the public sector to provide the necessary support to the private sector in order to operate a free market economy. The thinking of the government was that the free market economy would enable local industries become more competitive which would in turn make Nigeria also to be competitive in the global arena.

Some analysts contend that Nigeria's competitiveness is hinged on the government's industrial policy that encourages identifying and developing those sectors that Nigeria has some advantages.

The first problem for the government in carrying out an industrial policy is that little is actually known about identifying, before the fact, a "winning" industrial structure. There exist not a set of economics criteria that determines what gives different countries pre-eminence in particular lines of business... The winners emerge from a very individualistic search process, only loosely governed by broad national advantages in relative labor, capital, or national resources (Schultz, 1983:7-8, as in Miyajima, Kikkawa, Hikino, 1999).

Factor endowment

It is important at this point to note that just like every individual is endowed with all manner of gifts and capabilities so also every clan, every community, every village, every town, every city, every local government, every state, and every nation is endowed with various, gifts, capabilities, and resource endowments – both human and natural. Nigeria's economic and industrial development will only be made possible when the different tiers of government do an inward search to identify and exploit those natural and human resource endowments. Therefore, special priority needs to be accorded developing communities based on its resource endowment and encouraging of rural entrepreneurship.

For example, Uburu is a small town of about 100, 000 people or less including those who live in the town and majority who live and earn a living in other parts of Nigeria and the world. Uburu is a border town between Enugu State and Ebonyi State. The major occupation of the people living the town is farming and salt mining. There are quite a few other natural endowments found in Uburu apart from salt. There is a lake in the town with huge salt deposit which sustained the need of the people in the Eastern region before and during the Nigerian civil war, and still does to some extent. The salt deposit has the capacity to meet a greater percentage of the salt need of Nigeria and even for export. But unfortunately, politics has not allowed good economic judgment to prevail on the need to develop and commercially mine salt in that town.

Previous administrations in the region did not find it of interest to invest in the mining project because the whole of Ohaozara local government council has been under total neglect of the various governments, both states and federal, past and present. In fact, somebody described it as the "Niger Delta" of the old Eastern Nigeria. An attempt was made by this author to get the federal ministry of mines in Abuja in 2006 interested in the development and mining of the salt deposit in Uburu but was rebuffed by the staffers. In fact, the personal assistant to the then minister of mines bluntly told the author that it was better for the major salt importer to import salt from the Dead Sea than to develop and mine the Uburu salt lake. They didn't consider it "commercially viable." This is quite unfortunate. The former governor of Abia State, Dr Ogbonaya Onu, who is a son of Uburu made attempt to develop and mine the salt lake in the early 1990s through private public partnership with a foreign firm, but unfortunately his regime was cut short by General Sani Abacha's infamous coup d' tat. Ever since then the people have continued to mine salt through the crude method. Salt mining has been a major source of income for many families in Uburu. Many of the prominent people from the town were educated in the best schools in Nigeria and abroad with incomes earned from salt mining.

The point is that the factor endowment available in the town is unfortunately neglected and potentially wasted rather than developed and revenue earned by both the indigenes of the town and also Ebonyi State (through taxes that could have accrued) and the federal governments. Investing the salt mining project by would encourage other economic activities within the town, alleviate poverty and bridge the existing urban-rural migration "crisis" as a larger population of the indigenes resides outside the town – all in search of better standard of living.

This is just one case in point. Many Nigerian rural communities harbor over 60 per cent of the population and these people live under sub-human conditions without jobs and no capital to trade. The various government programs directed towards alleviating poverty have not been successful because it is not targeted at the right people it is supposed to benefit.

Competitive communalism

As mentioned above, the nation's industrial policies in the 1960s before the advent of the discovery of oil in commercial quantity and the complete abandonment of the farm as a result, seemed to have encouraged healthy competition amongst the different regions of the country. Since 2007 when Yar'Adua and his governors took over reins, there seemed to be a semblance of the type of competitive communalism amongst some of the governors. It was actually started by the former governor of Cross River State, Donald Duke, who reckoned that for that state to survive and compete in the national and international scene the state government needed to do something radically different. So his administration focused on attracting tourists to the state to generate revenues from the tourist visiting the state. To open up the state to tourism the government of Donald Duke revamped the moribund Obudu Cattle Ranch and turned it to a world class resort. In addition, the government also built Tinapa as a commercial venture and gave it export processing free zone status to enable companies located there to produce for export – duty free.

That kind of threw up a challenge to their neighbors, Akwa Ibom State, later set a golf course to position the state as an entertainment center. What that seems to do is to attract and encourage tourist visiting their neighbours to spend a little more time and money visiting Uyo which is about an hour's drive away to play golf and be entertained. In the West coast of the country the Lagos State governor, Babatunde Raji Fashola (SAN) announced that his government had a singular purpose of making Lagos a mega city and a financial hub in the sub Sahara Africa. His government has been doing new roads and reconstructing existing ones, greening the environment, and improving the transport system for easy movement within the state. The essence of all these is to create an enabling environment for businesses to thrive.

The Imo State Model

The present Imo State government under the able leadership of Ikedi Ohakim, seemed to have recognized the import of factor endowment and competitive communalism in his approach to the governance and economic development of the state. In a television interview anchored by Professor Pat Utomi and the Patito's Gang team and broadcast live on the Nigerian Television Authority (NTA) network, the governor revealed to Nigerians his strategy towards making the state economically viable and competitive. Owerri, the Imo State capital, is strategically located within South East and South-South regions. It is just about an hour's drive to PortHarcourt, Rivers State; Yenogua, Bayelsa State; Umuahia, Abia State; Warri, Delta State; and Onitsha, Anambra State.

The government of Ohakim since taking office in 2007 studied the economies of the states in the region and came up with a strategy on how to compete. Because of the state's closeness to the restive Niger Delta, the government focused on providing enough security for the protection of life and properties so that businesses can thrive within the capital city as well as the state as a whole. The state has been so positioned and fast being perceived as a safe place to visit and live. This attracted the hosting of the 2009 edition of the Most Beautiful Girl in Nigeria pageant for the first time in Owerri. Many tourists and visitors Rivers, Bayelsa, and other places within the region and even abroad looking for a place to spend the weekend or holidays visit the state regularly.

Businesses thrive and investors' confidence is higher in a guaranteed and secure business environment. The government invested in the provision of quality road infrastructure and networks. The idea was to provide road networks for people to travel from anywhere in rural and urban communities within Imo State to the state capital, Owerri, within a maximum time period of 45 minutes. This enhances on time delivery of goods and people, thereby improving and increasing productivity.

Beyond all these is strategic development plan of the government to identify and commercially exploit the existing natural and human endowments within the state in order to make it more competitive within the region. Three things are important to mention here. The first is the cashew orchard located in Okigwe. For many years travellers and passersby would stop there to eat as many cashew seeds as they wanted without paying for it. No investor was encouraged to increase or improve the value chain of cashew until the government decided to invest in the process of cashew for commercial purposes – for for domestic use and export to other countries. The plan is to make the state the largest producer and exporter of cashew in Nigeria.

Then there is the cassava farm in Ikeduru, near Owerri. The government has invested and encouraged farmers to invest in the production of cassava to also make the state the biggest supplier or exporter of the products in the country. The government invested heavily in improving the yield per square meter of farm land. The government has done a lot to return the state and Nigeria to the global palm oil map, as a major producer and exporter of oil palm (red oil as it is often referred to).

It is interesting to note that Imo State produces the highest number of Joint Admission and Matriculation Board applicants year in year out, and subsequently the highest number of graduates in Nigeria. Having taken cognizance of that fact, the Ikedi Ohakim government came up with a program which they aptly called "Finishing School" aimed at retraining of university graduate and equipping them with new skills relevant to today's workplace. When the fist set of over 63 people completed the five weeks intensive course, they were all snapped up by different organizations. The state is gradually being positions to start "exporting" quality human capital both nationally and internationally. Like the Philippines whose major source of foreign exchange earnings is their export of human capital, Imo State will soon start earning revenues from the export of their quality human capital. This could turn out to be a major competitive advantage for the state if well managed and stained.

Kano State model

The Kano State government, in recognition of the importance of ICT both in the knowledge economy both in governance service delivery and as economic boost to the state embarked on refocusing the state as a leading ICT service provider in Nigeria. The state used to harbor over 60 per cent of the industries in the northern part of the country, but due to the general neglect of the industrial sector of the nation's economy, the state experienced de-industrialization. To compete, the government decided to focus on ICT outsourcing to drive the state's economy. But why the ICT Park in Kano? That is the question every one would ask. The government believes that such ICT park would be a key service provider to the foremost commercial center in the North. A huge teeming population of about 10.6 million people is a huge market with serious potentials.

The government through ICT development policy established the ICT Park in 2004 with the assistance of the Malaysian government. In 2006, the government decided to make a serious commitment by awarding contract for the building of the structure. The government embarked on sensitization exercise to create awareness of the concept and to get the citizens interest and buy in. The main aim is to provide a serene environment that would stimulate the growth of the ICT industry in the region.

The concept of the Park basically "is to provide an enabling environment in terms of buildings, infrastructure, energy and fiscal policies that would promote the efficient production of ICT goods and services meant for local , national and international markets."

Some of the objectives of the ICT Park include the following:

   • Promote the use of ICT as an economic

development sector in the state.
- Create employment opportunities thereby reducing unemployment.
- Create conditions for the adequate supply of IT manpower for the state.
- Promote the penetration and use of ICTs in the state
- Provide opportunity for technology transfer and acquisition
- Attract foreign investment
- Making Kano a major outsourcing centre

To ensure the success of the project, the government embarked on a massive marketing of the Park and the state with the following unique selling points

- Major center of commerce especially in the North and the nation as whole
- International airport
- Good road networks to many states in the country
- Large enough population for a major local market
- A major center of learning
- A robust financial sector
- Attractive tax regime including EPZ
- Subsidy for rent and other services
- Joint marketing of products
- Patronage from government of ICT services

The three Cs of Competitive advantage are concept or ideas and innovation, competence, and connection. Innovation is what drives the new knowledge economy. Any nation or state or community that do not deliberately invest in innovation will not be able to compete in the national and global marketplace. The second C of competitive advantage (competence) has to do with the skills and capabilities available within a nation or community to get work done more or less. Competence comes through education and training among others. The western part of Nigeria has been able to dominate most aspect of the country's economy such as telecommunication, banking and financial services, insurance, oil and gas, manufacturing, etc because of the availability of highly trained and educated people in the region. The former premier of the western region, Obafemi Awolowo introduced free education policy for the citizens of the region to help build human capital for the future the country. That policy has paid off today as the evidence is quite glaring. Other parts of the country were not so lucky to have such visionary leadership.

The third C has to do with connection or put another way, strategic alliances or networks. Ideas, products, and services are being marketed globally today. The world has become flat, thanks to globalization. Whatever advantages nations used to have do not almost exist any more. Whatever advantage few nations still have will not be for long. The Internet is helping people and businesses connect with one another, and also it has become a major and powerful platform in the marketing of goods and services.

Comparative advantage (Ricardo's Comparative) states that a country should concentrate on its natural endowments and buys what it doesn't have. Competitive advantage on the other hand states that a country should make what it do better to have an edge over others. The most important thing of note is that a country can convert its comparative advantage into competitive advantage.

CHAPTER
TWENTY SIX

THE ENVIRONMENT OF
OUTSOURCING BUSINESS

The world economic and business environment is changing so rapidly that it has great impact on businesses – especially trade in services outsourcing. Many governments have liberalized capital flows, technology, goods and services, and even people. In addition, new technologies and improvements in information technology have brought about the death of distance as businesses can either run their operations from a distance or outsource some services locally and overseas. The erected barriers by different governments in most parts of the world seem to have crumbled or are crumbling in a faster rate than ever experienced in history. This has resulted in increased in competition. The increased competition has also led to improved quality and reduced costs. A new vista of opportunities has also opened up by way of new markets due to heightened global competition.

Environment, as defined by Donald A. Ball et al, is the sum of all the forces surrounding and influencing the life and development of the firm. These forces are in two categories: internal (controllable) forces and external (uncontrollable) forces. According to Ball et al, uncontrollable forces are external forces over which management has no direct control, although it can exert an influence. Controllable forces on the other hand are internal forces that management administers to adapt to changes in the uncontrollable forces. It deals also with the macro issues in an economy that affect businesses – large and small alike. Some of the internal or controllable forces include factors of production – people, capital, and raw materials

The ITO/BPO provider or business has three different kinds of environments to contend with. They are the domestic environment, foreign environment, and international environment.

Domestic Environment: The domestic environment has to do with all the uncontrollable forces originating in the home country that surround and influence the firm's life and development (Ball et al 2002). It is hoped that the managers of In-shoring businesses are and should be familiar with the domestic environment. This includes both the ones set up by the local entrepreneurs and or a foreign subsidiary. The impact of the domestic environment can also affect the operations of the foreign subsidiary in the sense that any unfavourable government policies could affect any planned expansion.

Foreign Environment: The foreign environment has to do with all the uncontrollable forces originating outside the home country that surround and influence the firm. It is important to note that both the domestic and foreign environments have the same characteristics but differ in three major areas – value, assess, and interrelatedness. In terms of force value, sometimes political force value could be diametrically opposed to each other. Take for example the embargo placed on Zimbabwe by George W. Bush, the former president of the United States of America due its bad human rights policies.

President Barack Obama also of the US, on assuming office, also upheld the embargo. What that means is that no United States based company is allowed by law to do business in or with Zimbabwe for as long as the embargo remains. Let us assume that there is a company based in Zimbabwe or even the Zimbabwean government that requires American products or services. Since the embargo prevents trade or any economic activity to take between the two countries that invariably means that that transaction will not take place. If an American company has a subsidiary located in South Africa, for instance, and does outsourcing business or any other business for that matter, the Zimbabwean company or government could order the products or services through the American subsidiary in South Africa since there is no such embargo placed on them by South Africa.

The political and legal elements of the foreign environmental forces are very difficult to assess. One of the challenges facing ITO/BPO users is whether the existing legal system will protect them in the case of breach of contract by a provider domiciled in a particular country. The political element may not pose much of challenge because of the awareness of the benefits of outsourcing to any economy. In fact, most closed economies are opening up to global competition at a faster rate. Some nations are creating an environment of attractive outsourcing destinations to outside world.

The only challenge will be when a law prohibits a 100% ownership of a company operating in that particular country. In the past, such law existed in Nigeria whereby foreign companies were not allowed to own more than 49 per cent, while local people own at least 51 per cent. That has changed since the democratic dispensation whereby foreign investors could have a 100 per cent ownership of a company within Nigeria.

The other challenge is that they are interrelated. Though the forces are interrelated but they are also often different in types and degrees of interaction. A typical example is the case where there is a combination of high-cost capital and abundance of unskilled labor. This is obtainable in many developing countries. This situation leads to the use of unsophisticated technology compared to the more advanced countries where labor is highly skilled. The management challenge therefore is to choose between installing costly and specialized machinery that requires fewer workers and installing less expensive, general-purpose machinery that requires a larger labor force. In a developing economy, the management will choose the less expensive, general-purpose machine with larger labor force.

International Environment: the international environment is the interaction between domestic and foreign environmental forces or between sets of foreign environmental forces; the interaction between the domestic environmental forces and the foreign environmental forces or the interaction between the foreign environmental forces of two countries when an affiliate in one country does business with customers in another (Ball et al, 2002). Let's take for example a manager that works in a company based in Ghana that provides ITO/BPO services to other companies also based in Ghana. This manager does not work in the international environment since he provides services within the country, Ghana. But when the company begins to provide services to companies in Kenya, then the manager works in an international environment because he is affected by both the domestic environment of Ghana and the foreign environment of Kenya.

Environmental forces: let's look at some forces in the environment that affect businesses. These forces could be classified as internal (controllable) forces and external (uncontrollable). Controllable or internal forces are forces that the organization must manage in order to adapt to changes in the external or uncontrollable forces. Example, in 1990/1991 the government of India decided to open the Indian economy, and encouraged Diaspora Indians and foreign investors to invest in India. Some laws were changed to accommodate this decision. That singular decision turned around the Indian economy and India became an outsourcing hub in less than a decade.

A similar situation occurred in Nigeria when the democratic government unbundled the telecommunication sector in 1999. Many players in the sector, including foreign players, invested heavily to make Nigeria's telecommunication sector the fastest growing in Africa, and one of the fastest growing sectors in the world.

Another example is the North American Free Trade Agreement – a political force – which has affected all controllable forces of companies that do business in Canada, Mexico and the United States of America. Businesses based in these countries had to rethink their businesses practices to benefit from the agreement. This agreement has generated big business for Mexico because many US firm, in order to take advantage of the lower wages in Mexico, have relocated their subsidiaries to that country. European and Asian companies were not left out in this. They also set up subsidiaries in this free trade zone to avoid paying import duties they would have ordinarily have paid if they are importing directly from their home country.

Uncontrollable forces on the other hand are external forces over which management has no direct control, although it can exert an influence (Ball et al, 2002). Uncontrollable forces consist of the following characteristics: competitive, distributive economic, socioeconomic, financial, legal, physical, political, socio-cultural, labor, and technological.

Competitive: It is important to note here that nations do not compete against or with each other.

It is their companies that do compete against each other. On the other hand, the nature of a nation's economic system, its social conditions, and political system affect the competitiveness of the nation's firms in the global marketplace. These are some of the factors that determine the competitive of nations at a macro level (or national competitiveness). National competitiveness is therefore the ability of a nation's producers to compete successfully in world markets and with imports in their own domestic markets (Ball et al, 2002).

Many countries are creating attractive business and investment environments for outsourcing. Competition has intensified following the huge success experienced by China and India as manufacturing and IT/BP outsourcing hubs respectively. Countries like Romania, Kenya, Nigeria, and South Africa are competing for dollar or business from Europe, USA and even India. In countries where hitherto there were virtually no or few outsourcing firms in the past, many have now sprang up. A number of foreign firms including multinational companies have set up firms or subsidiaries in countries with low cost advantage, efficient and skilled manpower, thereby competing with local firms. Some foreign outsourcing firms from the US and Nigeria (Socketworks) have set up in Ghana to take advantage of business opportunities, lower wage, availability of requisite skills, and good operating environment.

As markets become flatter resulting from crumbled trade barriers, competition will become more intense. It will get to a point where foreign firms can no longer be differentiated from local ones as they compete in every sector of the domestic economy, outsourcing inclusive. As the world progressively move deeper into the knowledge economy, the protections and advantages hitherto enjoyed by local firms will almost disappear. This will lead to improved quality of products and services and operational efficiencies. In this new knowledge economy, innovative capabilities and investment in research and development will improve a nation's competitiveness. Innovation is simply the transformation of knowledge into new products, services as well as process. Any nation that its firms are able to convert knowledge into products and services better than others will surely survive and thrive.

Economic: This has to do with economic variables that can easily influence the ability of a company to do business within country. Some these variables include the gross national product (GNP) of the country, the cost of unit labor as well as personal consumption expenditure. A country's GNP is the sum total monetary value of all goods and services produced for consumption within that country and also within a specific period of time. Outsourcing opportunities abound in countries with high GNP, lower labor cost per unit, and higher purchasing power. The personal ability to consume is dependent on the purchasing power of the individual.

All aspects of business – production, marketing, finance, and human resources – are affected by a nation's economic development. Economists have been able to group nations into different categories based on their levels of economic development. These categories are: developed, developing, newly industrializing countries (NIC), and newly industrialized economies (NIE).

Developed is a term used to describe the most technically industrialized nations, while developing is the classification given to those nations that have lower income and are less technically developed. The newly industrializing countries include countries such as the four Asian tigers and middle income economies of Mexico, Brazil, Malaysia, Chile, and Thailand. Newly industrialized economies on the other hand are fast growing upper middle-income and high-income economies of South Korea, Singapore, Taiwan, and Hong Kong.

It is important at this point to consider some dimensions of the economy and their relevance for businesspeople. Managers need hard and soft data of the rate of change and size of some economic and socioeconomic factors in gauging the market potentials of the markets they want to enter or outsource their businesses. Among these economic indicators important for consideration are the gross domestic product (GDP), gross national product (GNP), distribution of income, private consumption expenditure, interest rates, inflation rates, labor cost, exchange rates, individual ownership of goods, and private investment. Also equally important for consideration is the socioeconomic factors such as the total population, age distribution, rural-urban migration, and skilled labor supply (e.g. the number of working women compared to men).

Socioeconomic: What has population got to do with it? A lot! The distribution of human population is an influential factor. India has a large pool of skilled IT manpower which has given it a competitive advantage. What makes a population a large market is not just the numbers, but also if it has a high propensity to consume. For example, the United States is not the largest country in the world in terms of population, but it is the largest market because its population has high propensity to consume. It also has a large pool of highly skilled and competent working population.

Financial: This is another factor outside the control of businesses. Businesses thrive in an environment with low inflation rate, interest rate and taxation. Investors look out for low tax and interest rates environments that will make their return on investments worthwhile. High inflation rates will also wipe out any gain the company could make. That's why a major function of the national central banks is to bring about price stability or manage inflation.

Some of these financial forces, which are also uncontrollable, that affect businesses include foreign currency exchange risks, national balances of payment, taxation, tariffs, national monetary and fiscal policies, and inflation.

Legal: as the world economies open up or the world markets democratize and become more interlinked, a legislation considered a local issue could have a national and international dimension. The legal environment of business has to do with the legal system of a nation, and how they protect businesses.

For example, the user and provider of outsourcing services will be interested to know how the legal system of the country protects transactions (especially data protections or proprietary rights and enforcement of contract laws) and how long it takes the courts to dispose of cases in case of any breach.

Political: Businesses must deal with political forces to survive. The political forces include the type of government – capitalist or socialist or communist leaning – the country operates, the international organization, and the political climates. The political climate in Zimbabwe, for instance, discouraged many businesses from – local and foreign – from operating. Kenya had a post election violence that affected many businesses. Businesses thrive under conditions of stable political environment. Government ownership of businesses is equally an important factor affecting businesses. Several reasons could be adduced for government ownership of businesses. Some of them include extraction of more money from the company they consider may be concealing profits; government belief it run the company more efficiently and make more money; ideological differences and nationalization of some businesses; attempt to get votes during elections by pretending to save jobs by putting dying companies on "life support" and abandoning it after the elections; for putting money into a business, the government would want to have control. The bottom line is that to a certain degree, all governments are in business.

Sociocultural: This deals with elements of culture. Indeed culture matters. This is a title of a book that came out of Harvard University Colloquium on culture and economic development and edited by Lawrence E. Harrison and Samuel P. Huntington Some element of culture that affect businesses include attitude, beliefs and opinions among others. Culture simply means or implies the way we do things around here. Part of knowing your customer to understands his or her culture – beliefs, attitudes, religion, etc. Cultures are different for different countries and people. Taking time to study the cultures of your customers – whether domestic or foreign is important to business success. Culture affects finance, human resource management, marketing, and production.

Labor: The unit of labor has to do with the composition, requisite skills, and importantly the attitude. The attitude of workers is critical to the success and failure of the firm. Modern organizations hire now hire people for attitudes firstly before skills. People with the right work and life attitude can always be trained for skills. The argument has always been that a worker can have best skill in the world but he or she will not be of much use to the organization if she has the wrong attitude. The knowledge has brought with it high mobility of labor. People live and work in different countries of their choice. The recent US immigration law, due largely to the ageing workforce, has encouraged immigration into the United States. Approximately about 10.4 percent of people residing and probably working in the US are foreign born.

The outsourcing industry has also experienced a shift as well. There is more emphasis on workers possessing domain knowledge (specialized knowledge in a particular) than the general, routine work done in the past. For example, those companies outsourcing legal services require that some staff of the service provider should have in their employ some legal and/or paralegal personnel so that they can better understanding the work and perform it professionally. In this 21st century, businesses, especially those in industrialized nations, experienced labor shortage – in the area of skilled high-tech labor. To bridge the gap, American and European companies outsourced some of the functions to third party service providers, and also the government softened their immigration laws to admit into these countries highly skilled people.

Technological: The main driver of the knowledge economy is technology. Outsourcing is also technologically driven. Technology aids quality and efficient service delivery. Availability of high technical skills determines how resources are converted by firms to products and services. Technology helps in improved product and services as well in cost reduction. Technology is fast changing and becoming more sophisticated. The biggest challenge for developing nations, which is not a challenge to developed nations, is the affordability of these new technologies and the availability of skills required to use or operate them.

The Changing World Environment: Since the world entered the knowledge economy, the rate of change has accelerated faster than i previously was. The world environment – business, political, technological, etc – is not only changing linearly but exponentially too. The changing environment is world environment is also occurring both through evolutionary means in some countries, and in some other countries it is revolutionary. The question therefore is not whether it is occurring but at what rate it is occurring.

The flattening of the markets has affected foreign trade and investment in a positive sense. As more countries in different parts of the world democratize, and more and more trade wall crumble, many previously closed economies are opening up more than ever before, thus encouraging foreign trade and investment. Some of these environmental factors include the recent actions of various governments in different parts of the world to liberalize the flow of capital, technology, people, goods and services. In addition, there has been a great improvement in information technology such that it has become easier for managers of firms to run those firms from any distance without physically being there all he the time. Meeting could be held in different countries and in different time zones through teleconference and video conferencing. In other worlds, communication has shortened the distance or has brought about the death of distance.

The visible benefit of government liberalization and improved information technology include the increased competition which forced companies to improve quality and the same time reduces cost price of goods and services. As firms strive to reduce cost, they are forced to seek out locations anywhere in the world with the right environment where they can move their production activities to achieve the desired low-cost and economies of scale. The increased competition on the other hand will open up new markets for firms to offer their goods and services. Companies can either compete for market share in a highly competitive environment or locate where there is less competition. They have that choice to make. The firm also has to make a choice (strategy) of standardizing their products and services to be sold in the global markets or produce different products for to be sold for specific domestic markets.

Culled with permission of the International Trade Center, Geneva, from the book Destination Africa: Strategic Business Outsourcing by Dr Austin Nweze

CHAPTER TWENTY SEVEN

*THE FRESH GRADUATE AND
THE NIGERIAN SOCIETY:
TACKLING THE CHALLENGES
OF A DEVELOPING ECONOMY*

Early Years

In the 1970s and the early part of the 1980s Nigeria experienced the first oil boom. The economy was somewhat vibrant and the government went on a spendthrift. As a matter of fact, the then head of state, General Yakubu Gowon was quoted as saying that Nigeria's problem was how to spend her oil money. This period was considered a boom period for the fresh graduates and the undergraduates as well. Boom period because fresh graduates were almost sure of getting a decent job in the public or private sector with a car and accommodation attached to the job. They had better quality of life than compared to what obtains in today's

Nigeria.

Challenges

The good old days of the 1970s seem to have disappeared into thin air. The Nigeria Graduate today is faced with the hard economic realities that could be said to be recursive. The Nigeria fresh graduate is faced with several challenges, which include and not limited to the following:

What to do next or how and where to get a job

Where to live or locate

The trauma of being counted as one of the numerous unemployed

Lack of relevant skills for paid employment and self-employment

How to deal or cope with immediate family responsibilities

Lack of relevant work experience

The Modernization Paradigm

Several years ago, dissatisfied with explanations of why nations are poor I began to reflect on the subject. I generally found patterns of thinking, if you will, shifts in paradigm in the mode of Thomas khun's thesis of the structure of scientific revolutions.

Indeed the dominant paradigm at independence, influenced significantly the grants making and agenda setting function of the Social Science Research Council in the United States emphasized the need for cultural transformation for societies to move down a continuum bound at one end by the primitive and other by the modern. The modernization paradigm would eventually suffer much after the influence of economist like Walt Rostow and political scientist like William Siffin, whose Bazaar-canteen Model was a particularly graphic depiction of that paradigm.

Remhardt Bendix Embattled Reason is a remarkable reflection on the influence of the SSRC and the paradigm

Ascendance of Econometricians

By the 1980s the ascendance of the Econometricians and the increased involvement of the World Bank and the IMF in the policy process of transition economies especially because many had fallen into a debt trap and were under pressure to undertake structural adjustment programs.

The legacy of the involvement of the multilateral has largely been the emphasis on policy choice as the path to development.

For the most, this trust neglected even the role of institutions in making policy more efficacious in terms of implementation. By the late 1990s a gradual rediscovery of institutions was underway and even culture was rediscovered. A colloquium at Harvard on how values shape human progress resulted in the volume edited by Harrison and Huntington, Culture Matters, which brought culture back to the development agenda.

Growth Drivers Framework

My review has produced a framework, which considers some key independent variables, which include institutions, Human Capital, Entrepreneurship, Culture and Leadership in addition to policy choice.

Since then I have seen the increased popularity of two key elements of the framework: Leadership and Entrepreneurship. My hope is not a fad but a renewed commitment to these critical aspects of how human progress is achieved

The Way Forward

Create Culture Of Entrepreneurship
How can we create culture of entrepreneurship in Nigerian universities? A good starting point may be an observation of my experience in the USA. In graduate school in the US in the 1970s; I was struck by the culture of interviews and brushing up on CVs as spring came around for seniors. Many years later when I went back on sabbatical, I was equally struck at the shift from CV writing to business plan hawking.

The book Culture in an Age of Money- The Legacy of the 1980s in America edited by Nicolaus Mills indeed shows the triumph of the spirit of the times gave us the new more entrepreneurial American, even if it is somewhat critical of the culture of triumphalism and conspicuous consumption. Obviously, many reasons impacted this campus culture. They include the work of President Reagan's Competitiveness Commission, the growing influence of Business Schools and the transition to new technology- led age in which entry barriers fell than rise.

Parental Interventions

Parents can become "evangelical entrepreneurs" preaching the value of self-employment to their wards early enough in life. A recent study of 200,000 grades 6-12 students in the United States showed that more than 75 percent of the respondents had learned most of what they know about money from either of the parents.

Intervention of Civil Society Groups

Some civil society groups such as FATE Foundation, Center for Values in Leadership (CVL), STEP, and Entrepreneurship Resource and Development Center have been set up to provide skills on leadership and entrepreneurship to aspiring entrepreneurs or fresh graduates. The government and companies should support these organizations. Fresh graduates and students should also be encouraged to take the entrepreneurial path. Rather than looking for paid employment, they should create jobs. Rather than Peddle Resumes (CVs), they should be peddling business plans.

Change Campus Culture

I am convinced that to change campus culture we need a few things to take place:

1. Curriculum Changes
This will help solve the acute capacity gap and the existing mismatch between the available manpower and needs to achieve the set growth target of the economy. The National Universities Commission (NUC) report showed that out of the 913, 862 candidates that took the 2005 university Matriculation Examination (UME),
2.5 percent showed interest in education curses

0.7 percent in agriculture

24.8 percent in science

18.4 percent in administration

17.7 percent in science

The implication of this is that the interest in science related course is waning. No Nation can develop without science and technology

2. Breaking of the entitlement mentality of extant Nigerian Culture

3. Introducing more interdisciplinary orientation beyond General Studies

4. Developing Team Based evaluation of Work

5. Improving Town-Grown relationship such that business support more research that engage both students and lecturers and ultimately open up opportunities students can explore

I was enthralled to learn that some students of the University of Benin under the aegis of Achievement Consortium International, held a final year students to take up courses in entrepreneurship. Such efforts should be encouraged. With these and institutional arrangements aimed at spotting and supporting talents to capture business opportunities we will see progress. I will urge, however, that the essence of enterprise as value creation and an opportunity to collaborate with God to bring create to its perfection is the true value of an entrepreneurship orientation and not just a primitive search for material accumulation. The latter does not sustain motivation. The value creation on the other hand provides a more fulfilling basis for daring.

CHAPTER
TWENTY EIGHT

Book Review

BUREAUCRACY IN NIGERIA

A review by Florence James

I ntroduction
There is no gain saying that the day to day administration and management of the entity called Nigeria falls squarely on the shoulders of the government of the day. From independence in 1960 to date, we have has successive governments:- civilian and military, democratic and autocratic who have tried in their little way to steer the ship of state. In their bid to manage the vast human, material and natural resources bestowed on us by styles without success. However, irrespective of the government in power, one thing has remained constant: The administrative system of governance:- **Bureaucracy**

What is Bureaucracy?
The American Heritage Dictionary amongst other

things defines Bureaucracy to be any of the following:
"Administration of a government chiefly through bureaus or departments staffed with none elected officials".........

"Management or administration marked by hierarchical authority among numerous offices and by fixed procedures"........

"An administrative system in which the need or inclination to follow rigid or complex procedures impedes effective action"

From Max Weber, point of view "Bureaucracy is a system of carrying on the business of government by means of departments or bureaus each under the control of a chief, in contradiction to a system in which the officers of government have an associated authority and responsibility.

From the fore going, the key words in bureaucracy includes: "rigidity", "departmentalization", "administration", "procedures", "hierarchy" amongst others.

Characteristics and key features of Bureaucracy in Nigeria:

As practiced in Nigeria, bureaucracy has the following distinguishing features and characteristics:

- **Specialization and division of labor:**
  The structure of governance and administration in Nigeria is such that individual Ministries of government have specific goals and objectives they are created to cater for and achieve. Within the ministries and parastatals, we have departments that handle specific tasks and responsibilities. This has lead to division of labor

and specialization.

- **Employment based on technical qualification**

As a result of the bureaucratic structure in place in our government offices and ministries, the personal touch is lacking. Decisions are based on policies and laid down procedures. For instance in the area of employment, recruitment is based on technical qualifications.

- **Hierarchical Arrangement:**

In most government offices in Nigeria, there is a strict hierarchical system of administration in place. This ensures clearly defined routes of reporting, seniority, authority, channel of communication etc. this ultimately ensures respect, orderliness and discipline.

- **Promotion based on seniority, achievement or both:**

More often than not promotion is based on seniority and availability on the top, not necessarily on competence and technical skills. This promotes laziness and de-motivates the hardworking staffs, who to the best of their knowledge feel promotion is based on length of service and not on job output.

- **Standardization:**

Bureaucracy leads to standardization as there are many standard policies, procedures and guidelines already put in place which staff must follow in their day to day affairs in the office.

- **Protection against arbitrary dismissal: (Job Security)**
  Unionism, Standardization, specialization and rules/regulations in force at government agencies and parastatals ensures that there is job security in a bureaucratic setting.

Advantages of Bureaucracy:
A well practiced bureaucracy has the following advantages.

➢ Impartiality and fairness
➢ Rules are known and codified
➢ Defined system of authority and communication
➢ Division of labor
➢ Easy coordination
➢ Rationalism

In spite of the numerous advantages inherent in a bureaucratic setting the following issues stand out as minuses to bureaucracy:

- **Conflicts due to specialization:**
  Specialization in a bureaucratic setting as ours in Nigeria often leads to conflict especially where there is interdependence in the work place. In a case where Mr. A's job depends on the output from Mr. B's job and Mr. B refuses to perform, this could lead to tension and misunderstanding.

- **Individual initiative and development are stifled:**
  Due to standardization, rules and regulation as

well as policies and guidelines necessary for decision making in the bureaucratic government setting in Nigeria, individual initiative and development are stifled.

- **Delay and red tapism**
This is one of the greatest setbacks in the concept of bureaucracy especially as practiced in Nigeria. There is unnecessary delay and bottlenecks in approval/execution process. Even when jobs are done by external consultants, payment is often a Herculean task.

- **Rules are regarded as ends instead of means.** Bureaucracy as practiced in Nigeria has turned staff into robots that do not like thinking for themselves but would rather follow the rules to the letter forgetting the saying that rules are made by man and not man by rules. There is dogmatism and stiff nakedness. This leads to a stiff and rigid way of doing things.

Some other glaring disadvantages in the bureaucratic setting in Nigeria include the following:
➢ Outdated Controls
➢ Poor conflict resolution strategies between ranks and functional groups
➢ Long chain of command distorts communication
➢ Sub-optimal utilization of human resource
➢ Rigid, change resistant, non-innovative
➢ Bureaucrats are conditioned to behave and act along given patterns.

Conclusion

From the fore going, Bureaucracy of well practiced has its positive and negative sides, with the positive out weighing the negative. The bottom line is management at all levels is good and efficient leadership and sound managerial skill which unfortunately many of our government officials and leaders are lacking.

CHAPTER
TWENTY NINE

CONFRONTING REALITY

I've avoided the temptation of talking about the current global economic situation, especially trying to predict what the future will look for Nigeria and the rest of the world. As a commentator on national, global, economic and business issues I find myself always being dragged into discussing it both in the electronic and print media.

I've listened to and read the commentaries of some renowned economists and analysts in Nigeria and globally but I seem to be getting conflicting reports. There seems to be two schools of thought concerning the current global environment and how it affects or impacts on Nigeria. The debate raging from the two camps sometimes remind me of a song done by the Afro music exponent, Fela Anikulapo Kuti, in which he captured the typical Nigerian way of debating national issues, like corruption. People are busy arguing and none is focusing on addressing the main issue. The debate has been whether Nigeria is in recession like the rest of the world or experiencing economic slowdown. The Central Bank Governor was almost taken to the "gallows" for saying that Nigeria is insulated from the global crisis by those who think otherwise.

Those who believe Nigeria is experiencing economic slowdown hinged their argument on the performance of the non-oil sector of the economy like agriculture and the likes. The issue shouldn't be whether Nigeria is in recession or not but rather how prepared the country is to handle the either situation. Some are even calling for government bailout of some sectors of the economy just because the US, Europe and other countries of the world are bailing out banks and other essential sectors of the economy without understanding the economies of these countries and how they function. Some have argued for the bailout of the textile industry, largely located in the Northern part of the country. The federal government planned a N70 billion bailout of the sector. The economics of the bailout of that sector does not favor doing that. The reason is simple. If you give money, call it a loan, to the textile companies to revitalize their businesses without fixing the energy (power) issue and other infrastructural challenges bedeviling the sector, then that will be tantamount to throwing money away. We need to understand that energy – power – constitute at least 30 percent, next to machinery or equipment, of the manufacturing component.

Nigerian made products are 35 percent to 40 percent disadvantaged compared to imported products due to high cost of doing business a major component of which is power or energy. The only form of bailout that will make economic or business sense is to fix the infrastructure and power (energy) challenge. No nation has ever industrialized without power (energy), and Nigeria cannot be an exception. The more a nation industrializes the more their energy needs. Take China and India as examples. Because of the massive industrialization of these two nations in the last decade or so, their energy demand help fuel the high oil prices experienced before the global recession that brought oil prices down from almost $150 per barrel to $40 per barrel.

For a bailout to make sense there has to be provision high quality infrastructure – good quality road infrastructure, good transportation system, water, power and other utilities. Otherwise the bailout money would be used for the provision of these amenities or what I call running your own mini (or local) government. A bailout that will benefit the common man is for the government to invest heavily in construction and reconstruction of roads, schools, and other infrastructure. These will improve businesses and put more people back to work.

The Nigerian condition was triggered by the mismanagement of the economy by the various governments that ruled over the years. The economic strategies of the various governments have been poorly executed. The financial and economic crises in Nigeria are partly due to the global crisis but mainly as a result of the mismanagement of the economy many years before now. Nigeria has never been lucky to have any leader that understood how to or was willing to properly manage the economy even when they surround themselves with the "best" economists and economic managers. The issue of politics and other self interests had always drowned sound management of the economy. There has always been structural imbalance. We should not forget the issue of weak institutions. Part of the US government's attempt to resuscitate their economy was the strengthening of their weak institutions.

In the book which I co-authored with Prof. Pat Utomi, we made the point of how strong institutions can foster economic growth. Here are the excerpts from the book: "The importance of Institutions for economic growth is now widely accepted. But there is no blue print for building institutions and that seems sometimes to make donors pretend they do not matter that much. In our view, weak institutions and culture are the silent giant killers of reform for growth. They are silent because people often focus on the more physical and glamorous aspects of nation building.

Colonial hegemony usually is accompanied by attempts at transplanting institutions. The effectiveness of these new institutions in setting boundaries for conduct, so that uncertainty is reduced and economic intercourse possibilities increase, is not well established. Examples in fact abound of pre-colonial institutional arrangements that continue to be more effective than the transplanted institutions. The incidence of Moral Hazard in modern banking in countries like Nigeria as compared to traditional banking arrangements like the etsu-tsu cooperatives is good illustration.

Thanks to Douglass North, the view of institutions as evolutionary, organic and therefore able to adapt with infusion from elsewhere should encourage commitment to search for local partners who can graft attributes from other experiences unto local platforms. Civil society and the strengths of associational life and horizontal linkages or networks are of high value here. The assimilation of Fulani Institutions into Hausa structures in Northern Nigeria is one of the finest examples of what is possible. This is usually a function of the public square and the quality of contestation of ideas in the public arena by civil society.

Aid that supports growth of the civil society and the expansion of the public space ultimately facilitates the building of institutions. In this sense some of the aid money of the last decade which support African NGOs may be right headed, in general, even if some may have been poorly targeted in terms of the motives of some the entrepreneurs of voluntarism. Support for enshrining democratic accountability; leadership and entrepreneurship development; promoting property rights will ultimately strengthen capacity for growth.

Recent experience has shown that until vertical accountability takes root a country can slide towards anarchy or failed state status without loud alarms going off. Liberia and Somalia and the 'revenge of the poor' (Kaplan) in Sierra Leone advertise the desperate need to commit strongly to institution building. As institutions matter for peace and stability so do they matter for effective policy implementation?

A typical cliché in Nigeria is that Governments make

great policies but the policies fail because of a certain monster called implementation. The naked fact is that the absence of accountability has taken away from shared values and left a society in which the disconnect between the state and society, the leaders and the citizen is such that policy objective of attitude change is unlikely to come from the leadership being able to persuade the people to take ownership of change initiatives.

Where yesterday's Nigeria had the challenge of two publics, as Peter Ekeh's seminal essay offers, it today can be said to have two nations in which a rentier state with its political and monopolistic business groups hold sway, out of touch with, and almost contemptuous of the Nigerian people, as the conduct of elections in Nigeria show. Continued failure of policy has produced growing inequalities with Nigeria now in the league of the 20 worst cases of income inequalities in the world and 71 percent of the population living below the poverty line.

In Nigeria's Two Publics there is identification between the masses of the people and the elite from their clan, and those elite with the norms of their primordial base, so that the man who would not steal from the Village Development Association Fund gives no thought to any wrong in emptying the government Treasury and can expect the support of his people if he is caught. In the emerging two nations view of society this emotional link is eaten away by the desperation to monopolize access to rent and the failure to open up opportunities. Constricting democratic space, as the elite tend to seek to do, as with elections in Nigeria, against a popular desire for democratic expression, invariably results in popular disaffection that makes policy implementation problematic and ultimately pushes men to rebel.

Aid aimed at civil society or Private Development Agency initiatives to broaden opportunities at the Bottom of the Pyramid will invariably be smarter aid. To prevent the two Nations from engaging in a manner that leads down a path to anarchy, as in Sierra Leone, interventions at the levels of civic education, entrepreneurship development and capacity building in the second nation where poverty and powerlessness seem to dominate, by private development agencies, and civil society, is key. The state, which is seen as Game caught by hunters in the triumphant part of the political elite, is too preoccupied with managing the booty sharing between competing factions of the elite to play well the role of reducing the daily troubles of the second nation citizens and far too distrusted down there to be effective.

Assistance from abroad driven by human solidarity is then best channeled through the PDAs to where need exits without the interception of state actors who would sooner turn to such flows and add those resources to the bounty pool for prebendal 'judicious' allocation to first nation citizens.

The scourge of poverty flowing from these conditions is such that the governments of Nigeria will be lacking in both the capacity and character to make a significant difference. Whether it be in terms of systemic corruption ambushing the budget or the sensitivity to the cry of the majority of the people, an army of Easterly's 'searchers' and social entrepreneurs may be better assurance of escape from dehumanizing conditions with better support. That might indeed be smarter aid."

Someone made the point that Nigerians have been in perpetual recession mode since the 1980s due to the peculiar structural problems of the Nigerian economy, one of which is the weak institution mentioned above. Others include short-term planning mentality (or better still, shortsightedness) of the economic planners and policy flip-flop. When this crisis was brewing, the government and policy makers were playing "Ostrich," pretending that whatever was happening out there in the world would not affect Nigeria. We have since found out the opposite was the case. The reality of the crisis has dawned on the government. The expected revenues in the 2009 budget have been drastically reviewed downward due to the falling and volatile oil prices. The government and policy makers have just been confronted with the reality of the impact of the global financial and economic crises on the national economy. It is and will never be business as usually for some time to come.

What the government and policy makers should be concerned with now is how to confront the reality before them. It will be fool hardy for them to use old thinking in dealing with the current reality. The situation in the capital markets all over the world has shown that investors' appetite is waning. When the global financial crisis came to fore, hedge fund investors who invested in emerging markets like Nigeria pulled out their funds from the Nigeria capital market. As at the first quarter of 2008, the market had lost about 69 percent or 70 percent of its value and to 35 percent in 2009.

In the global arena, the situation is not any better, in some cases even worse. The difference is on how these countries have confronted or are confronting reality. In 2008 or there about, one chief economist at Goldman Sachs stated that China was going to bail the United States out of the recession. Don't forget that China is a major exporter to the US market, and they invested heavily in the US economy.

But we have seen that rather than bailout the US, China itself succumbed to the global recession together with most other countries. The Chinese government projected a 10 percent growth in the GDP for 2009 and later lowered it to 8 percent. In April 2009, China recorded only 6 percent growth in the GDP. The World Bank expected that China's recovery could begin in 2009. It's expected that if that happens, it will help other Asian countries recover from their slowdowns. In March 2009, China experienced a little growth in after about six months of no growth. Areas with noticeable increase are car sales, property transactions, domestic investment, and domestic loans. All these grew faster than official targets.

Though the World Bank sounded optimistic about China's quick recovery, but Andrew Gordon (in Investors Edge online) thinks otherwise for the reasons he listed below:

- 45 percent of China's economy relies on exports. Its exports have plunged with global demand falling off a cliff. Thousands of factories making for-export items have closed. Will one of those people singing the praises of China's massive stimulus package explain to me how building roads in Jiangxi Province will help factories in Guangdong Province making toys and clothes and tea pots get back on their feet?

- China importing more commodities is not a sign that the economy is picking up. My contacts tell me that China is simply taking advantage of low prices.

- Explosion of loans is going to bite China in the back-end. When China issued directives to its state-owned banks to open up its vaults and lend, lend, lend, it was an open invitation for local big-wigs to drag out their favorite pet projects. The vetting of this latest mega-round of loans was short and sweet. We've seen in the U.S. how a critical mass of bad loans can take an economy down. China's willingness to go down this road can mean only one thing. Their political leadership and economic elite are even more arrogant than the US.

- Then there is the issue of inflation.

This global economic crisis has been described as worse than the great depression of the 1930s. during that period of depression world leaders gathered in Brenton Wood in the US to deliberate on how to solve the global economic crisis at that time. That meeting gave birth to two institutions we have today - the World Bank and IMF – otherwise known as the Brenton Wood institutions. At that meeting Africa was completely absent. It almost happened in the 2009 edition when the G20 met in the UK to fashion out ways to revitalize the world economy. The G20 agreed to inject about $5 trillion by 2010 into the various economies to cushion the effects of the global financial and economic meltdowns – create jobs, make credit more available or restore lending, and bailout essential institutions.

When the meltdown came to the fore in 2008, I had this gut feeling that this could achieve two things: reforming of the World Bank and IMF to provide better supervision of global finance or a new global institution could be established to supervise global finance. The reason is simple. Global crisis of this nature requires global solution. Since finance is global, it makes sense that monitoring and supervision should be global. Therefore, monitoring and supervision should not be left completely to the various national central banks to do. Not quite long after I made that comment at a public forum, the British Prime Minister advocated the need to globally monitor or supervise global finance. The result of the crisis was the setting up of the United Nations Experts Commission on the global economic crisis headed by Joseph Stiglitz, an American renowned economist and Nobel Prize winner. The UN Commission has it medium-term initiatives to create a global economic coordinating council with the responsibility of coordinating economic policy and access impending problems and institutional gaps. The G20 agreed to work out ways to restore confidence, growth, and raise output by 4 percent. In addition, the G20 greed to establish a new Financial Stability Board (FSB), reshape the regulatory systems and strengthen the global financial institutions.

What has happened as a result of the crisis is that things have fallen apart and the center can no longer hold. This crisis has changed the world for good. Things will never remain the same again. A new world economy has emerged with new players coming from the unexpected and unlikely parts of the world. A new protectionist regime has emerged and Keynesian brand of economics hold sway. Like Joseph Stiglitz once said, "we're all Keynesians now." China and few other countries like Venezuela are now calling for the move away from dollar as the global currency for international trade. My thinking is that as the world moves towards the next phase of globalization, which is the globalization of culture (including one universal language), one universal currency (or one world currency) is around the corner.

Beyond the Meltdown

What should countries like Nigeria be looking at or be doing when the crisis finally blows over? I think the government, the economic planners or economic policy makers should be thinking of how to reinvent the Nigeria economy. With better management of the budget deficit as well as the current account deficit Nigeria's economy could be steered away from deep crisis. The crisis also spells opportunity for Nigeria. To borrow from Rahm Emmauel, President Barack Obama's chief of staff "never waste a great crisis." Though some Americans criticized him for making such a statement at a time where American people were going through tough times, but there is a lot of sense in what he said. This is actually a time of opportunity for individuals and nations who have the entrepreneurial mindset to seize the moment. Philip Humbert, PhD made the following suggestions on how organizations and individuals can survive and thrive in economic crisis:

1. Use crises for life management. There's a huge difference between observing a storm around you, and being threatened by it personally. Life is full of storms and some people seem to plan ahead, navigate skillfully and handle them just fine. When we are secure and know our loved ones are well protected, watching the power and drama of a storm can be great fun. But when we're getting wet and the roof is threatening to blow away, storms are terrifying. How are you handling the current "storms" and is there anything you want to learn or do differently in the future?

2. Use crises for personal clarity. When families flee in the face of a hurricane or the brush fires that strike California periodically, people grab their most important essentials first. Some take family pictures or heirlooms. Some take birth certificates or other documents. Most try to grab a few clothes or other possessions. Times of crisis invite us to notice what we value most, what is truly at the core of our lives. In times of crisis, we get very clear about who we are, what we love, and where we're going in life. Use this crisis to re-examine your life and (if appropriate) make new choices.

3. Use crises for tactical advantage. In times of upset and chaos, some panic while others thrive. When the old ways no longer work and the "ordinary" can no

longer be trusted, those with the most energetic and innovative solutions always come out on top. During this economic crisis I think it's wonderful that many people are starting businesses they "always dreamed of" but never pursued in more peaceful times. Others will find new niches or unique value-added opportunities. Some will unfortunately suffer and be victimized by powerful forces beyond their control. That's a shame! Instead, learn to use the wind and rain, the lightning and turbulence to your advantage.

I'm told the Chinese symbol for crisis involves two characters, one for "danger" and another for "opportunity." I love that! I certainly agree with the observation that we live in dangerous times. Things are changing and not always to our immediate advantage. But there is also a freedom and energy and "yeasty ferment" about these times. Find and seize your opportunity!

Look inside to clarify your values, priorities, hopes and aspirations. Notice what's important. Notice what you've been neglecting in the boom times of recent years, or anything these recent storms may have uncovered on the shores of your own life. And take action! Try stuff! Try some new ways, some new approaches, and some new directions. Use these crises to your advantage. They're too valuable to waste!

On a national level, the government should strengthen financial and regulatory institutions to perform their regulatory and supervisory roles better. Adopt expansionary regime to put money in the hands of the people, especially the middle class. Above all, the government should diversify and decentralize the economy by making policies that will stimulate the manufacturing sector or improve the productive sector. Without a good industrial base, the economy will continue to be in a limbo. Cue should be taken from China. The Chinese government, over the years made policies and encouraged manufacturing. China's export strategy has helped the country's economy even in times of economic crisis. They have the highest foreign reserve in the world – over one trillion dollars. There is also an urgent need to encourage and promote entrepreneurship and entrepreneurial development. There is no gainsaying the fact that entrepreneurship is the engine growth of any economy. Once the economy is diversified away from oil and gas and also decentralized, economic or entrepreneurial activities can take place in communities and villages thereby helping solve the problem of urban-rural migration. In order words, rural entrepreneurship should be encouraged. Rural entrepreneurship is simply means the establishment of industrial units in rural areas. Note that over 60 percent of Nigeria's population dwells in rural areas with agriculture as their major occupation. The 2009 economic outlook showed that agriculture is projected to contribute about 42.02 percent to the Nigeria's economy (or output). This makes a strong case for rural industrialization.

Entrepreneurship thrives where there is good governance and strong institutions are in place. Institutions are systemic frameworks or value systems used by society to set limits to acceptable conducts. Institutions exist to constrain behavior in a way that facilitates social intercourse and economic exchange relations.

There should be a national strategy on human resource development to feed the real sector as well as the informal sector and governments with high quality personnel to enhance productivity and provide good governance and management of organizations. This involves investing in improving the educational system and provision of schools and good health care facilities. Nigeria ranks 38 (or less than 50) in the Human Development Index of the United Nations. In all of these, leadership is central and a very critical factor. Without good and authentic leadership organizations as well as nations will fail. Unfortunately, leadership is in high demand but in short supply.

Investments in key infrastructure such as power, energy, roads, etc, should be emphasized as growth enablers. Going forward, special attention should be paid to growing the industrial sector of the economy. This will ensure provision of jobs to the millions of people and the rebuilding of the middle class. The middle class is critical to the sustenance of the real economy and growth.

CHAPTER THIRTY

First world creditors versus Third world debtors: A review of

The Debt Threat

By Noreena Hertz'
Reviewed by Omena Abenabe

I NTRODUCTION
Noreena Hertz' *The Debt Threat* is a reminder to
countries who are into the habit of borrow that
nothing is free in Freetown; everything has a price but
also that the creditor owes a debt. In it, she takes a
historical approach to tracing the debt burden which
has become an albatross in to the global community,
threatening the sovereignty of nations and threat to the
human race.

With very clear historical details, facts and approach,
and with euphemistic yet poignant points, Hertz in this
four-part book makes it clear that the West was culpable
in the debt which threatens the livelihood of the poor
as poor nations poorer, the sick left for dead and
children are kept out of schools as governments in these

countries, in a bid to keep up with their inconvenient obligation of debt repayment consistently cut back on budgetary allocation meant for this group of people. She however strikes hard at the lending nations, attempting to prove that their claimed intentions for giving loans have no virtue but just a strategy to enslave weak nations. But, she doesn't stop there; otherwise, it would have been a book of many complaints. She goes on to proffer a blueprint for social regeneration.

OVERVIEW

The year of Jubilee is the year of freedom and people always want freedom. Bono, lead singer for U2, didn't think it was unfair that while they in the West celebrated abundance, down in Africa, people were sinking further into the abyss of misery. If jubilee was to have any meaning, it must much all of humanity. Debt has become a time bomb and he set to defuse it but, in the real world of politics, how was this ever going to play out? Hertz explores, tracing the foundation of debt from the Cold Ward to the current era.

A cold debt

It all began with the Cold War. Political leanings and ideologies differed and getting new allies was necessary for future survival, therefore, countries in need were not necessary given loans based on their needs but based on geopolitical interests. It was a time of democracy versus the communist other. While some were wise in borrowing in this period, others were not. Mao Zedong of China needed the money to build back his county. Clear, focused, he did and repaid the loan before it ever had the chance to become and albatross on the neck of his people. No so with so many others.

The foray of the West into Africa therefore has little to do with development and more to do with geopolitical interest as a British Foreign Office document quotes in the book shows: "If Africa is remain loyal to the Western cause, its economic interests must coincide with, and reinforce its political sympathies... If the Western Powers are unreasonably insensitive to the economic aspirations of independent Africa, the Governments of the new states may be compelled t turn to the soviet union for the assistance they will certainly need." This insight made the west overlook any nobility of will and they began borrowing blindly to corrupt and dictatorial regimes such as Zaire's Mobutu SeseSeko, and Iraq's Saddam Hussein.

Hertz then outlines why nations went on a borrowing spree, first the loans could easily go unaccounted for, second, the some countries needed it as domestic savings were not meeting their plans for development (in this however, as with Mao Zedong, the debtor showed foresight in borrowing) but most important, in the ideological battle between the East and the West, the developing countries were caught in between and they believed that the courting phase would never end. With this, the strong nations set the agenda for underdevelopment in weak nations. "It is absolutely clear," Hertz writes, "that the lender is not an almsgiver and the world of real politik. The agenda is to serve the perceived self-interest of the lender, debt to be granted and withdrawn as he sees fit."So once the Cold War ended, the courtship with the developing nations also ended as they became less useful the East and the West.

All that was left in between was a cold debt which would set the foundation on which all other debts built their sordid tales.

Appearance and reality

In chapter three, *Backing the Bad Guys,* Hertz traces the economic trapset for the weak nations by the powerful ones through the various Export Credit Agencies (ECA). Export Credit Agency is"a financial institution or agency that provides trade financing to domestic companies for their international activities. Export credit agencies (ECAs) provide financing services such as guarantees, loans and insurance to these companies in order to promote exports in the domestic country. The primary objective of ECAs is to remove the risk and uncertainty of payments to exporters when exporting outside their country. ECAs take the risk away from the exporter and shift it to themselves, for a premium. ECAs also underwrite the commercial and political risks of investments in overseas markets that are typically deemed to be high risk". (investopedia.com). Virtually all industrialized nations have them. Their aim is to encourage companies within their countries to carry out business abroad and they do this by lending to these companies or by insuring their loans. These agencies also lend moneys directly to developing nations. However, it is a clear tool for 'corporatocracy', and the disguise is to act like they are in a nation to help. The 2002 G8 Africa Action Plan state: "We commit to... helping Africa attract investment, both from within Africa and from abroad and implement the policies conducive to economic growth – including facilitating and financing of private investment through increased us of development finance institutions and export credit risk-guarantee agencies."

Noble in concept but Hertz notes that the operational reality was a far cry from its intended line of action. These loans served geopolitical interests, the interest of commercial banks. The presence of the ECAs led to an increase in reckless borrowing, as someone put it, 'we cannot lose'. With this mindset, the risks were uncalculated. Moreover, loans from the ECAs went into lining the pockets of corrupt government officials in lending countries. Also, Transparency International established that the process itself was corrupt as contract figures are inflated by 10-2- per cent. And by keeping to corrupt practices, such a good idea contributed greatly to the legitimization of corruption and stunted economic growth. Practice also showed that they finance environmentally unfriendly projects and also use the ECAs to finance arms sales. This ECA story, Hertz calls a 'barefaced hypocrisy'.

Banking on oil
World economics is never complete without the oil story and in the case of debt threat, one would expect that bankers will offer some form of professional lead in its financial dealings. Not so. In chapter four, Hertz however reveals how the complicity of oil price, alongside the careless handling of the lending process eventually culminated in the recession of the 80's, turning developing countries into economic slaves of the IMF and World Bank. And Nigeria plays a major role in this part.

Karl Ziegler of First Chicago, fresh from business school jets off to Kenya to head his banks' syndicate loans division. His job, he says, was to 'sell money'. With such a clear focus in a highly competitive market, and a rather myopic one at that, it is clear to see why and how this problem came about. Too much money had come into the banks from oil sales. The rise in oil price had been unprecedented and unforeseen and the banks were left to recycle these funds. With a simple objective such as 'sell money' many things were over looked. In essence, for them, it was a case of the end justified the means. Business ethics disregarded. There was no yardstick for borrowing, none. It was the wild in the west. Of the total sum borrowed by commercial banks in this era, Nigeria accounted for 20% of the ROI of all lending countries. The rationale behind this reckless process was that 'Sovereign countries do not go bankrupt' (64). The profit was there for all to see but the problem is; they were looking at the wrong indices.

Lack of due diligence was another reason. While one bank gave out loan on judgment from a single newspaper article, another did so based on the fact that the country was owning, and Ziegler reveals that although the Nigerian government was neck deep in corrupt practices and the country had no clear need for the loan, they went ahead to 'dump' the loan of the country whose leadership had no sense of good judgment. For them Ziegler and First Chicago, it wasn't about the wellbeing of the country in question, it was just another good deal, placing them ahead of competition. This lack of due diligence was a careless move as history was there to guide their steps.

Hertz goes back in time to the early 19th century, revealing a turn of events which showed how such careless act once led to an economic depression. As That happened in the 19th century. 65-66. There was a turn of events, as should have been expected. Oil prices again soared. In 1982, Mexico went flat broke and was the first to announce, in a series of countries, that it was d that it was going to default in its loans. Other Latin American countries followed also defaulting. But Hertz also reveals in this chapter that the lending nations are not the only ones who suffer bad fate. The more oil-importing countries borrowed the greater the impact in the developed countries as the felt the impact on consumer goods, leading to inflation and also showing that no one was isolated from the effect of such reckless action. And when everyone was tired of the commercial banks, they turned to the capital market. Little did they know what awaited them.

'Capital has no soul'
The cold war era was past, so was the era of the ECAs. Then came the capital market and the countries fell, head over heels for the new suitors, not calculating what risk lay ahead of them. Hertz explores the reason this new turn and also analyses the risk and how it came about. Hertz gives at least three reasons countries went to the capital market:

- They need some form of external funding, being unable to raise domestic capital. Domestic capital means a raise in taxes which would make a government unpopular, therefore, they preferred to raise the extra funds needed from outside the county.
- They believe it will be cheaper to borrow abroad as the interest rates tend to be lower than domestic interest rates
- The loans on offer were often more attractive

than commercial loans
- Borrowing governments had lesser restrictions on how they spent as bond covenants were less restrictive
- Also, in times of crisis, commercial banks have been more troublesome than bondholders.

But the deal was not as smooth a sail as it seemed. It came with its own set of conditions:

- **Currency inflation**. Bonds are denominated in hard currency, exposing borrowers to substantial currency risk. This means the value of the currency determined the value of the bond. The fluctuation was rather hurtful to the economy as was the case with the Asian region when currencies of the various countries there plummeted to less than 50% against the dollar.

- Theabsence of the Bretton Wood institutions, IMF and World Bank doesn't free them as they are left to the soulless bond market which is still being controlled by the IMF and World Bank. And the bond market intimidates by fixing its own interest rate. So, if a country is considered irresponsible, the interest rate is increased. This inconsistency prevents proper planning and means that the lenders are more at an unknown risk.

Irresponsibility, or vice versa, is determined by a country's ability to stick to IMF's policy in fiscal terms, balanced budget, and low inflation, as well as adopted policies of privatization, deregulation, liberalization, and the reduction of trade barriers. In essence, the country has to surrender its economic sovereignty, whether or not it decision is hurting the economy. An example with Brazil which was doing all right, had sound economic promise but a deviation from the World Bank and IMF's idea of what their policy should be, so they were in that regard, irresponsible.

How is this judgment made? What are the parameters? They rely on two main sources:

- Reports published by influential banks or security firms
- Rating from ranting agencies

Hertz points out that both sources are "capable of distorting the way the market reads how 'responsible' or 'trustworthy' a country is.When a country is termed 'irresponsible, interest in its loans are raised and the marketers fix the price of bonds based on market forces. To forestall these arbitrary conditions, these countries must again turn to the IMF and World Bank.

The world meets at Bretton Woods

History tells tales from which lesson can be drawn. Now out of the Great Depression, the industrialised nations sought a way to ensure that such a problem does not repeat itself. It sought a system which would ensure that and the developmental banks were born. Hertz traced the true intent at inception, to the reality within which they now. At inception, at Bretton Woods, both institutions were set up for three key deliverables:

- To help war-ravaged Europe rebuild itself
- To ensure that the world does not again face a 1930s-type depression
- To at the same time have full employment and world trade

Two men we at the fore: John Maynard Keynes, a Brit; and Chief International Economist of the U.S. Treasury, Harry Dexter White. They both put forth their ideas and in the end, theInternational Bank for reconstruction was born, soon known as the World Bank. Their two-step approach was:

- The World Bank should return to the gold standard to prevent countries from devaluating their currencies at will
- A rethink of the management of balance payment of payment of deficits

To achieve the second proposition, there was the need for another institution, but there were two approaches proposed.

Keynes sought equilibrium, noting that both deficit and surplus countries should share a part of the responsibility. He proposed that surplus should be discouraged and funds provided for countries running at deficit should have little or no conditions and repayment plan should not be time-bound. Dexter thought otherwise. To him, "not only should the burden of preserving global financial equilibrium fall on the deficit countries alone, but that loans should only be temporary and be accompanied by demands for 'adjustment'" (pg 95). To achieve the equilibrium proposed by Keyes, countries running on surplus would save and countries on deficit can borrow. In the end, Dexter's 'adjustment' proposition carried the day, as Hertz notes, mostly because at the time, America had a stronger financial clout. And that has been a problem since. MONEY.

As the economy at the First World nations got better, the need for both institutions diminished and they had to look elsewhere. The Third World country needed them. In theory, it was a need. When it concentrated on projects which will benefit the masses, it was welcomed. However, the Brazil and Nigeria examples show that these moneys went pumped into projects which endangered the ecosystem and hands which knew nothing but corruption and tyranny as a way of life as theAbacha example reveals. They cared less for impact and value system and more for who can pay and who can – and should – be caged. As a result, countries which had begun to industrialise, under the 'adjustments' had to go back to becoming commodity suppliers, creating an imbalance in their system and engendering poverty again. In Hertz words, this advice "resulted in many countries losing the self-sufficiency they once had in feeding their own population." And it resulted in the case of robbing Peter to pay Paul as countries in a bid to service or repay loans borrowed from the IMF to pay the World Bank what the owed – or simply to service their loan. Soon, the inhumane mode of operation came fully to the fore as Hertz shows in the second part of the book.

Jubilee is a mirage

Hertz's conversation with a Rwadan top official nails the point of how far both institutions had gone from their original intent and purpose. An institution which was set up to help "war ravaged Europe rebuilds itself" denies a loan to a country recovering fromgenocide."The streets of Kigali were littered with dead bodies, The previous regime had looted the coffers... So we went to the World Bank, that first week, and we said we desperately need some help. And you know what the World Bank said to us? Not until you have paid your outstanding debt." The 'developmental finance' companies had lost its moral fibre, so much so it would make such a proposition. Another proof is the fact that when James Wolfensohn, former MD at World bank who is seen as a reformist saw that the debt owed by developing countries had become too much of a burden and made a recommendation for debt relief, it was thrown aside. But by early 1990's it was obvious to both institutions that their wrong policies had resulted in the quagmire they found themselves in as they gave loans as well as set a one-size-fit-all economic policy for all the countries, disregarding the fact that the economic realities were different. By 1995, the G8 meeting at Halifax accepted that the Paris Club agreement with defaulting countries was solving no problem and something needed to be done.

In 1996, the Paris Club set up the Heavily Indebted Countries Program (HIPC) "to reduce the external debt of eligible countries as part of strategy to achieve debt sustainability" (pg114). It was remarkable, being the first time the World Bank, in its 50-year history, was committing to a debt relief scheme but Hertz says it was seriously flawed. The amount of debt to be cancelled was based on overoptimistic growth projections. The reason for this flaw, as is with Washington's 'development template' was that the people who owed these monies were hardly thoroughly involved in plans. Her claim was substantiated by the fact that in 2002, both institutions confessed that they had been overly optimistic in their projections as they proved to be grossly inaccurate.

Karma

There is a natural sequence of cause-and-effect in life. Hertz explores the effect of this rather off-handed approach to borrowing and the effect it eventually had on both parties, first rationalizing the reason for this careless serial act. First, she outlines the human flaws which led to it – both internally and externally. First were the internally forces of greed, myopic governments, and delusional leaders. For instance, President Mehnhem of Argentina – out of greed - borrowed money and lined the pockets of senators before the elections. Ukraine president then, Kuchma allegedly financed a pro-government presidential bid with a Eurobond issue. Second, governments make myopic decisions borrow to dodge savings, budgetary prudence, or seeking our new ways of generating revenue internally. Unfortunately, they live with excessive optimism that they have the capacity to service the debt. That is delusional.

Having outlined what could have been done from within, Hertz also looks at the external forces which prevented countries from fulfilling their debt obligation:

- Terror. The war on terror is not yet won which means it impossible to give, with all the negative implications for the developing world's ability to export successfully and generate the requisite foreign exchange to service the debt that this brings
- US Deficit. The implication of this is that a rise in US Deficit is a rise in interest rate, thereby making it impossible for the countries to meet their mark.
- Fluctuating - and ever rising - oil price.

This keeps importing/developing countries perpetually in debt as they might be pushed to borrow to meet the financial implications of unforeseen increase in oil price.

But while one might argue that loans in themselves are good, Hertz has been able to analyze how they become bad debt. She however highlights what the problems are with sovereign debt:

- There is no organized bankruptcy procedure in place for sovereign default and, for the bond holders, attempts by creditors to get back their money usually gets messy.
- For the commercial banks, as was popular in d 80's, one country's default can jeopardize the credibility of the entire financial institution is questioned
- Default is costly for business. Foreign companies, having nationals from the developed countries, suffer the effect as the ECA cannot fulfill its insuring promise all the time. This is made worse as the debt profile increases.
- Emigration to developed world for greener pastures. As it gets harder, people leave home for the developed world. If the drift is too much, it creates a burden for the developed world themselves

But that is only for the developed world. For the developing world, the implications are:

- It is impossible for the defaulting country to get new credit as there is an immediate freeze on borrowing
- If a significant amount of sovereign debt

is in the hands of domestic investors, writing down a significant percentage count wipe out most of the domestic financial institutions, leading to a collapse of the domestic banking system. This will increase the rate of poverty, and ultimately...

- Leads to social unrest and domestic economic crisis and
- Rise in social vices and violence against women: rape, kidnap, loss of job, trafficking. Women are often the backbone of their families and this means there will be an imbalance in the ecosystem of society and family life. Chaos. Women need to be empowered.

Loans are however still needed as they are needed for expansion in emerging markets but should it go? Hertz believes the pros and cons should be weighted, considering all the conditions that come with it and the borrowing nation should be certain that it is making the decision at the right time. Lack of understand, she says, becomes a grenade and in the next chapter explores the far-reaching implications.

'Turning and turning in the widening gyre'

Hertz asserts, "Disease, a manifestation of the dark side of debt, can fast become a developed-world problem, put its safety at risk and, hurt in its pocket. The rich world's negligence also has the potential to corrupt its very soul." Corroborated by Lawrence Summers' assertion which is the verse for opening the book: "If developing countries scourged by disease do not develop, they cannot contribute to the broader global growth in which we have such a stake, at a time when more than 40 per cent of our (their) export already goes to developing countries. The national economic distress and political instability that inevitably accompany this... can cause greater damage to the global system as a whole".

To meet World Bank and IMF's conditions, developing countries often have to cut back on social expenditure. SAP is enforced, exposing the countries to the risk of bankruptcy and even more economic hardship as SAP does not engender industrialization, instead it creates a dependency economy.

Budgetary provisions for education, healthcare, suffer cutbacks as there as the country strives to meet its debt servicing obligations. For many of these countries, high interest rate and fluctuating currency rates also means that the gap in exchange rate has become so wide and high, the developing countries are left perpetually servicing their debt, never even getting to the point of repaying the original debt. A country which wants to take the responsibility of clearing its debt is left with the option of cutting down on budgetary allocation for social welfare. This in turn means that the society's chance for growth is stunted. Low budget allocation for education means that parents have to pay for their kids' education. This in turn affects health as the populace is not knowledgeable on the simple things as that. As the health status diminishes, it worsens as people have to pay for healthcare. Payment for healthcare also means that they will rationalize spending even further. Resources become scarce and Summers' assertion plays out.

The threat for the developed world as history has

shown us is that this social degeneration affects them. Dengue fever connected France Alabama, France, Berlin (the Ebola case), and so on. This is made possible as poverty in countries lead to migration. Migrants are often, unfortunately, agents of these problems. Besides migrants, neighbouring nations also quickly feel the effect of especially disease, water and airborne diseases. Human trafficking, tourism, international trade all means that agents of diseases in these regions are also moving around.

Hertz up until this chapter has been discussing 'grenade' in the metaphorical sense. In the next chapter, she makes it real.

Osama lives on

Hertz believe growing debt leads to disaffection as nations feel cheated. The social unrest caused by the trend means that someone must vent and as the whole world grows smaller in the process of globalization, so does the treat to world peace. This the CIA foresaw this and noted, "The rising tide will create many economic winners, but it will not life the beats... Regions, countries and groups feeling left behind will face deeping economic stagnation, political instability and cultural alienation. They will foster political, ethnic, ideological and religious extremism, along with the violence that often accompanies it."

Poverty forces people to lose their soul. The economic instability causes people to become desperate and the result is in the way they act. Politicians use it to score cheap political scores; Mugabe used the anti-IMF song to garner support. It is also used to legitimize acts of militancy and terrorism. As Michael Fortin notes, "We have to recognize that this deplorable act of aggression may have been, at least in part, an act of revenge on the part of desperate and humiliated people, crushed by the weight of the economic oppression practices by the people of the west." (161). Militancy, as in Nigeria's Niger Delta case, provides lucrative opportunities for desperate people in the population. It does not justify the act but must be investigated and combated, having been identified as a resultant effect of sovereign debt.

Debt erodes the fabric of society as its attendant evil leads to desperation and loss of humanity. Then corrupt men, who have made their money through illegal means now invest in social welfare projects and gain cheap popularity. Morality is then lost as in the case of Rafael Caro of Mexico. The truth is, these people end up meeting the basic human needs of people in the society, therefore, people look up to them. But, Hertz say, "The danger of extremism or drug running taking holds in these weak environments is all too clear". True. Soon, failed states emerge. Empirical evidence is there to show that most of the failed or quasi failed states are highly indebted: Angola, Afghanistan, Burundi, and Somalia. Their indebtedness can be traced to the Cold War loaning era. They not only pose a danger to themselves but to their neighbors.

Then comes the ecological threat:

Relying on commodity market, weak countries are forced to exploit their natural resources as a means of Internally Generated Revenue (IGR). This is inevitable as IMF and the World Bank conditions means they have to rely on commodity economy. This is how the problem plays out:

- Weak nations exploit their natural resources
- They inevitably cannot afford to be environmentally responsible
- It inspires short-termist behaviors. Selling of rights that make them indebted in the future as a short term way of raising money.
- Loans provided for are sometimes for environmentally dangerous projects

And the air we breathe in, globally, becomes unsafe. This terror is worse than a singular act perpetuated by Osama Bin Laden.

It would seem that we have a nuclear threat created by both weak and strong nations in coalition. Having established the culpability of both parties, Hertz sets out to write a reconciliatory blueprint.

Let's begin again

She says first step is face the truth

- Regimes who borrowed these monies had no democratic consent
- They were hardly used to projects which improve the lives of the populace
- The lender was aware of the fact that the money being borrow would be used irresponsibly.

Based on these parameters, she notes that these debts can and should be considered illegitimate. But, in her view, all three must be together. Therefore if it was borrowed by a military regime and used for projects which had direct bearing and benefits for the people, it is legitimate.

If however, the debt cans be said to be legitimate from foregoing, Hertz believes there are other ways to establish that the debt is illegitimate: when, as a result

of the debt, the country
- Is unable to cater for subsistent levels of food, water, clothing, shelter, basic healthcare and education of its citizens
- Destroys its environment to increase revenue to service its debt,

These are based on the principle that the debtor's right should not override fundamental rights.

Truth accepted, Hertz calls for reconciliation; debt cancellation through ad hoc arbitration tribunals. This is to ensure that the interest of all aides is balances. Then one can be assured of hope for regeneration. But that is not all. It is important that the ball is set rolling for a new spate of development.

Put in place a mechanism to ensure that the resources freed are not wasted but are invested in aspect of the budget which will strengthen the social fiber of society. She advocates for National Regeneration Trusts which will be used to channel the monies accrued into developmental projects. And she outlines the proposed composition and mode of operation:
- The trustees majority nationals with proven records in delivery and integrity
- Nominal trustees from United Nations bodies, e.g. UNICEF or WHO
- Government officials in the board must be in the minority
- The inflow and outflow of income must be made public
- Putting the money into public trust is the only condition for eligibility in this scheme
- The only condition for the relief is, the countries ensure that the money meets the

needs of the sick, uneducated, the poor, and the environment and are not stolen and kept in some foreign banks or invested in some white elephant project or civil wars

- To ensure countries do not have to take from their budget to put into the trust, thereby defeating the aim of the trust, international donor organizations will pledge to keep funding the flow and they must not be empty promises. Commitments must be made

Hertz believes such a trust is more likely to deliver on promise. But she doesn't leave the ball in the court of strong nations; she suggests five principles by which weak nations can maintain a healthy financial status:

- Improve mobilization of domestic resources through better tax collection and less spending on frugal matters
- Transparency of borrowing for all classes of lenders
- Developing countries borrowing from the capital market must be allowed to control in and our flow of capital
- A complete overhaul of the West's ECAs to stem the tide of reckless borrowing to weak nations
- The roles of the Bretton Wood institutions must be recast

But this does not automatically mean that the developed nations will maintain stability. It only gives them a balance. It does not solve the problem of poverty, inequality, disease, and insecurity. Hertz goes further to highlight the need for a level playing ground between developed countries and developing one:

- Get more money to those who need it and provide a foundation for a country which engenders long-term investment
- Cut back on military expenditure and seek other similar avenues where resources can be freed
- Encourage free trade on fair terms

As Hertz points out in closing, her proposal will not be easily accepted but it is important to deal with this issue because, there are powerful individual, institutions profiting heavily from sovereign debt, however it has become imperative and inevitable because sovereign debt now poses a threat on human existence.

TREATMENT OF THEME

Hertz shows great balance in the treatment of her theme. She doesn't condemn loans as she concretely cites instances when they have been used for the good of the nation. In chapter four, 'pushers and junkies', she notes that though most Latin American loans were given "for general purposes", some governments spent wisely. Argentina, Brazil and Mexico invested some of its borrowed funds in infrastructure. This enabled the government of the day to maintain support from the masses as borrowing meant that they did not have to increase taxes.

She however makes too much of a case for the borrowing countries, almost absolving them of their irresponsibility and lack of foresight. Her words "the fact that the loans were being sold so hard was just too much of an allure to be able to resist.' And she corroborates it with the assertion of a finance minister in Latin America who said: "I remember how bankers tried to corner me at conferences to offer me loans, They would not leave me alone. If you are trying to balance your budget it's very tempting to borrow money..." This is a clear case of irresponsibility and no excuses can be made for them. It was just a lack of vision and strong will. After all, Hertz had earlier cited the example of Chinese, Mao Zendong, who was wise in spending and repaying.

He also had loans shoved down his throat at, perhaps, a more tempting period in their national life but he was wise because he was on a mission to lead his people out of the conflict period. Truth is, the onus is more on the lender to calculate the risk. In a situation where there was so much money in the hands of the banks and they needed to recycle this money, their strategy will be to wear out a potential borrower, using all marketing gimmicks which would be helpful in forcing the money down their throat. Why? Because their objective, really, is to sell this money. The potential borrower however has the responsibility to calculate the risk involved. In this case, however, it would appear they smiled like a potential bride whose price was yet to be paid but based on the assumption that it would be paid, moves to the 'husband's' house. Hertz makes a case for – or probably just tries to empathise with – the developing countries who just kept borrowing. She gives the following reasons:

- A desire to ensure the country's future development (however, there was no empirical evidence of a plan set in place to ensure this
- For oil-importing countries, this was a huge relief in a time when budget benchmarks had

been rubbished owing to the unprecedented soaring oil prices
- African commodity exporters, anticipating a continued stable export market thought it was safe to borrow
- A Latin American finance minister noted that it was 'just too good to resist' the hard sell
- The World Bank and foreign governments from industrialised economies, sold the idea that it was the road to 'accelerated development'
- The IMF also sold its own idea, that the debt was a good foreign policy between the lending and the borrowing countries.

Perhaps, only the oil-importing countries could be justified but the others were simply irresponsible, lacking strong will and good judgment. These are not signs of good leadership, but then, not much is expected from bad leaders. It is also a lesson for Africa and other developing nations that economic policies should not be based on ideological speculations, instead and they should be made on empirical realities. The IMF and World Bank sold their ideas based on a bias for the countries and power bloc they represent but governments in the developing countries did not seem to have the financial intelligence to decide how this wound play out in the future.

DISCORDANT TUNES
Not everyone agrees with Hertz.
Coyle (2004) says it is "another pamphlet disguised as a book. It pretends to weigh up the details and evidence, but its tone implies that anyone who disagrees is

stupid or bad" He adds: "cancelling all debts owed by poor countries - the aim of this campaign bandwagon - is neither easy nor right. Nor are HIV/Aids, the loss of Amazon rainforests and terrorism caused by these debts, which is the facile claim Hertz makes.It's alarming anybody might think debt cancellation would solve these problems, or even a simpler one such as the failure of some poor countries to achieve development. History in this field is littered with the wrecks of old panaceas. The idea that all "we" have to do is cancel unfair debts is as inadequate as any other idée fixe, whether aid or multinational investment."

Adams (2005), lead columnist at the Guardian UK says: "It is deeply wrong that countries ravaged by Aids spend more on debt servicing than on healthcare. But to blame everything - from climate change and al-Qaida to (bizarrely) falling sugar maple yields - on debt, as Hertz does, is to lose perspective. While no one can doubt Hertz's good intentions, the road to hell is paved with books like IOU. Developing-world debt is a serious issue, and it deserves more judicious treatment than this."

CONCLUDING THOUGHTS

Hertz told a story out of personal conviction while establishing her ideas with facts. She successfully traces the beginning to the future of debt and that makes the book good resource for political economy and the topic of sovereign debt. Even her critics agree that this debt is a threat. However, her points are overstated and I find her blueprint rather idealistic in proposition.

REFERENCES

Mueller, Dennis C. Constitutional Democracy. Oxford. Oxford University Press. 1996.

Hertz, N. The Debt Threat: How debt is destroying the developing world. New York. Happer Collins Books. 2004.

Kaplan, Robert D. The Coming Anarchy: Shattering the dreams of the post war. New York. Vintage Books. 2000.

Ake, C. Democracy and Development in Africa. Ibadan. Spectrum Books Ltd. 2003.

Adams, R (2004).Hard to credit (book review)
> http://www.guardian.co.uk/books/2004/
> oct/30/highereducation.news

Hinmashu (2008). The Debt Threat – Noreena Hertz (a review).
> http://
> himanshuonbooks.blogspot.com/2008/07/
> debt-threat-noreena-hertz.html

Definition of ECAs: http://www.investopedia.com/terms/e/export-credit-agency.asp#axzz290glyHmO

Cole, D (2004).I.O.U: the debt threat and why we must defuse it by Noreena Hertz: Facile claims on debt that don't add up (boor review)
> http://www.independent.co.uk/arts-
> entertainment/books/reviews/iou-the-debt-
> threat-and-why-we-must-defuse-it-by-
> noreena-hertz-6160982.html

Aiyede E.A
2006; *The role of INEC, ICPC and EFCC in combating political corruption.*
department of political science, university of Ibadan (Nigeria).

Akerele, Taiwo
2006; 2007: *confronting the challenge of weak institutions*
Businessday. March 28th 2006. page 44

Akam, Christian
2002; *Corruption in Nigeria (The Niger Delta Experience)*
fourth Dimension publishers, Enugu, Nigeria

Alam, Shahid
1989; *Anatomy of corruption; An approach to the political economy of underdevelopment.*
American Journal of economics and sociology

Asobie, Asisi
2005; *a contribution at an anti-corruption summit in kaduna.*
www.vanguardngr.com . read on the 18th of October 2006

Ajayi, Rotimi
2005; *Can the war against corruption succeed?*
www.vanguardngr.com.   Read on the Friday 22nd September 2006

Businessday Nigeria
2007: *Soyinka charges FG to release Asari-Dokubo, Uwazurike*
Thursday February 22. page 6

Daniel Kaufman
2004; *cost of corruption*
www.worldbank. Com/wbi/workingpapers

Dan, Isaacs
2006: *the different faces of the corruption war in nigeria*

www.BBConline.com. Read on the 16th of November 2006

Gboyega, Alex
1996; *corruption and democratization in nigeria as in Aiyede E.A*
(2006; the role of INEC, ICPC and EFCC in combating political corruption
Department of political science, university of Ibadan, Nigeria).

Ike, Naijaman
2003 ; *Nigeria's fight against corruption.*

www.zmag.org. read on the 17th of October 2006

Independent Commission Against Corruption ICAS
2006; *forms of corruption.*

www.icas.org. read on the 15th of December 2006

Komolafe, Kayode
2006; *Beware of Politics of anti-corruption*

www.dawodu.com. Read on the 17th October 2006

Kofarmata, Dan Azumi
2005; *state governor's and Nigeria's anti-corruption war*

www.elendureports.com . read on the 15th of November 2006.

Obasanjo, Olusegun
2003; *Nigeria; from pond of corruption to island of integrity*

www.nigerianvillagesquare.com. Read on the 15th of November 2006

Osoba, Olusegun
1996; *Corruption in Nigeria; a historical perspectives*
   Review of African political economy; vol 23. no 69

Ribadu, Nuhu
2004; *The role of the EFCC in sanitizing the Nigerian economic environment in a democratic setting. A paper presented at a summit in Adamawa state*

www.efccnigeria.org. read on the 1st of November 2006.

Senan, Murray
2005: *politics and corruption in Nigeria*

www.bbconline.com. Read on the 16th of October 2006

Saturday SUN
2007; *On performance, IBB deserves merit award –Kasim Afegbua*
Saturday, June 23. page 14.

Tanzi, Zito (see Aiyede E.A)
2006; *The role of INEC, ICPC and EFCC in combating political corruption*
Department of political science, university of Ibadan (Nigeria).

The Nigerian Guardian
2007; *Protests as Govt. declares public holidays*
Thursday, April 12. pages 1 & 2

The Nigerian Guardian
2007; *Tinubu accuses Obasanjo of plot to derail polls*
Saturday, February 10. page 3

The South African Institute of International Affairs (SAIIA)
2005; *Is Nigeria's anti corruption crusade for real?*

www.saiia.org.za. Read on the 14th of December 2006.

Thisday Nigeria
2007; *24 candidates to bid for presidency, Atiku out*
Friday, march 16. page 1

Thisday Nigeria
2007; *Obasanjo: Atiku cautions visiting American Editors*
Saturday, January 27. page 3

Thisday Nigeria
2007; *Atiku: I can't see Obasanjo eye to eye*
Thursday, march 1. page 18.

Thisday Nigeria
2007; *Indicted candidates must be disqualified-Ribadu*
Sunday, February 11. page 6

Thisday Nigeria
2007; *Appeal court Annuls Dariye's impeachment*
Friday march, 9. page 1& 6

www.transparency.aman.palestine.com

www.taipei.ethics.gov

www.sida.gov.corruption/publication

www.saharareporters.com

Zeller, Tom

2006; *Is Nigeria's anti-corruption commission corrupt?*

www.newyorktimes.com. Read on the 15th of January 2007

The Dynamics of Privatization and Public Enterprises By Yakubu Sankey A. Thesis Submitted to A.B.U Zaria 2001 for the award of PhD.

The Dynamics of the Nigerian Economy By Oladele Olashore

The Punch Newspaper

The Dynamic of Nigeria Economy By Oladele Olashore

The Oxford Advanced Learner Dictionary

The 'NEEDS' Document, 2004

The Punch Editorial

www.Dawodu.com

Public Finance in Theory and Practice by Richard Musgrave international Student Edition McGraw Hill 1976

ABOUT THE AUTHOR

Dr. Austin Nwezez

For many years Dr Austin Nweze published Successful People magazine, the first Nigerian magazine focused on the promotion of entrepreneurship, which contributed to the recent interest and attention being given to the subject  and sector by the government, universities, NGOs, and the private sector. For over 15 years he consulted for corporate organizations and government establishments in the areas of management, finance, marketing, strategy, and performance acculturation.

He is a commentator on national issue, economy and business in the print and electronic media and the founding President of Association of Outsourcing Practitioners of Nigeria (AOPN). He teaches Business Journalism and Economic and Business Environment at the School of Media and Communication (SMC), Pan African University, Lagos, Nigeria, and the Principal Consultant, Bellwether Consulting.